Insurgency & Terrorism

Titles of Related Interest:

Alexander & Latter   TERRORISM & THE MEDIA: DILEMMAS FOR GOVERNMENT, JOURNALISTS & THE PUBLIC

Alexander & Picard   IN THE CAMERA'S EYE: NEWS COVERAGE OF TERRORIST EVENTS

Bacevich et al.   AMERICAN MILITARY POLICY IN SMALL WARS: THE CASE OF EL SALVADOR

Blackwell & Blechman   MAKING DEFENSE REFORM WORK

Charters & Tugwell   ARMIES IN LOW-INTENSITY CONFLICT: A COMPARATIVE ANALYSIS

Collins   GREEN BERETS, SEALS & SPETSNAZ: U.S. & SOVIET SPECIAL MILITARY OPERATIONS

Hilsman   AMERICAN GUERRILLA: MY WAR BEHIND JAPANESE LINES

Mallin   TANKS, FIGHTERS & SHIPS: U.S. CONVENTIONAL FORCE PLANNING SINCE WWII

Paschall   LIC 2010: SPECIAL OPERATIONS & UNCONVENTIONAL WARFARE IN THE NEXT CENTURY

Radu & Tismaneanu   LATIN AMERICAN REVOLUTIONARIES: GROUPS, GOALS, METHODS

Shaker & Wise   WAR WITHOUT MEN: ROBOTS ON THE FUTURE BATTLEFIELD

Simpkin   RACE TO THE SWIFT: THOUGHTS ON 21ST-CENTURY WARFARE

Taylor   THE FANATIC

Towle   PILOTS AND REBELS: THE USE OF AIR POWER IN UNCONVENTIONAL WARFARE

*Related Journals**

Armed Forces Journal International
Defense Analysis
Survival

*Sample copies available upon request

Insurgency

&

Terrorism

Inside Modern Revolutionary Warfare

Bard E. O'Neill

BRASSEY'S (US), Inc.
Maxwell Macmillan Pergamon Publishing Corp

Washington • New York • London • Oxford • Beijing • Frankfurt
São Paulo • Sydney • Tokyo • Toronto

Brassey's Editorial Offices: Brassey's Order Department:
22883 Quicksilver Drive   P.O. Box 960
Dulles, Virginia 20166   Herndon, Virginia 20172

Brassey's books are available at special discounts for bulk purchases for sales promotions, premiums, fund-raising, or educational use.

Library of Congress Cataloging-in-Publication Data

O'Neil, Bard E.
     Insurgency & terrorism / Bard E. O'Neil.
     p. cm.
     Includes bibliographical references and index.
     ISBN 0-08-037456-5
     1. Guerrilla warfare—History—20th century. 2. Insurgency—History—
     20th century. 3. Terrorism—History—20th century. 4. Military history,
     Modern—20th century. I. Title. II. Title: Insurgency and terrorism.

U240.054   1990
355.02'18'0904—dc20   90-36727
                                                                CIP

British Library Cataloguing-in-Publication Data
O'Neil, Bard E.
     Insurgency & terrorism : inside modern revolutionary warfare.
     1. Terrorism
     I. Title
     322.42
     ISBN 0-08-037456-5

10 9 8 7 6 5 4

Printed in the United States of America

CONTENTS

FOREWORD

THE FOCUS OF AMERICAN NATIONAL SECURITY EXPERTS since the end of World War II has been on the containment of the Soviet Union and the containment of the spread of communism. Our alliances, our military forces, our security assistance, our doctrine, and our tactics have all been based on this containment ethos. Even though most of the conflicts in the world during the past 45 years have involved insurgencies, the U.S. armed forces have been primarily organized, equipped, and trained to respond to the strategic and conventional threat of the Soviet Union and its Communist allies. A secondary purpose for the forces created to counter the Soviet threat was to be able to handle effectively all forms of lesser conflict. The fig leaf of containment is rapidly disappearing as a rationale for our military needs. The question that is being debated by national security strategists today is, "After containment, what?"

There are several preliminary answers to this question. Clearly, the United States and its allies must retain adequate strategic and conventional forces to provide insurance against a resurgence of the Soviet military threat—a threat that has been significantly altered by world events of the past year. Equally it is clear that if we are to succeed in this changing world, the last decade of the twentieth century must be characterized as the period during which the low end of the spectrum of warfare became a distinct and critical element in American military thinking.

Fortunately for all of us, Bard O'Neill's book arrives during this period of reexamination. *Insurgency & Terrorism* provides a means whereby those interested in understanding the nature, the environment, and the impact of conflicts at the low end of the spectrum of warfare can begin to piece together a national security strategy that does not address as an afterthought the main source of future conflict.

For O'Neill, insurgency and terrorism are not afterthoughts. He has been intimately involved in the study of these matters for over 20 years. His book represents a primer on insurgency and terrorism for those who have focused on conventional and strategic warfare in the past. It provides much more for those who are seriously concerned with our national security strategy and our efforts to carry out that strategy in the future. *Insurgency & Terrorism* gives them a means whereby they can understand insurgencies with all the attendant political, economic, and social issues that such matters bring to future national security planning. It is the understanding of these issues and how they vary, region to region and nation to nation, that should form the foundation of our future national security policies. Insurgency, terrorism, the illicit drug trade, and other forms of incitement to conflict will be in the forefront of our national security concerns in the future. Bard O'Neill has done our nation a service by providing a way to analyze these issues so they can be understood and objectively addressed during this period of reexamination.

As the fog of containment drifts away, Bard O'Neill's *Insurgency & Terrorism* will bring our national security requirements for the future into clearer focus by providing invaluable insights into how to answer the question, "After containment, what?"

GEN. EDWARD C. MEYER, USA (Ret.)
Arlington, Virginia

PREFACE

TWENTY YEARS AGO I DEVELOPED WHAT BECAME A LIFE-long interest in the subject of insurgency. I was interested in both particular cases and, most especially, how to analyze them. As I pored over the literature, it became evident that there were two kinds of writings on the subject: descriptive and theoretical. Seldom did the two come together, and the theoretical materials often focused on only parts of the problem. The more I read, the more I became convinced that there was a need for a comprehensive framework for analysis that integrated and added to the collective understanding and insights about insurgency.

My observations led me to devise a framework for analysis in 1970. Since then, it has appeared in several iterations, each of which sought to build upon and improve the previous one. After countless case studies—written and oral—and numerous visits to countries facing insurgencies, I decided the time had come to pull together what I had learned and develop a book that would be useful to various individuals and groups interested in the subject, be they participants, observers, scholars, students, or government analysts.

I have kept two subsidiary aims in mind: to keep the book succinct and to avoid being overly theoretical. This is by no means to dismiss the value of more theoretical works, such as Ted Robert Gurr's *Why Men Rebel*. To the contrary, as the reader will soon discover, I have incorporated a number of ideas from these important works. My purposes, however, are different from theirs. Whereas the theoretical works were intended primarily for academics, I am writing for a more general audience. Hence, while obviously concerned about explicit and structured analysis, I have tried (not always successfully) to tilt away from social science jargon, not because it lacks utility but because it tends to turn off more general readers.

The study of insurgency is fraught with perils, because of the zealotry and partisanship that surrounds the subject. There is no poverty of commentary on issues having to do with supporting or opposing particular insurgencies or broader phenomena such as "revolution" and "counterrevolution." Suffice it to say that I am not interested in taking positions. I am concerned with straightforward, dispassionate analysis of the status of insurgencies that "tells it like it is." The difficult task of giving informed policy advice and of making decisions is gratefully left to others.

A number of colleagues gave their time to read and critique all or portions of the manuscript. Among those who made constructive suggestions were Dr. William Heaton; Mrs. Margaret Dean and Mrs. Ruth Van Heuven, Department of State; Ms. Alice Maroni, Congressional Research Service; and Colonel Michael Diffley and Colonel Terrence "Rock" Salt, U.S. Army. Dr. John Schulz's editorial assistance and substantive suggestions were invaluable.

Administrative support was provided by a number of people. Early drafts were typed by Mrs. Myra Evans and Ms. Mary Ellen Feldcamp, and the final draft was completed by Mrs. Myra Simons. Mrs. Simons, a particularly bright and energetic secretary, offered numerous constructive suggestions along the way.

I would also like to acknowledge the generous assistance of Mrs. Johanna de Onis and Mrs. Mary Quinteros, two dedicated librarians whose efforts saved me countless hours of additional work. Finally, I would like to thank Colonel Roy Stafford, dean of faculty and academic programs at the National War College, and two former commandants, Major General Perry M. Smith and Rear Admiral John Addams for encouraging and supporting me in this undertaking.

Responsibility for this effort is, of course, solely my own. The views expressed herein do not necessarily represent those of either the Department of Defense or the U.S. government.

BARD E. O'NEILL
Washington, D.C.

I Insurgency in the Contemporary World

THE LAST CHAPTER OF THE TWENTIETH CENTURY IS JUST starting to unfold. If the past is prologue, we are in for continued rough times. For years now, we have been faced with an unstable, dangerous, and frequently violent international political environment. In fact, since World War II there has been an average of eight wars going on somewhere in the world at any given time. Casualties have been counted in unnumbered millions.

For those interested in international affairs, this state of affairs should come as no surprise, since the media remind us daily of the carnage. What is striking about the violence is that so much of it occurs in the context of internal wars or insurgencies. Pick up a copy of either the *New York Times* or the *Washington Post* on any day and you are likely to find several articles on insurgencies. Yet seldom is the broader context understood.

These so-called small wars, which can be found on virtually all continents, are often very costly and frequently involve major interests of regional and global powers. Because of their continuing importance, insurgencies deserve serious and systematic analysis, and in this book I set forth a way to do precisely that.

Insurgency, of course, is hardly a new phenomenon, as Roman armies could have reported from Gaul, Judaea, or elsewhere. Indeed, insurgency has probably been the most prevalent type of armed conflict since the creation of organized political communities. It would be difficult and perhaps impossible to find many volumes on political history that do not mention rebellions, revolutions, uprisings, and the like.

Our contemporary era is no different; since World War II, terrorism and guerrilla warfare have been predominant types of political violence. Between 1969 and 1985, the number of major international terrorist incidents alone jumped from just under two hundred to over eight hundred

1

per year, sparking international headlines and leaving people everywhere bewildered, polarized in their opinions, and often afraid. Most of those incidents were the handiwork of insurgent groups seeking to achieve a variety of objectives. Consequently, to understand most terrorism, we must first understand insurgency. We begin the quest for understanding with some preliminary comments on international and domestic factors that have accounted for the prevalence of insurgency since the early 1950s.

The International System

The structure of power in the international system that emerged after World War II was asymmetrical and bipolar, divided between Western and Eastern blocs, led by the United States and the Soviet Union, respectively. The United States enjoyed a clear advantage because of its enormous economic capacity and nuclear weapons superiority until the 1960s. The Soviet Union, meanwhile, acquired recognition as a superpower by virtue of the perceived threat posed by its larger land forces and the tight control it appeared to have over Communist parties around the world, particularly in Eastern Europe. This bifurcation of power and the ideological hostility between the two sides gave rise to a global struggle for power and influence that persists, despite structural changes in the international system that became evident by the 1970s.

Europe was the most immediate arena of the struggle for power in the postwar era. Nations such as France, Italy, and Greece—suffering from postwar political instability and severe economic dislocation—were believed vulnerable to Communist political inroads. While the conflicts in France and Italy centered on the fear that well-organized Communist parties might come to power through domestic political processes, a civil war in Greece prompted concern that violence might also play a part in Soviet designs. As things turned out, the reality of Moscow's commitment to the Greek Communists was less than originally perceived and proved to be short-lived. As for the rest of Europe, the aid provided by the Marshall Plan, together with astute political and economic leadership in the European countries, led to a dramatic recovery and gradual stabilization.

As the threat in Europe receded, attention shifted to the newly emerging countries that were products of the rapidly disintegrating European colonial empires. Although some of these countries achieved independence peacefully, others such as Vietnam and Algeria underwent a lengthy period of violent conflict. In cases where the anticolonial insurrections were led by Marxist parties (e.g., Vietnam and Malaya), the prevailing perception of the bipolar international structure of power led to fears that victories by the insurgents were tantamount to losses for the West, due in part to the fact that international struggle for power was considered a zero-sum game.

Within this context, the policies of the West in general and the United States in particular were widely seen as oriented toward, or actively supporting, the status quo, while the Soviet Union and its allies were perceived to have the revolutionary mission of upsetting the existing order and structure of power.

Both ideological predispositions, dating back to Lenin's critique of imperialism, and the fragility of the new, less-developed countries, which came to be known collectively as the Third World, led Soviet and, shortly thereafter, Chinese leaders to the conclusion that the Achilles' heel of the West was in the Third World. Accordingly, Moscow and Beijing extended moral, political, and material support to both "progressive" governments and Marxist insurgents in the Third World. The underlying assumption behind support to various insurgents was that deplorable economic, social, and political conditions in many of the new nations were the products of imperialist or neo-imperialist exploitation by Western countries, and this made insurgent leaders natural allies of the Communist bloc. Neither Moscow nor Beijing foresaw that in later years their clients would jealously guard their newly won independence and be as defiant toward them as they were toward the West. But while they may have miscalculated the eventual relationships they would have with their clients, the Soviet Union and the People's Republic of China (PRC) correctly assessed the opportunities inherent in the unstable domestic situations of many Third World countries.

The Domestic Context

In general, two fundamental challenges confronted most Third World nations following independence: lack of national integration and economic underdevelopment. The lack of national integration was rooted in societal divisions along one or more lines—racial, ethnic, linguistic, or religious— and in the absence of a political tradition that included legitimate centralizing values and structures that transcended parochial loyalties. Accordingly, it was not surprising to find intergroup antagonism and distrust eventually giving rise to insurrections directed at governments dominated by personalities from rival groups in such places as Burma, Malaya, India, Pakistan, Ethiopia, Nigeria, Iraq, and the Sudan, to note but a few. Moreover, even in countries where group rivalries did not lead to major outbreaks of violence, these rivalries were often just one of several impediments to economic development.

As noted by many scholars, the obstacles to economic development go beyond the lack of national cohesion to include such things as a dearth of requisite human, capital, and natural resources; psychocultural resistance to change; corruption; nonexistent, poorly trained, or cumbersome, inefficient bureaucracies; the lack of an adequate communications and transportation infrastructure; and the disadvantageous competitive position of less-developed countries vis-à-vis the major powers in the international economic system. Further exacerbating this situation was the frequent misuse of foreign assistance on showplace projects, conflicts with regional rivals that devoured already scarce resources, and frustrations engendered by political leaders who failed to make good on promises that they would improve the standard of living of their peoples. Such failures normally had one or more causes. Leaders were incompetent, saw their own power base as threatened by needed changes, or were simply overwhelmed by the magnitude of their problems and their lack of resources.

The clustering of factors that gave rise to insurgencies varied from case to case. Particularly violent situations arose where societal divisions were cumulative and were combined with economic and political disparities. In the Sudan, for instance, the bloody conflict between the black insurgents of the south and the Arab government in the north was an outgrowth of racial, ethnic, linguistic, and religious differences, as well as political and economic discrimination against the southern populace. While there were some specific differences, essentially similar situations arose in Iraq, where Kurds revolted against the Arab government in Baghdad; in Ethiopia, where Eritreans initiated a long, bitter struggle against Amhara-based regimes in Addis Ababa; and in Sri Lanka, where Tamil Hindus attacked the Sinhalese Buddhist ruling establishment.

In addition to insurgencies rooted in intergroup antagonisms, there are those that had as their main cause socioeconomic disparities between classes. Whether it was the Philippines in the early 1950s, Cuba in the late 1950s, Laos and Vietnam in the late 1950s and 1960s, or El Salvador, Guatemala, and Nicaragua in later years, the story was a familiar one: small ruling establishments, supported by vested interests (e.g., landowners, the military, or religious leaders), controlled the lion's share of economic wealth and political power. In a few cases, such as the Philippines, modest reforms were inaugurated and played a role in undercutting the insurgencies, but in most situations staunch resistance to reform and change, accompanied by repression, fueled and prolonged hostilities. Where colonial powers and colonists constituted the ruling elite, as in Algeria, Rhodesia, Angola, and Mozambique, a nationalist dimension merged with socioeconomic disparities and caused prolonged conflicts.

The insurrections based on socioeconomic disparities and concomitant demands for political change opened the door to local Communist party involvement. The parties articulated an ideology that identified the source of deprivation (class exploitation and imperialism or neoimperialism) and promised a new political and economic order that would address popular needs and usher in a new era based on a fair distribution of socioeconomic resources. Equally important, the Communist parties provided sophisticated organizational formats and a flexible approach that brought together Communists and non-Communists in what they called national liberation or democratic fronts. Finally, they enjoyed various kinds of support from the Soviet Union and the PRC.

The Domestic-International Interplay

While all insurgencies were potentially disruptive as far as international order was concerned, those based on class conflicts and led by Communist parties appeared to pose a significant threat to the overall balance of power between East and West. As the major Communist powers gradually extended various types of support to insurgent movements, the Western powers, most notably the United States, increased their aid to beleaguered governments. By the early 1960s, public pledges of assistance to wars of liberation by both Chinese and Soviet leaders led President John F. Kennedy and his national security advisers to conclude that special counterinsurgency forces and doctrinal principles would be necessary to stabilize friendly governments threatened by Communist insurgents. They stressed the combination of political, military, social, psychological, and economic measures.

Although the United States preferred to keep its troops out of insurgencies, deteriorating situations in Laos and Vietnam prompted U.S. leaders to send advisers and, later, regular military forces to Southeast Asia. Closer to home, the United States began extensive training and advisory efforts to shore up Latin American regimes increasingly threatened by Marxist insurgents in the wake of the Cuban revolution. The direct and indirect involvement of Washington, Moscow, and Beijing in Third World insurgencies led many to conclude that the East-West struggle was being waged through proxies in the less-developed nations.

The involvement of the major powers in various internal conflicts and their ability to produce and rapidly transport weapons and other assets around the world resulted in a general trend toward the internationalization of insurgencies. Despite the eventual American setback in Southeast Asia and alterations in the international structure of power that had become evident by the time Richard M. Nixon became president in 1968, this trend continued.

In the late 1960s, the Nixon administration presented a more sophisticated conceptual framework than its predecessors in its analyses of international politics. This framework, articulated principally by Henry A. Kissinger, special assistant for national security affairs, depicted a new pentagonal structure of power comprising the United States, the USSR, the PRC, Japan, and Europe. Although Washington and Moscow maintained military preeminence, the other actors asserted considerable influence because of their economic or demographic resources. While the U.S. administration acknowledged the emergence of smaller regional powers like Brazil and Iran, the key arena for international politics consisted of relationships among the major powers. President Nixon and his advisers saw America's role and power in that arena threatened by the debilitating effects of the Vietnam War on the U.S. economy and social cohesion.

The administration therefore sought to disengage from Southeast Asia in order to concentrate on "more important" areas like Western Europe. As is well known, the disengagement process was not an easy one, given the persistence of North Vietnam, the failure of South Vietnam to defend itself, and Washington's commitment to achieve "peace with honor." The phrase "peace with honor" did not refer to prestige per se; it meant leaving Vietnam with America's credibility intact.

As things turned out, the Vietnam War actually intensified for a period of time, bringing increased public and congressional protests in the United States. Though peace accords were negotiated and the American troop withdrawal began, Hanoi eventually renewed large-scale fighting and South Vietnam fell. The negative experience in Vietnam reinforced the administration's view that American involvement in Third World insurgencies should be more selective and limited to aid and military assistance. Furthermore, Congress, reflecting public opinion, tried to forestall future debacles like Vietnam by passing the War Powers Act and specific pieces of legislation like the Clark amendment, which ended U.S. support for insurgents in Angola. The Department of Defense, meanwhile, concentrated its attention on nuclear and conventional warfare and de-emphasized the role and capability of its special forces. The administration was not entirely comfortable with these developments. It still perceived potential threats by Marxist insurgent groups or governments in Third World countries but was unable to turn the situation around. Furthermore, the Defense Department continued to downplay special forces during the first three years of the Carter administration.

The American desire to avoid future Vietnams did not mean an end to international involvement in insurgencies. To begin with, Moscow, Beijing, and Cuba continued to aid insurgents in places like Eritrea, Thailand, Oman, El Salvador, and Nicaragua. At times Soviet and Chinese support was as much, if not more, a product of a growing Soviet-Chinese rivalry than it was a product of continued antipathy toward the West. Whatever the motivations of the Communist states, their involvement frequently generated a negative reaction by powers that felt threatened by their activity. In a number of cases, countries other than the United States became involved in counterinsurgency on the local government side. In Oman, for instance, Jordan, Iran, Saudi Arabia, and Great Britain supported the sultan against the Popular Front for the Liberation of Oman, which was backed by the Soviet Union and, for a time, the PRC.

Another development that fostered continued international involvement in internal conflicts was the appearance of new regional actors motivated by realpolitik, ideological considerations, or a combination of both. To achieve their aims against regional rivals, various governments backed insurgent groups across their borders and sometimes beyond. For example, the Shah of Iran gave aid to Kurdish rebels in Iraq to gain leverage against Baghdad in negotiations over land and border disputes; Algeria assisted (some would say "created") the Polisario rebels in the Western Sahara, who were fighting against Morocco, Algeria's rival for hegemony in the Maghrib; and the Republic of South Africa–backed UNITA (National Union for the Total Independence of Angola) insurgents in Angola as part of an overall security policy aim of weakening neighboring states that threatened both South Africa's position in Namibia and its apartheid policies at home.

The actions of some governments were inspired by ideology. Libyan leader, Muammar el-Qaddafi propagated what he called his "third universal theory," a blend of populist, Islamic, Pan-Arab, and socialist tenets that he believed should be adopted everywhere. Identifying the principal obstacles to the spread of his ideas as the imperialist powers, Israel, and reactionary Arab regimes in the Middle East, Qaddafi sought to undermine them by sponsoring and aiding insurgents of various stripes who shared his opposition to these enemies. In the late 1970s, the Iranian revolution brought to power an Islamic government that also sought to spread its doctrines and ideas through the support of insurgents in various Middle Eastern countries (e.g., Bahrain, Kuwait, Saudi Arabia, and Lebanon).

An important point worth noting is that even though the United States partially retreated from involvement in insurgencies during the 1970s, the international dimension of insurgencies remained important because of the continued involvement of the Communist powers and the actions of regional states. In the 1980s this trend was reinforced by renewed American involvement in situations involving insurgent groups.

Renewed American Involvement

During the Nixon years, the administration's move away from entanglement in foreign insurrections was reflected in the Nixon Doctrine, which allowed for advice and assistance to friendly governments threatened by insurgents but precluded military involvement. As noted earlier, this policy was the result of both the public aversion to "new Vietnams" and the administration's strategic assumption that the East-West conflict should be addressed primarily in terms of major-power politics, with less attention paid to peripheral, Third World areas.

The Nixon Doctrine notwithstanding, flexible response remained the conceptual cornerstone of U.S. defense policy. Although this strategy meant that theoretically the United States should be able to respond differentially and proportionately to threats on the nuclear, conventional, and insurgent levels of conflict, the attention and resources devoted to the insurgent level of conflict diminished considerably in the Nixon, Ford, and Carter years. But, as is so often the case, at the very time this trend was dominant, new events in the international arena were slowly giving rise to a countertrend that eventually refocused American attention on insurgent conflicts. Among these events were transnational terrorism, the oil embargo and production cutbacks of 1973, the Iranian revolution, and the 1979 Soviet invasion of Afghanistan.

The upsurge of transnational terrorism came in the wake of Jordan's rout of the Palestinian guerrillas in 1970 and 1971. Motivated by a variety of aims, the Black September Organization and other Palestinian groups carried out a series of bombings, assassinations, kidnappings, skyjackings, and the like. Their acts, together with similar ones by a growing number of ideologically disparate insurgent groups, compelled the United States to adopt political and military countermeasures to protect its citizens.

The renewed attention to insurgent conflicts created by terrorism was reinforced by the oil embargo of 1973 and subsequent price increases, which made the West acutely aware of its vulnerability to disruptions in the supply and price of vital raw materials. Of the many dangers to the supply of raw materials that defense planners envisaged, one of the most troublesome was the threat posed to governments of oil-producing states by insurgents hostile to Western interests. As analysts looked at the problem, questions reminiscent of the Kennedy years began to resurface: Which regimes are vulnerable? Is their existence vital to American interests? What are the social, economic, and political sources of instability? What American policies could prevent or mitigate political upheaval? Under what circumstances should the United States intervene? How should it intervene?

Whatever fears the West had about the potential of insurgent movements to threaten its interests were realized by the overthrow of the seemingly durable Shah of Iran and the establishment of an Islamic regime antipathetic to both the United States and neighboring Arab oil producers in the critical Persian Gulf. Before long, Teheran became a center for various insurgent groups opposed to governments in the area that were either major oil producers (Saudi Arabia) or contiguous to the major producers (Oman).

The renewed concern about insurgent warfare increased further with the Soviet invasion of Afghanistan in December 1979. In this case, however, attention was focused on how effectively insurgency might be used against the Soviets by rebels who were already actively opposing the Marxist regime that had seized power in April 1978.

When the Reagan administration came to office in the wake of these events, the differences became sharper between those advisers who wished to avoid involvement in insurgencies and those who felt it might not be possible. The latter's attitude was due, in large part, to the convergence of two factors: the general threat perceptions of the president and the growing insurrection in El Salvador. As far as President Reagan and most of his advisers were concerned, the Soviet threat was paramount because a long-term nuclear- and conventional-arms buildup by the Soviet Union had shifted the superpower military balance in its favor and enabled it to expand its influence geographically through the deployment of its own personnel, or surrogates, to places like Angola, Afghanistan, Ethiopia, Libya, Syria, South Yemen, and Vietnam. The Reagan administration further believed that unless the Soviets were checked, they would continue this process of expansion, using in some cases the instigation of, or support for, insurgencies in countries that had pro-Western governments.

Even though the Soviet threat was uppermost in the minds of the Reagan defense establishment, there was increased concern that serious threats to American interests could be posed by radical insurgents independent of Moscow. But, even in these cases, there was still a fear that the Soviet Union would benefit from a diminution of Western power, which could result from insurgent victories. In light of its assumptions about the Soviet Union's improved capability to project military power and its proclivity to exploit Western vulnerabilities, that the Reagan administration exhibited fears about revolutionary insurgencies in Guatemala and, especially, El Salvador was not surprising. From the administration's point of view, both situations were part of a Soviet design to spread Marxism in the western hemisphere, and they had to be contained. Consequently, the United States gave strong moral and political support to the threatened governments, increased military and economic assistance, established a counterinsurgency training program for the Salvadoran military, and dispatched advisers to the area. Pressure, albeit uneven, was exerted on El Salvador to implement human rights reforms and land redistribution. Although American combat units were not directly engaged, it had become clear that the post-Vietnam aversion to involvement in insurgencies had been overtaken by events.

Despite its very busy domestic agenda and immersion in relations with the Soviet Union and the Middle East, the Reagan administration's involvement with insurgencies during its second term in office did not change perceptibly. Attention and various forms of assistance were directed not just to governments like those of El Salvador and the Philippines, which were threatened by Marxist insurgents, but also to rebels who were fighting Marxist regimes in Angola, Nicaragua, and Afghanistan. Moreover, the regional conflicts became an important part of the diplomatic discussions between the superpowers, while the Department of Defense, as part of its overall buildup, once again devoted increased resources to special forces of various kinds.

Insurgencies were not the only concern of the national security policy community, however. Drug dealers and international terrorists acting on behalf of governments posed new threats. Their actions and those of insurgents hostile to the West were viewed as manifestations of "low-intensity conflicts" that could threaten the security interests of the United States and its friends. This led various U.S. government agencies dealing with national security policy to search for doctrinal principles and organizational formats for waging low-intensity conflicts.

As of this writing, the search for a general, cohesive doctrine and organization for dealing with low-intensity conflict has not been notably successful, largely because drug dealing, international terrorism, and insurgency differ substantially with respect to purpose, modus operandi, and vulnerability to various countermeasures. In view of these differences, there is no effort to lump them together in this book. Instead, I will focus exclusively on insurgency, which by itself is a multifaceted and complex subject.

Purpose

This brief summary of the role of insurgencies since World War II is not intended as a moral or political critique of past roles played by internal and external participants in these conflicts. Its purpose is to underscore the persistent importance of insurgency as a type of conflict in the international system. Insurgency will likely continue to be prominent because there are no signs that the problems of national cohesion and economic development that give rise to these conflicts will be solved. Moreover, while Soviet involvement may diminish as a result of the changes in Soviet foreign policy stemming from Mikhail Gorbachev's "new thinking," rivalries between and among major and regional powers will doubtless continue, and subversion of adversaries will be viewed in many countries as an attractive and rational alternative to the costs of major interstate wars.

The persistence of many current insurgencies and the emergence of unforeseen ones mean that participants, journalists, students, government analysts, and scholars in many parts of the world will be spending considerable time trying to better understand and evaluate them. The main purpose of this book is to provide a method of analysis that will be helpful in these endeavors. The framework is designed to bring together factors that can have a crucial bearing on the progress and outcome of insurgent conflicts. These factors, which are set forth in succeeding chapters, focus attention on key questions that should be asked about all insurgencies, regardless of time and place.

The components of the framework are not the product of a random selection process. They were abstracted from an exhaustive review of the literature, including theoretical and historical writings by scholars and articles, books, and monographs by participants, journalists, and other observers. Once these components were identified, the literature was again reviewed to collate, compare, and synthesize various insights regarding them. The framework for analysis was then applied to a wide range of cases to test for consistency and validity. Although I try throughout the study to identify, define, and suggest relationships among the factors, I make no pretense that I am providing a formal theory or model. The framework does, however, provide a systematic, straightforward format for comprehensively analyzing or comparing insurgencies.

There is no assumption that all concepts, definitions, propositions, hypotheses, and examples in the framework are flawless. My experience with both this framework and other conceptual devices in the social sciences suggests that all conceptual schemata should be open to refinements, deletions, additions, and qualifications. Accordingly, case studies are crucially important because of what we learn about the particular situations under consideration and because of ideas and findings that will improve the framework. The framework used in this book is the product of an evolutionary process, involving many changes suggested by numerous case studies. While I believe its value has thus been improved, I fully anticipate the evolutionary process to continue, for there is much still to be learned.

I make no effort to pass judgment on whether such things as particular insurgencies, governments, strategies, forms of warfare, types of organization, and external support are inherently good or bad, moral or immoral. The object is to develop concepts that can be used to pose essential questions.

The concepts used in the framework will be defined, discussed, and illustrated extensively. Definitions are, of course, somewhat arbitrary and, with respect to insurgency, can be quite contentious. Terms like *insurgency, guerrilla warfare, terrorism,* and *revolutionary* have not only been defined in various ways but have often been used interchangeably. To avoid the confusion and obfuscation that are inevitable when definitions are unclear, I have set forth what I mean by the various terms and then tried to use them consciously and consistently in case studies. This does not mean the definitions cannot be changed or refined at some point; they can and have been. But analysis, communications, and mutual understanding are all served by adhering to common concepts, however imperfect, until such time as they are redefined.

The discussion of the concepts is based on a wide variety of written works, including my own. The examples and illustrations are drawn from both these sources and extensive case studies completed by either graduate students at civilian universities or highly select groups of midcareer government officials. Some cases, such as the insurgencies in Eritrea, the Western Sahara, El Salvador, Northern Ireland, Guatemala, Angola, Afghanistan, Nicaragua, Italy, and the Philippines, have been analyzed at various times in the last twelve years by more than twenty different groups, all of which used continually updated information. Other cases—such as the ones involving the Tamils in Sri Lanka, Sendero Luminoso in Peru, South-West African People's Organization in Namibia, the Monteneros in Argentina, and the Thai National Liberation Front in Thailand—have been examined by more than ten independent groups. Many of the strong points of consensus among these groups are reflected in the commentary and illustrations in the pages ahead.

The presentation of the framework begins in chapter two with a definition of insurgency and a discussion of various goals insurgents pursue, types of insurgencies, and forms of warfare. Chapter 3 deals with different strategic approaches insurgents may adopt and suggests the relative importance they ascribe to the environment, popular support, organization and unity, external support, and government response. In chapters 4 through 8, each of those factors is discussed separately and a number of relationships between and among them are drawn. I believe this framework can assist readers concerned with this vital subject, whatever their specific interests.

II   The Nature of Insurgency

INSURGENCY MAY BE DEFINED AS A STRUGGLE BETWEEN A nonruling group and the ruling authorities in which the nonruling group consciously uses *political resources* (e.g., organizational expertise, propaganda, and demonstrations) and *violence* to destroy, reformulate, or sustain the basis of legitimacy of one or more aspects of politics.[1] Legitimacy and illegitimacy are terms used to determine whether existing aspects of politics are considered moral or immoral—right or wrong—by the population or selected elements thereof. For present purposes, politics is defined as the process of making and executing binding decisions for a society. Generally, the major aspects of politics may be identified as the political community, the political system, the authorities, and policies. Any or all of these may be considered illegitimate by insurgents, and it makes a great deal of difference precisely which one is at stake.[2]

Aspects of Politics

THE POLITICAL COMMUNITY

The political community consists of those who interact on a regular basis in the process of making and executing binding decisions. These interactions may consist of active participation in the policy process or simply passive acceptance of the decisions. Although political communities have varied in size throughout history, with some even being empires, in the contemporary international system the political community is, for the most part, equivalent to the state. Most citizens in the Western blocs take the political community for granted, although their respective countries may contain a multiplicity of ethnic, religious, and racial groups. Even where group animosities and conflicts over political and material resources are strong (e.g., the Flemings and Walloons in Belgium), people have been accustomed to being part of geographically distinct states that enjoy historical continuity and international recognition. There are, of course, exceptions, such as the members of the Basque Homeland and Liberty (ETA, from its Basque name) in Spain and of the Irish Republican Army (IRA) in the United Kingdom, both of which violently reject the idea that they should be in the political communities of which they are nominally a part.

While violent rejection of the political community is the exception rather than the rule in the Western and Soviet blocs, the Third World has experienced substantial conflict related to the legitimacy of political communities. This is not surprising, since the boundaries of many states in the developing world were established by former imperial powers with little regard to the distribution of ethnocultural groups. Thus, in Africa, the Middle East, and Asia, it is not uncommon to find major ethnic and religious groups either living in two or more contiguous states (e.g., the Pathans in Afghanistan and Pakistan; the Kurds in Iraq, Iran, Turkey, the Soviet Union, and Syria; and the Baluchi in Afghanistan, Pakistan, and Iran) or being incorporated into political entities in which they are subjected to rule by rival groups (e.g., the subordination of the Islamic Moros to Christian rule in the Philippines and the Eritreans to Amhara rule in Ethiopia). In all these examples, as well as in a number of other situations, violent conflict over the legitimacy of the political community has occurred at some time or another in the past few decades.

THE POLITICAL SYSTEM

Where a consensus on the legitimacy of the political community exists, there may be other grounds for internal warfare. A case in point is violent discord over the political system—that is, the salient values, rules, and structures that make up the basic framework guiding and limiting the making and execution of binding decisions.* "Values" are general ideas of the desirable, such as equality, justice, liberty, and individualism, whereas "rules" encourage desired patterns of behavior (e.g., prohibition of private property is a rule that supports the value of equality). Over the years, political scientists, anthropologists, and sociologists have used many different terms and concepts (e.g., *high and low authoritarian, pluralistic, polyarchic, traditional, autocratic, oligarchical, monarchical,* and *totalitarian*) to describe and contrast political systems. From several that could be adopted, I have

---

*In previous iterations of the framework, the term *regime* was used to refer to salient values, rules, and structures. However, since the term *regime* has sinister connotations, I have chosen to replace it with *political system.* Although *political system* is often associated with all aspects of politics, the more restricted definition used herein should be less distracting to the general readership for whom this book is intended.

chosen four models developed by Charles F. Andrain. Although they are ideal types from which actual systems may diverge in specific ways, they nonetheless capture the basic differences between systems.

The first political system, *traditional autocracy,* is one in which elitism, ascription (birthright), and personalism are key values. Top decisionmakers are drawn from a small group—a family, clan, or lineage—that is considered to have the exclusive right to rule. The personal traits of the top leader are extolled and his right to rule is further legitimatized by sacred (religious) values that often portray him as divinely anointed. Government is marked by limited institutional development. Such groups as the clergy, landowners, and the military provide support for the regime and in return gain security and various socioeconomic privileges. And, while local leaders are left to control affairs at the lowest levels, they play little or no role in national-level policymaking. The general public, meanwhile, is expected to be apathetic and loyal.

While in the past there was little attention to economic modernization and bureaucratic development, in today's world traditional leaders are compelled to pay more attention to these matters because of the rising expectations of their populations. When this occurs, as it did in Saudi Arabia and Iran, traditional autocracies may be forced to transform themselves into a second type of system, *modernizing autocracies,* which like traditional systems, are characterized by elite rule. While political systems in transition from traditional to modernizing autocracies may continue to stress birthright and religious values as a basis for rule, building state power is the highest value of the modernizing autocracy. As this value is pursued, rule becomes more bureaucratic and impersonal and the structure of power evolves into a hierarchical one, with a president, military officer, or similar personage at the top. The leader functions as a patron who dispenses favors to military, police, bureaucrats, and landowners in return for their support. Unlike the traditional system, a more complex administrative apparatus manages affairs. While the state may control or even own more economic enterprises, a good deal of regulated private activity is permitted. Changes tend to be directed from the top, and the masses do not actively participate in the political process.

The third and most authoritarian political system is the *totalitarian* one. Its goal is to control completely all aspects of the political, economic, and social life of its citizens. Accomplishing this goal is, of course, far from easy, especially in developing countries, with their weak technological and/ or bureaucratic infrastructures. Whatever the case, the values of consensus and equality are primary in totalitarian regimes. And while populist rhetoric is commonplace and mass participation is encouraged in the process of reconstructing society, participation is controlled and orchestrated by a leadership elite, usually organized in a vanguard party that claims to represent the popular will. The top leaders use a complex bureaucracy, the media, the educational system, and a host of societal groups (e.g., peasant, workers', writers', and women's organizations) to carry out and control ambitious socioeconomic programs. With few exceptions, economic activity is in the hands of the public sector.

The fourth type of political system, the *pluralistic* (i.e., democratic), differs substantially from the authoritarian types. The principal values are individual freedom, liberty, and compromise. Numerous political structures exist within, and outside of, government. Those outside, such as political parties, the media, and interest groups, act autonomously. While precise institutional arrangements vary among pluralist systems, in all cases limits are placed on the powers of the top leaders by written or unwritten constitutions, which provide mechanisms for their periodic approval or removal.

No doubt the most notable contemporary examples of insurgencies motivated by a rejection of the political system are those led by Marxists, who view traditional and modernizing autocracies, as well as pluralist systems, as basically exploitative of workers and peasants because the values, norms, and structures of such systems serve the interests of feudal or capitalist classes. The Popular Front for the Liberation of Oman (PFLO), for example, accepts the political community, but utterly rejects the traditional autocracy led by the sultan. Through political efforts and through violence, it seeks to expunge the values of elitism, birthright, and religion (in this case, Islam) and the patrimonial structures of the sultanate and to replace them with a system in which binding decisions would be made by a single mass party that extols the values of equality and populism.[3] Traditional systems are not the only ones targeted by insurgents. Modernizing autocratic systems in Syria and Iraq are opposed by Muslim insurgents; pluralist systems in West Germany, Belgium, France, and Japan are confronted by anarchist and Marxist insurgents, and totalitarian systems in Angola, Cambodia, and Vietnam are also under attack. The common goal of the insurgents in all these and similar cases is to radically transform the political system.

THE AUTHORITIES

Another aspect of politics that may lead to insurrection involves the *authorities*. While some groups may not quarrel with the political community or the system, they may consider specific individuals illegitimate because their behavior is inconsistent with existing values and norms or because they are viewed as corrupt, ineffective, or oppressive. This situation is normally exemplified by coups in which insurgents seize top decision-making offices without changing the system of their predecessors. The well-known Latin American cases of the 1950s and the 1970 overthrow of the Sultan Said bin Taimur of Oman by his son Qabus provide illustrations.[4]

POLICIES

Finally, nonruling groups may resort to violence to change existing social, economic, or political policies that they believe discriminate against particular groups in the population (e.g., ethnic, religious, racial, and/or economic). A recent example is the terminal phase of the insurgency in the Sudan in the 1960s, where blacks in the south demanded a change in policies related to economic power and resources; another is the periodic attempts by moderate Shiite and Druse elements in Lebanon to redress the perceived maldistribution of political and economic assets that until now have favored the Christian community. While policies are clearly the major focus of the insurgents, in some cases they may also seek to displace authority figures they consider uncompromising.

The important thing to bear in mind is that insurgency is essentially a political legitimacy crisis of some kind. The task of the analyst, therefore, is to identify exactly what is at stake. To do so, it is necessary to ascertain the long-term goal of the insurgents and the relationship of that goal to the aspects of politics (the political community, political system, authorities, and policies).

Types of Insurgencies

When we look at the ultimate goals of insurgent movements and the aspects of politics they focus on, some very important distinctions emerge. If we fail to see the fundamental differences with respect to goals, we make a major mistake because, as we shall see later, differentiating among goals has not only academic value but some vital practical implications for those involved in insurgent conflicts. So the first question an analyst must answer is, What type of insurgency are we dealing with? In answering that question it is useful to be aware of the several types, their differences, and their goals.

Our research suggests seven types of insurgent movements—anarchist, egalitarian, traditionalist, pluralist, secessionist, reformist, and preservationist. The first four are all revolutionary because they seek to completely change an existing political system.

ANARCHIST

Without doubt the most far-reaching goal is espoused by the anarchist insurgents, who wish to eliminate all institutionalized political arrangements because they view the superordinate-subordinate authority relationships associated with them as unnecessary and illegitimate. Various groups in czarist Russia and Europe near the turn of the century fall into this category, as do several groups in more recent times, such as the Black Cells and the Black Help in West Germany in the 1970s. None of the contemporary groups have been particularly significant, however. Egalitarian insurgents, by contrast, have been quite prevalent, largely because Marxists fall within this category.

EGALITARIAN

Egalitarian insurgent movements seek to impose a new system based on the ultimate value of distributional equality and centrally controlled structures designed to mobilize the people and radically transform the social structure within an existing political community. This type of insurgency has been a familiar part of the post–World War II international political landscape and is epitomized by violent Marxist groups such as the Malayan Communist Party, the New People's Army (NPA) in the Philippines, the Viet Cong in South Vietnam, the Thai National Liberation Front, the Japanese Red Army, the Fedayeen-i-Khalq in Iran, the PFLO in Oman, the Democratic and Popular Fronts for the Liberation of Palestine, the Sendero Luminoso (Shining Path or SL) in Peru, and the principal groups in the Farabundo Martí National Liberation Front (FMLN) in El Salvador. Non-Communist egalitarian insurgents are exemplified by Ba'athist groups in the Middle East, especially those that seized power in Iraq and Syria.[5] Despite their populist rhetoric, egalitarian insurgents who come to power normally establish political systems that are authoritarian, repressive, and elitist.

TRADITIONALIST

Traditionalist insurgents also seek to displace the political system, but the values they articulate are primordial and sacred ones, rooted in ancestral ties and religion. The political structures they seek to establish are characterized by limited or guided participation and low autonomy, with political power in the hands of an autocratic leader supported by the nobility, army, and clergy. While the majority of the population may enjoy some autonomy at the local level, widespread participation in national politics, especially by organized opposition groups, is discouraged. In the present era, traditionalist insurgents generally struggle to restore a system that existed in the recent or distant past. Recent and current traditionalist insurgents include those who supported the return of the Imam in the Yemen Arab Republic (North Yemen) in the 1960s, groups in the Contra movement in Nicaragua, and moderate Islamic groups in Afghanistan, such as Muhammad Gailani's National Islamic Front for the Liberation of Afghanistan. Within the category of traditionalist insurgents one also finds more zealous groups seeking to reestablish an ancient political system that they idealize as a golden age. We refer to this subtype as *reactionary-traditionalists*. The Muslim Brotherhood in Syria, Islamic Jihad and Takfir wa Hejra in Egypt, Hezbollah in Lebanon, and the Hezb-i-Islami (Party of Islam) of Gulbuddin Hekmatyar in Afghanistan exemplify the reactionary-traditionalist subtype because they wish to establish Islamic political and social arrangements in accordance with either Sunni or Shiite visions (frequently distorted) of what the ideal past was really like.[6] Since reactionaries believe they are repositories of the truth, their rhetoric is dogmatic and they are intolerant toward those who do not share their views. Like the more pragmatic traditionalists, the reactionaries believe that economic and technological progress can take place in a traditional political setting. (Hekmatyar, for example, argues that unlike Christianity, there has never been a conflict in Islam between science and religion.)

PLURALIST

The last of the four insurgent groups seeking a revolutionary transformation of the political system, the pluralists, are not authoritarians. The goal of pluralist insurgents is to establish a system in which the values of individual freedom, liberty, and compromise are emphasized and in which political structures are differentiated and autonomous. While the history of Western civilization is marked by a number of such uprisings, in recent times there have been few if any insurgencies that we could confidently classify as pluralist. Case studies of almost every major insurgency since the mid-1970s suggest that while many groups use pluralistic rhetoric, their ultimate goals and behavior are anything but pluralistic. It remains to be seen whether UNITA in Angola, which calls for elections and power-sharing, and the National Resistance Movement in Uganda, which advocated human and civil rights during its struggle, will prove to be exceptions.

SECESSIONIST

The ultimate aim of secessionist (separatist) insurgents is even more far-reaching than the revolutionary goals espoused by the four types of groups we have just discussed. Secessionists renounce the political community of which they are formally a part. They seek to withdraw from it and constitute a new and independent political community. A classic example was the Confederacy during the American Civil War. In the contemporary international system, secessionist insurgent groups are especially prevalent and can be found in all corners of the globe. In Africa examples include Eritrean and Afar liberation organizations in Ethiopia, the Front for the Liberation of Rio d'Oro and Saguia el-Hamra (Polisario) in the Western Sahara (controlled by Morocco) and the South-West African People's Organization (SWAPO) in Namibia (controlled until 1990 by the Republic of South Africa). Asian secessionists include radical Sikhs of the Khalistan Liberation Front in India; the Liberation Tigers of Tamil Eelam (LTTE) in Sri Lanka; Shan, Karen, and Kachin groups in Burma; and the Baluchistan National Liberation Front in the Pakistan-Iran-Afghanistan triborder region. In the Middle East, Kurdish insurgents in Iraq and tribal rebels in Oman's Dhofar province have, at times, articulated secessionist aims. The Front for the Liberation of Corsica and the Brittany Liberation Front in France, Tirol and the Sardinian Armed Movement in Italy, and the Quebec Liberation Front in Canada are examples in Europe and North America.[7]

The type of political system that secessionists would establish varies between groups. The Sikhs in India and most of the Kurds in Iraq, for example, would no doubt opt for a traditional system, while the Eritrean Popular Liberation Front favors a Marxist-egalitarian system. Whatever the type of system they favor, the primary goal that inspires their efforts is secession. Regardless of their size and whether their focus is regional, ethnic, racial, religious, or some combination thereof, secessionists consider themselves nationalists. Accordingly, bona fide wars of national liberation such as China's anti-Japanese struggle and the Vietnamese and Algerian wars with France fall within the secessionist category because the *primary* aim was independence, not the establishment of an authoritarian political system of one sort or another. The PFLO in Oman and the NPA in the Philippines, by contrast, would not be secessionists, since they are seeking to change the political system rather than to achieve independence from rule by foreigners.[8]

REFORMIST

The sixth type of insurgency, the reformist, is the least ambitious. Exemplified in the early 1980s by the Kurds in Iran and the Miskito Indians in Nicaragua, reformists want more political, social, and economic benefits for their constituencies without rejecting the political community, system, or authorities. They are primarily concerned with the existing allocation of political and material resources, which they consider discriminatory and illegitimate.[9] Insurgents who demand autonomy, as opposed to separation, fall within the reformist category.

PRESERVATIONIST

The seventh and final type of insurgent movement is preservationist. Insurgents in this category differ from all the others because they are essentially oriented toward maintaining the status quo because of the relative political, economic, and social privileges they derive from it. Basically, preservationist insurgents seek to maintain the existing political system and policies by engaging in illegal acts of violence against nonruling groups and the authorities who are trying to effect change. The Afrikaner Resistance Movement in South Africa is one example, as is the insurrectionary movement that emerged in the early 1970s in Ulster, where Protestant organizations such as the Ulster Volunteer Force and the Ulster Defense Association have used political tactics and violence to retain a political system and policies that they believe are threatened by the IRA, Catholic moderates, the Irish Republic, and "British capitulationists." Right-wing "death squads" in Latin American countries, which are neither sanctioned by, nor have ties with, the ruling political authorities, also fall within this category. Those connected with the authorities are considered state-sponsored terrorists rather than insurgents.[10]

Identifying Insurgent Types: Four Problems

GOAL TRANSFORMATION

Although identifying types of insurgent movements may seem to be relatively easy, four complications should be kept in mind. First, some insurgent movements experience goal transformation because new leaders emerge with other goals in mind or because existing leaders calculate that less ambitious aims stand a better chance of being accomplished than old ones. The evolution of the Dhofar insurgency in Oman from a secessionist to an egalitarian one as the result of a Marxist takeover illustrates one reason for change, while the transformation of the Sudanese insurrection carried out by blacks in the southern area in the 1960s from a secessionist to reformist insurgency provides an example of lowered ambitions.

GOAL CONFLICTS

A second complication for the analyst occurs in situations where distinct groups or factions in an insurgent movement have different and at times mutually exclusive goals. One recent case is the uprising against the Marxist regime in Afghanistan, which involves reactionary-traditionalist, egalitarian, and pluralist factions. A second case is the Palestinian resistance, which contains egalitarian, traditionalist, and perhaps pluralist elements. In such circumstances, it is important to identify the lack of consensus concerning goals because of the significant effects this can have on the progression of the insurgency, not the least of which is internecine fighting, which can significantly undermine its capability.

MISLEADING RHETORIC

The third difficulty confronting a researcher is the frequent masking of ultimate goals by democratic rhetoric. When this occurs, it is particularly important to examine carefully the public and internal documents of the insurgents and the way the movement is governed before rendering a judgment about their primary or essential aspirations. The democratic pronouncements of movements that are politically pluralistic, like the Jewish Agency in Palestine during the 1940s, are far more convincing than those of centrally controlled and authoritarian organizations, such as Marxist and religiously inspired ones that claim to monopolize the truth. In the Jewish case, democratic values were actualized by the multiparty structure of the Jewish Agency, which became the basis for a democratic system once statehood was achieved. In sharp contrast is the Popular Front for the Liberation of Oman, which imposed harsh centralized rule in liberated zones during the 1960s, despite its democratic verbiage. This clearly suggests that any assessment of insurgent goals should include careful attention to how insurgents actually conduct their own political affairs.

GOAL AMBIGUITY

The final complication that may arise when trying to identify insurgent goals is ambiguity. This occurs when two or more aims may be evident, neither of which clearly predominates. Pinning down the precise aims of the Red Brigades in Italy and Sendero Luminoso (SL) in Peru, for instance, has proven difficult. In the case of the Red Brigades, the temptation to classify them as egalitarians because of their Marxist-Leninist rhetoric is mitigated by their emphasis on destroying the existing political system and the paucity of comments on what will replace it. Hence, the Brigades might be considered as anarchistic as they are egalitarian, if not more. Likewise, the SL's goal in Peru is not as clear as its Maoist ideological pronouncements might suggest, because Indian mysticism and symbols are extolled in what seems to be an attempt to synthesize traditionalism with egalitarianism.

Goal Identification

It should not be inferred from the preceding discussion that all insurgent movements are difficult to classify. To the contrary, the goals of many are straightforward, consistent with behavior, and easy to identify. Whatever the difficulty in ascertaining the goals of insurgent organizations, it is a crucial first step in any analysis; aside from its academic merits, it has a number of significant practical implications, which should become evident at various points later in this study. For now, a few general comments may help clarify this point.

To begin with, different goals place different demands on insurgents with respect to resources. Since secessionist and most especially anarchistic, traditionalist, pluralist, and egalitarian aims are by their nature not amenable to compromise, they normally result in strong resistance from authorities. This, in turn, means that in nearly all cases the insurgents must mobilize greater support and be prepared for a sustained commitment if they are to have any hope of success. Some egalitarian movements, like the Thai National Liberation Front, which are based on geographically isolated minority groups, are at a tremendous disadvantage initially because of their limited ability to mobilize support from the majority group, which sustains the political system and authorities. In contrast, reformist and preservationist groups may find that limited insurgent activity can convince the authorities to make concessions. This is because their aims do not require the political system to collapse or the authorities to abdicate. In response to reformist insurgents, the authorities may decide to cut their losses by agreeing to a more equitable distribution of political and economic benefits (e.g., the accord between the government and the southern rebels that ended the Sudanese insurrection in the 1960s). As far as preservationist challenges are concerned, the authorities may simply steer away from basic changes in the system (e.g., the British in Northern Ireland) in order to terminate or mitigate violence.

We can also see the practical importance of clarifying insurgent goals and ambitions when we look at outside powers that are thinking about becoming involved on one side or the other. Indeed, an argument can be made that the fears, commitments, and tendency of the United States in the 1960s to intervene in local conflicts was in part the result of an inclination to equate insurgency with the revolutionary aspirations of egalitarian movements. It is thus worth pointing out that calculations about intervention that gloss over ultimate insurgent aims can lead to ill-informed and costly entanglements and the creation of enemies where none existed before.

The Means: Politics and Forms of Warfare

POLITICAL MEANS

Insurgent movements use political resources and instruments of violence against the ruling authorities to accomplish their goals. Political activity includes such things as the dissemination of information (propaganda) through meetings, pamphlets, media broadcasts, and the like, arranging protest demonstrations, recruiting cadres (insurgent officials), training and infiltrating agents into the official establishment, persuading outside powers to extend various kinds of assistance, raising and managing finances, creating supportive groups (e.g., workers', farmers', women's, writers', and youth associations), providing services to the people, and devising and implementing strategies and plans. The importance of activities like these has led many analysts to characterize insurgency as primarily a political phenomenon and to attribute the success of individuals such as Mao and Ho Chi Minh more to their political acumen than their prowess as military leaders.

Success in marshaling and utilizing resources depends on effective organization. On a general level, there are two types: *selective*, where small elite groups threaten or carry out violent acts, and *mobilizational*, where insurgent elites attempt to actively involve large segments of the population on the behalf of their cause.[11] While a mobilizational organization is the most familiar to students of insurgency, because of the well-known Chinese, Vietnamese, Cambodian, Algerian, and Portuguese colonial conflicts, there are numerous examples of selective insurgencies, such as the Red Brigades in Italy, the Red Army in Japan, and the Muslim Brotherhood in Syria. Because some selective groups gradually evolve into mobilizational movements, the two are best viewed as ends of a continuum, with many cases falling between them.

The organizational effort necessary for coordinating both violent and nonviolent activity is not as demanding for a selective organization, because there is far less concern with linking the insurgency to the masses. But, in the long term, this neglect of the population often renders such groups impotent and, as a result, continues to be one of the contentious issues dividing leaders of insurgent movements. We will elaborate on this theme when we look at insurgent strategies, popular support, and organization.

The other aspect of insurgency, the use of violence, sets it apart from political protest movements like Gandhi's in India, Khomeini's in Iran, Solidarity in Poland, and the civil rights movement in the United States. One need not dispute the prominence of the political dimension of insurgencies in order to call attention to the important role that violent acts play, whether they are small-scale or take place in the context of large-scale warfare. It is not a matter of *either* politics *or* violence, but rather a matter of *both*—and the relative part they play in different situations.

FORMS OF WARFARE

The violent aspect of insurgency is manifested in different forms of warfare. A "form" of warfare may be viewed as *one variety of organized violence emphasizing particular armed forces, weapons, tactics, and targets.* Three forms of warfare have been associated with insurgent conflicts: terrorism, guerrilla war, and conventional warfare.[12]

Terrorism is a form of warfare in which violence is directed primarily against noncombatants (usually unarmed civilians), rather than operational military and police forces or economic assets (public or private). The active units of terrorist organizations are normally smaller than those of guerrillas, being composed of individuals organized covertly into cells. Their actions are familiar, consisting of such things as assassinations, bombings, tossing grenades, arson, torture, mutilation, hijacking, and kidnapping. While the targets of such violence may at times be arbitrary, often they are carefully chosen in order to maximize their political impact.[13] Although such terrorism has generally occurred within the borders of the state whose community, political system, authorities, or policies have become the focus of insurgent violence, there has been an increasing tendency since the mid-1970s to strike at targets outside the country. Because these acts are carried out by autonomous, nonstate actors, they have been referred to as *transnational terrorism* to distinguish them from similar behavior on the part of individuals or groups controlled by sovereign states *(international terrorism.)*[14]

Insurgent terrorism is purposeful, rather than mindless, violence because terrorists seek to achieve specific long-term, intermediate, and short-term goals. The long-term goal is, of course, to change the political community, political system, authorities, or policies. The intermediate goal of terrorism is not so much the desire to deplete the government's physical resources as it is to erode its psychological support by instilling fear into officials and their domestic and international supporters.

Though the general purpose of terrorism has been to alter the behavior and attitudes of specific groups, this has not excluded the simultaneous pursuit of one or more proximate objectives, such as extracting particular concessions (e.g, payment of ransom or the release of prisoners), gaining publicity, demoralizing the population through the creation of widespread disorder, provoking repression by the government, enforcing obedience and cooperation from those inside and outside the movement, fulfilling the need to avenge losses inflicted upon the movement, and enhancing the political stature of specific factions within an insurgent movement.[15] So when we look at the multitudinous aims that terrorist acts may serve, it becomes clear that we must take great care when generalizing about them. This is especially important, since similar actions may have quite different objectives. The hostage and barricade incidents in the Israeli towns of Qiryat Shemona and Ma'alot in the spring of 1974 illustrate this point well. While the release of Palestinian prisoners was demanded in each case, other, more important aims were revealed by insurgent statements. At Qiryat Shemona, the Popular Front for the Liberation of Palestine-General Command, an extreme hard-line group, sought to sabotage the peace process by increasing tensions, whereas at Ma'alot the Democratic Popular Front for the Liberation of Palestine was seeking to ensure its participation in any negotiations that might occur.

The upsurge in terrorism since the late 1970s notwithstanding, the most familiar kind of violence used by insurgents has been *guerrilla warfare*. The essence of guerrilla warfare is highly mobile hit-and-run attacks by lightly to moderately armed groups that seek to harass the enemy and gradually erode his will and capability. Guerrillas place a premium on flexibility, speed, and deception. The following comments by Mao provide an excellent summary of the basic features of guerrilla warfare:

> What is basic guerrilla strategy? Guerrilla strategy must be based primarily on alertness, mobility, and attack. It must be adjusted to the enemy situation, the terrain, the existing lines of communication, the relative strengths, the weather, and the situation of the people.
>
> In guerrilla warfare, select the tactic of seeming to come from the east and attacking from the west; avoid the solid, attack the hollow; attack; withdraw; deliver a lightning blow, seek a lightning decision. When guerrillas engage a stronger enemy, they withdraw when he advances; harass him when he stops; strike him when he is weary; pursue him when he withdraws. In guerrilla strategy, the enemy's rear, flanks, and other vulnerable spots are his vital points, and there he must be harassed, attacked, dispersed, exhausted, and annihilated.[16]

While victories are always important, they consist of relatively modest engagements followed by withdrawal and dispersal, rather than large positional battles designed to seize and hold territory. Guerrilla warfare differs from terrorism because its primary targets are the government's armed forces, police, or their support units and, in some cases, key economic targets, rather than unarmed civilians.[17] As a consequence, guerrilla units are larger than terrorist cells and tend to require a more elaborate logistical structure as well as base camps. Moreover, their locus of activity is almost exclusively in the rural areas.

Like terrorism, guerrilla warfare is a weapon of the weak; it is decisive only where the government fails to commit adequate resources to the conflict. Although Mao's ideological frame of reference led him to associate successful guerrilla warfare with left-wing revolutions and to dismiss its use by traditionalists as a contradiction of the "law of historical development," its successful use by traditionalists in Afghanistan suggests that such a limited perspective is myopic, to say the least.

Whether or not guerrilla warfare alone can be successful is another matter. In many cases, it has been necessary to combine guerrilla warfare with other forms of violence or to make a transition into *conventional* warfare (the direct confrontation of large units in the field) to achieve success. In most, but not all, insurgencies in which conventional warfare has been used, mobility has received great emphasis. Whether the transition to conventional warfare takes place depends on the strategy of the insurgents and judgments about the vulnerability of the government's armed forces to conventional attacks.

Three points should be kept in mind when identifying the forms of warfare used by insurgents. First, insurgents may use more than one form of warfare; the combination of terrorism and guerrilla warfare is the most common. An example would be indiscriminate bombings in civilian areas (terrorism) and guerrilla attacks in the countryside by the *mujahidin* in Afghanistan. Where this occurs, the analyst will want to ascertain what the most prominent form of warfare is.

The second point is that although many actions of insurgents are often categorized very easily, others may not be; they fall into gray areas. As noted, terrorism is primarily directed at unarmed noncombatants, while guerrilla warfare is aimed at the government's military and police forces. With this in mind, it is easy to designate indiscriminate bombing by the IRA of civilians in department stores, pubs, and the like as terrorism. But the bombings of military barracks and vehicles and sniper attacks on police and military officers by the IRA and by other groups, such as the Basque ETA in Spain, are more akin to guerrilla warfare. Indeed, these same acts in rural settings have always been subsumed within the context of guerrilla warfare.[18] In the IRA case, of course, the setting is urban and the size of the armed units is smaller. In addressing the differences between guerrilla warfare in rural and urban settings, Che Guevara pointed out that guerrilla operations in cities are less independent than those in rural areas and units that are very small (four or five men) because in urban areas the government's vigilance is greater and the possibilities of betrayal and reprisals increase enormously.[19]

The third thing to remember when dealing with forms of warfare is that *terrorism* is a highly politicized and emotive term. Nobody wants to admit that his or her group or the group he or she supports engages in terrorism. As a result, groups that carry out terrorist actions call themselves "freedom fighters." From our perspective, the dichotomy between terrorist and freedom fighter is a false one because the term *freedom fighter* has to do with ends (e.g., the secessionist goal of freeing one's people from control by another or the egalitarian aim of freeing workers and peasants from the oppression of an exploitative political system), while *terrorism* connotes means. Hence, one can be a freedom fighter who uses terrorism to achieve his purposes. The analyst, of course, must depict things as they are, regardless of his feelings about the insurgents. For the neutral or outside analyst this is easier than for an analyst who supports insurgents. But for the partisan analyst it may be more important because prolonged and indiscriminate terrorism can (as we shall see later) undercut support for insurgents, and ignoring or refusing to admit it means insurgents never address the problems or come to terms with the counterproductive aspects of terrorism as an instrument for furthering their cause. In short, the partisan analyst may fail to identify correctly and promptly the problems that the use of prolonged terrorism will eventually cause the movement. All analysts need to be scrupulously objective. If insurgent actions meet the criteria of terrorism as it is defined above, then they are using terrorism as a form of warfare.

Summary

When seeking to understand an insurgency, the first consideration is the nature of the insurgency. It is essential to ascertain first what type or types of insurgents one is dealing with, by carefully examining their ultimate goals and the means they are using to achieve their goals. It is especially important to distinguish among forms of warfare because they not only differ in terms of their purposes, targets, activities, and scale of organization but also with regard to the problems they pose for, and the requirements they place on, both sides.

Once the type of insurgency and forms of warfare have been identified, the next step is to address the various strategic approaches that insurgents adopt to maximize the effectiveness of political techniques and forms of warfare in their quest for victory. The strategies vary as to the relative importance they ascribe to six general variables: environment, popular support, organization, unity, external support, and the government response.

In the next chapter we will therefore address the crucial question of insurgent strategies.

Notes

1.   The definition of *insurgency* here is similar to that characterizing civil war in J.K. Zawodny, "Civil War," in *International Encyclopedia of the Social Sciences* (New York: Macmillan 1968), Vol. 7, p. 499, as cited in Sam C. Sarkesian, "Revolutionary Guerrilla Warfare: An Introduction," in Sam C. Sarkesian, ed., *Revolutionary Guerrilla Warfare* (Chicago: Precedent Publishing, Inc., 1975), p. 4. The use of violence by opponents of the government distinguishes insurgencies from sociopolitical protest movements, such as those led by Gandhi in India, Khomeini in Iran, and Solidarity in Poland. Those interested in systematically analyzing such movements will find Jerrold Green's use of the concept "countermobilization" in the Iran case very helpful; see his "Countermobilization as a Revolutionary Form," *Comparative Politics* (January 1984). The centrality of legitimacy in insurgencies is noted by Harry Eckstein, "On the Etiology of Internal Wars," *History and Theory* 4, no. 2 (1965): 133.
2.   On the question of legitimacy and parts of the political system, see Charles F. Andrain, *Political Life and Social Change*, 2d ed. (Belmont, Calif.: Duxbury Press, 1974), pp. 150–159; and David Easton, *A Systems Analysis of Political Life* (New York: John Wiley and Sons, 1965), pp. 171–219.
3.   Andrain, *Political Life and Social Change*, pp. 7, 191–262.
4.   Military coups fall within the broad scope of the definition. Even though those who engineer coups may occupy supportive roles in the political system, they are not, strictly speaking, part of the "ruling authorities." Indeed, one of the reasons for coups is to seize control of the highest offices or create new ones.
5.   The term *revolution* as used in this book refers primarily to political revolution. Whether or not it will be followed by a social revolution that drastically changes the class stratification system will depend upon subsequent actions by the new revolutionary elite and the response to those actions. The importance of value changes and the relationship between values and structures is the principal focus of Chalmers Johnson's *Revolutionary Change* (Boston: Little, Brown, 1965), a seminal work on the application of systems theory to revolution. For a comparison and evaluation of the explanatory power of Johnson's work vis-à-vis several other approaches, see Waltraud Q. Morales, *Social Revolution: Theory and Historical Explanation* (Denver: Denver University, 1973).
6.   For a discussion of the utopian (golden age) conceptualization of Islamic groups, see Gilles Kepel, *Muslim Extremism in Egypt* (Berkeley: University of California Press, 1984), pp. 226–240.
7.   Readers interested in secessionist groups will find *Conflict* 8, nos. 2/3 (1988), very informative because it contains several good articles. These include Wade Wheelock, "The Sikhs: Religious Militancy, Government Oppression or Politics as Usual," pp. 97–109; Vittorfranco Pisano, "Terrorist Ethnic Separatism in France and Italy," pp. 83–95; Robert C. Oberst, "Sri Lanka's Tamil Tigers," pp. 185–202;

and Paul Henze, "Ethnic Strains and Regional Conflict in Ethiopa," pp. 111–140.
8.   The difference between secessionists and other types of insurgents is exemplified in the following comments by Yasir Ahmad, a member of the Afar Sultanate
Liberation Front in Ethiopia, a Muslim organization that seeks to separate from
Christian-controlled Ethiopia:

> We are not a revolution that broke out to change the existing regime or cor-
> rupt rule. We have existed as a distinct nation, with its people, land, leader-
> ship, and culture, for centuries. We are a nation which was exposed to a
> crusader invasion, followed by a Communist invasion with the support of a
> superpower. We are resisting this invasion with the faith we derive from our
> Islamic belief.
>
>   We fought the Abyssinian empires until they became exhausted. We
> imposed a peaceful-coexistence agreement on them under which we allowed
> them safe passage through our territory to the sea in return for money. They
> exploited our goodwill, and through the help of the crusader states they in-
> cluded our territory in the map of the empire.

See "Afar Liberation Leader Interviewed on Struggle," *Al-Qabas* (Kuwait;
June 10, 1988), p. 7; repr. in *Foreign Broadcast Information Service Daily Report,
Africa*, no. 88114 (June 14, 1988), p. 2.
9.   While the Kurds in Iraq at one time had a secessionist goal, their demands
during the mid-1970s were essentially reformist (to wit, increased revenues from
oil, more social services, and a substantial degree of political autonomy within the
framework of Iraq). The current Kurdish insurrection in Iran also has reformist
aims, despite claims by the government that they are secessionist.
10.   Quite often the term *counterrevolutionary* is used to refer to preservationist
insurgents. See, for instance, Don R. Bowen, "Counterrevolutionary War: Missouri,
1861–1865," *Conflict* 8, no. 1 (1988): 69–70. Some scholars have analyzed preservationist insurgents within the context of "vigilantism"—that is, acts or threats of
coercion that are conducted by individuals and groups seeking to defend the existing
order against subversion and that transgress the accepted normative restraints on
coercion in a polity. See H. Jon Rosenbaum and Peter C. Sederberg, "Vigilantism:
An Analysis of Establishment Violence," in H. Jon Rosenbaum and Peter C. Sederberg, eds., *Vigilante Politics* (Philadelphia: University of Pennsylvania Press, 1976),
pp. 4–5. The concept of vigilantism is broader than the category of preservationist
insurgency in that it encompasses coercion that receives support from the ruling
authorities, but we are interested only in cases where it is applied by autonomous
groups. Otherwise put, we concentrate on insurgent vigilantism. For an incisive
commentary on the Protestant preservationist insurgents (regime control vigilantes),
see Richard Ned Lebow, "Vigilantism in Northern Ireland," also in *Vigilante Politics*, pp. 248–250. Also see Julian Braum, "Northern Ireland's Fighting Protestants,"
Christian Science Monitor, March 31, 1988.
11.   On this distinction, see Ted Robert Gurr, *Why Men Rebel* (Princeton, N.J.:
Princeton University Press, 1970), pp. 10–11. I have substituted the terms *selective*
and *mobilizational* for *conspiratorial* and *internal* war to avoid confusion, since I
use the latter terms for different purposes later in the book.
12.   Samuel P. Huntington, "Guerrilla Warfare in Theory and Policy," in Franklin

Mark Osanka, ed. *Modern Guerrilla Warfare* (New York: The Free Press of Glencoe, 1962), p. xvi; Arthur Campbell, *Guerrillas* (New York: The John Day Company, 1968), p. 3.

13.   The attributes of political terrorism are analyzed cogently by Paul Wilkinson, *Political Terrorism* (New York: John Wiley and Sons, 1974), pp. 14–18.

14.   See U.S. Central Intelligence Agency, Research Study, *International and Transnational Terrorism: Diagnosis and Prognosis* (Washington, D.C.: CIA, April 1976), pp. 8–9. The University of Oklahoma Study Group on Terrorism subsumes both international and transnational terrorism within a broader category that it calls "nonterritorial terrorism." See Charles Wise and Stephen Sloan, "Countering Terrorism: The U.S. and Israeli Approach," *Middle East Review* (Spring 1977): 55. Needless to say, actions by governments may also be considered terrorist acts.

15.   On terrorist aims, see Brian Jenkins, "International Terrorism: A Balance Sheet," *Survival* (July/August 1975): 158–160; Bard E. O'Neill, "Towards a Typology of Political Terrorism: The Palestinian Movement," *Journal of International Affairs* (Spring/Summer 1978): 35–37, 42; and Brian Crozier, *A Theory of Conflict* (New York: Charles Scribner's Sons, 1974), pp. 127–128. Although much attention has been given it, a precise definition agreeable to all or most scholars has remained elusive. For a representative sampling of recent attempts to grapple with the definitional problem, see Wilkinson, *Political Terrorism*, pp. 9–31; David Fromkin, "The Strategy of Terrorism," *Foreign Affairs* (July 1975): 692–693; H. Edward Price, Jr., "The Strategy and Tactics of Revolutionary Terrorism," *Comparative Studies in Society and History* (January 1977): 52–53; Jay Mallin, "Terrorism as a Military Weapon," *Air University Review* (January–February 1977): 60; Central Intelligence Agency, Research Study, *International and Transnational Terrorism: Diagnosis and Prognosis*, pp. 8–9; Jordan J. Paust, "A Definitional Focus," in Yonah Alexander and Seymour Maxwell Finger, eds., *Terrorism: Interdisciplinary Perspectives* (New York: John Jay Press, 1977), pp. 19–25; and Martha Grenshaw Hutchinson, "The Concept of Revolutionary Terrorism," *Journal of Conflict Resolution* (September 1972):383–385. The last mentioned is a particularly admirable effort to define terrorism, albeit only in its revolutionary variation.

16.   Mao Tse-tung, *On Guerrilla Warfare*, Samuel B. Griffith, trans. (New York: Fredrick A. Praeger, 1962), p. 46. On the attributes of guerrilla warfare, see Julian Paget, *Counter-Insurgency Campaigning* (New York: Walker & Co., 1967), p. 15.

17.   This definition is similar to the one Robert B. Asprey uses in his *War in the Shadows*, 2 vols. (Garden City, N.Y.: Doubleday, 1975). Whereas Asprey identifies the target of the small-scale attacks as "orthodox military forces" (Vol. 1, p. xi), we have expanded it to include police and key economic targets. Further insights concerning guerrilla warfare may be found in Edward E. Rice, *Wars of the Third Kind* (Berkeley: University of California Press, 1988), pp. 61–66; and *Guerrilla Warfare*, John Pimlott, ed. (New York: Bison Books, 1985), pp. 34, 44–45.

18.   *New York Times*, August 23, 1988. My own research on the ETA, which included conversations with both Spanish and American officials in Madrid in the spring of 1988, uncovered a strong consensus that ETA targets were primarily military and Guardia Civile personnel.

19.   Che Guevara, *Guerrilla Warfare* (New York: Vintage Books, 1961), pp. 29–31.

III   Insurgent Strategies

THE PREVIOUS CHAPTER DISCUSSED GOALS AND FORMS OF warfare insurgents may adopt. How their ends and means are related brings us to the crucial matter of strategy. For our purposes, *strategy* is defined as the systematic, integrated, and orchestrated use of various means to achieve goals. What kinds of goals are chosen, which means are emphasized, and how systematic the plans are will differ considerably from case to case.

Strategies also vary in terms of conceptual sophistication, ranging from the clearly and carefully articulated to the inchoate. Moreover, like the grand strategies of states, insurgents implement their strategies in less than ideal fashion because of the interplay of conflicting political interests, limited material resources, and unanticipated events or because insurgents sometimes adopt strategies that others have used successfully but that are inappropriate for the different environment in which they are operating. One reason for the latter phenomenon is that the previously successful insurgent leaders were able to convince others that their strategy had universal applicability.

Strategic Approaches

To make it easier to understand and evaluate insurgent strategies, we will concentrate on four broad strategic approaches that have provided guidance, if not inspiration, for many recent and contemporary insurgent leaders. Where appropriate, we will examine the importance of popular and external support, organization, cohesion, the environment, and the government's role (the strategic factors that comprise the criteria for evaluating insurgencies that we will discuss in later chapters). We will also look at significant shifts in emphasis and new ideas within the contexts of the four approaches.

THE CONSPIRATORIAL STRATEGY

Perhaps the oldest and least complicated insurgent strategy is the conspiratorial one, which seeks to remove the ruling authorities through a limited but swift use of force. Conspiracies are basically coups led by either military officers, who are not part of the ruling elite, or civilians. In many cases the removal of the authorities is considered necessary to achieve the real goal, which is to change policies and/or a political system that insurgents consider illegitimate. In other situations, the aim may be to replace the authorities either because they are threatening to undertake major policy initiatives that will upset the existing distribution of social, economic, and political privileges (preservationist insurgents) or because the leaders are perceived to be corrupt and inefficient (and are thus opposed by reformist insurgents).

Whatever the ultimate goal may be, the crucial instrument for seizing power is a small, secretive, disciplined, and tightly organized group. The decisive arena for insurgent activity is the major urban centers, especially the capital city, where political and economic power is concentrated. Conspiracies based on the military pay little or no attention to the organized involvement of the public. To the extent that the views of the masses are taken into consideration, calculations center on assuring public acceptance of the outcome. Like popular support and organization, external support is not a major consideration. While environmental factors, such as economic regression and maldistribution, political disorder, and corruption, may be the underlying causes of the insurrection, the defection of military officers is the crucial variable. Although military insurrections have occurred throughout history and are hardly uncommon now, the fact remains that in many cases where governments face severe social, economic, and political problems, they still manage to retain the loyalty of the military. When this happens, civilian-led conspiracies may be hatched. The continued loyalty of the military to the governing authorities is a formidable obstacle for civilian insurgents, who must then engage in more extensive political activity and preparations for using violence. Part of their effort involves attempts to infiltrate and subvert the military, particularly rank-and-file officers and enlisted personnel.

The most striking contemporary example of this situation is the 1917 Bolshevik insurrection in Russia, which popularized the conspiratorial strategy, particularly among Marxist revolutionaries. Lenin, the key Bolshevik strategist and tactician, was convinced that the ultimate seizure of power depended on a highly organized political party that would obtain support from certain discontented social groups such as the rank-and-file military and the workers, especially in the capital city (which in the Russian case was Petrograd). A critical part of Lenin's conspiratorial strategy was the assumption that the government was undergoing a general crisis and was alienated from significant sectors of the population (workers, soldiers, and peasants) and that it would capitulate when confronted with low-level violence, subversion of the military and police, and the final seizure of the media, government offices, and other state-controlled institutions. In the words of John Shy and Thomas W. Collier, in this scheme battles were "conceived as brief, climactic encounters fought for control of the nerve centers of a modern society."[1]

Although segments of the population beyond the party were organized into soviets (committees) to play a role in the Bolshevik scheme, Lenin's strategy was essentially elitist. As Lenin bluntly put it, "We are apprehensive of an excessive growth of the Party, because careerists and charlatans, who deserve only to be shot, inevitably do all they can to insinuate themselves into the ranks of the ruling party."[2] He had no intention of mobilizing the general population within the framework of an extensive shadow government. And although there was always a readiness to exploit mass grievances where they existed, there was no systematic effort to solicit them. In fact, one of the reasons for creating the vanguard party was Lenin's lack of confidence in the ability of the workers to understand either their own predicament or the requirements for a successful revolutionary insurgency; this was something that only the intellectual elites of the party could do.

Although Lenin denigrated the idea of enduring alliances with non-Bolshevik dissidents, he argued strenuously that under certain circumstances it was necessary to pursue "united-front tactics" by cooperating temporarily with groups he despised, such as "reactionary trade unions" and the Social Democratic and Socialist Revolutionary parties. At all times, however, a limited group of dedicated activists, whose activities could be more easily controlled and coordinated, was to constitute the vital leadership echelon.[3] Lenin placed a premium on ideological, strategic, and tactical unity; deviations were unacceptable. While a key aim of the leadership elites and cadres was to exploit mass discontent, only segments of the population, mainly in the urban centers, became the targets of proselytization, infiltration, manipulation, and, ultimately, control. Although scattered terrorist acts took place, violence was basically confined to the direct seizure of key government facilities. Neither systematic terrorism nor guerrilla warfare was important. In theory, there was little need for external support, because deteriorating social and economic conditions and the government's political and military ineptitude made it vulnerable to a quick, decisive, and forceful move by the insurgents. Although foreign financial inputs and sanctuaries across the borders were not unwelcome, their importance was downplayed or denied altogether.

Because of Lenin's success in Russia and its profound historical impact, there was a belief that his conspiratorial strategy could be effectively followed by other revolutionary insurgents. What was overlooked, of course, was the fact that the czarist regime had been toppled (March 1917) because of its own blunders and a spontaneous uprising of the citizenry of Petrograd, events that had little or nothing to do with Lenin *or* his strategy. In fact, Lenin, who was in exile, initially refused to believe reports that the Romanov dynasty had fallen, and accepted them only after he read about the events in the Zurich newspapers. From that moment onward, Lenin concentrated his efforts on overthrowing the provisional government.

When the provisional government proved to be incapable of establishing its authority and failed to extricate Russia from its disastrous and unpopular involvement in World War I, Lenin and his cohorts, particularly Leon Trotsky, who joined forces with Lenin and became chairman of the Military Revolutionary Committee, eventually carried out a coup on November 7 (October 25 o.s.), 1917. It is worth recalling that the coup took place after several months of hesitation and indecisiveness by Lenin and came in response to a weak crackdown by the Kerensky government. Robert H. McNeal has thoughtfully summarized the import of these events:

> The October Revolution conformed to Lenin's conception of proletarian revolution. Unlike the March Revolution (or the mass upheavals of May and July), it was not a spontaneous upsurge of the proletariat but a *coup d'état* in which the "vanguard of the proletariat" had organized and directed elements of the lower classes. The party of Lenin's design had shown little ability to topple the tsarist government under normal conditions, and it is highly unlikely that it could have done better in a parliamentary democratic system. But in the crucible of revolution the party had proven its strength.[4]

It does not detract from Lenin's historical stature to point out that the success of his strategy depended as much on events beyond his control as it did on his considerable conceptual, organizational, and political acumen. Yet, when it came to replicating his strategy in other countries, especially in Europe, where the Bolsheviks had great hopes, the main problem was the absence of the particular combination of political, economic, and social factors that in Russia had created a vacuum with respect to political legitimacy and authority. In spite of the psychological aftershocks of World War I and the traumas of the Great Depression, the political systems of the West retained their legitimacy, and governments continued to exercise control over critical institutions, such as the military and the police. Even in China, where the decay of the traditional system, the diffusion of power to warlords, widespread corruption, and socioeconomic problems had led some Marxists to believe they could seize power in the late 1920s, the various ruling authorities proved resilient. As a consequence, the Chinese Communists were compelled to devise a markedly different strategy for insurgency, one that emphasized prolonged armed struggle based on mobilizing mass support.

THE STRATEGY OF PROTRACTED POPULAR WAR

The strategy of protracted popular war articulated by Mao is undoubtedly the most conceptually elaborate and perhaps the most widely copied insurgent strategy. It was a response to conditions in China, which differed substantially from those which faced Lenin and his cohorts in Russia. In contrast to the Bolsheviks, who confronted a feeble provisional government, the Chinese Communists had to overcome adversaries who enjoyed obvious superiority during the 1930s and 1940s—first the Japanese and then the Kuomintang (Chinese Nationalist Party), led by Chiang Kai-shek. Under such circumstances it became apparent that although a strong, well-organized party along Leninist lines would be necessary for success, a quick victory based on support from the urban proletariat was not feasible. In spite of contrary views held by fellow Chinese Communist leaders and Soviet advisers, Mao came to the conclusion that the revolutionary struggle would be a long one and that the peasantry, not the urban proletariat, was the most important revolutionary class. As things turned out, the Chinese Communist insurgents did engage in a long conflict, during which they mobilized substantial popular support by means of extensive organizational efforts. Militarily, the struggle consisted mainly of hit-and-run guerrilla attacks in the countryside, which eventually gave way to mobile conventional warfare.[5]

Although Mao eventually succeeded, his road to power was not an easy one. During the 1930s he experienced not only battlefield setbacks but also opposition from comrades who resisted his strategy and influence within the party. Nevertheless, the tenacity of Mao and his followers enabled them to survive the celebrated Long March (a costly and arduous retreat to Shensi in the north), to establish control over the party, and to carry out operations against the Japanese invaders.

The Japanese occupation was fortuitous for Mao because it provided a nationalist appeal around which support could be rallied and also because it diverted the attention of the Kuomintang away from Chinese Communist insurgents. Moreover, as the war dragged on, Mao's stature as a heroic nationalist was enhanced, while the dislocation and costs of the fighting further weakened Chiang Kai-shek's position. Indeed, there is reason to question whether Mao's strategy would have been successful against the Kuomintang if the Japanese had not invaded China. The fact remains that Mao did win, and his strategy became increasingly attractive to insurgents around the world because it offered them a cohesive, systematic blueprint for their own struggles against colonial occupiers or oppressive indigenous regimes. The Chinese, of course, welcomed the emulation of their strategy and were vigorously encouraging it by the time the Cultural Revolution began in the 1960s.

The Maoist version of the protracted popular-war strategy, which was used in both the anti-Japanese and anti-Kuomintang wars, consists of three sequential phases, each of which differs with respect to the correlation of forces. First is the *strategic defensive,* a time when the enemy is on the offensive and the insurgents must concentrate on survival, political organization, and low-level violence. As the insurgents gradually gain support and achieve military successes, they enter the second and longest phase, the *strategic stalemate,* which is characterized by guerrilla warfare. Further escalation and victories, which lead to demoralization, lethargy, and defections on the government side, usher in the *strategic offensive,* during which the insurgents move from guerrilla warfare to mobile conventional attacks on a large scale, and the political and psychological effects of the insurgent victories lead to a collapse of the government.[6]

The three stages in Mao's scheme have specific objectives, involve different combinations of political and military actions, and depend on the outcomes of preceding stages. The *strategic defensive* phase emphasizes political mobilization. In Mao's words:

> This move is crucial; it is indeed of primary importance, while our inferiority in weapons and other things is only secondary. The mobilization of the common people throughout the country will create a vast sea in which to drown the enemy, create the conditions that will make up for our inferiority in arms and other things, and create the prerequisites for overcoming every difficulty in the war. To win victory, we must persevere in the War of Resistance, in the united front and in the protracted war. But all these are inseparable from the mobilization of the common people. To wish for victory and yet neglect political mobilization is like wishing to "go south by driving the chariot north," and the result would inevitably be to forfeit victory.[7]

Pursuant to political mobilization, cellular networks are created, political organizers engage in propaganda activities to win popular support, and terrorists carry out selective acts of intimidation against recalcitrant individuals. At this point, fronts composed of various social groups (e.g., religious, occupational, youth, and women's) may be organized along with pressure groups and parties to gain popular support. Simultaneously, insurgents usually try to infiltrate enemy institutions; foment strikes, demonstrations, and riots; and perhaps carry out sabotage missions.

As part of their political effort, the insurgents stress appeals based on both ideology and material grievances and try to provide some social services and engage in mutual self-help projects (e.g., harvesting crops or building schoolhouses) to demonstrate their sincerity and to gain acceptance and support. A key objective at this time is the recruitment of local leaders, who, once in the organization, play a key role in detaching the people from the government. To institutionalize support, insurgents begin to construct shadow-government structures (parallel hierarchies) that will provide de facto control of the population. If the government fails to react, it will lose by default; if it responds successfully, the insurgents may suffer a decisive fate similar to that of the Tudeh Party insurgents in Iran during the shah's reign.[8]

Selective terrorism during this period serves many purposes, including the attempt to gain both popular and external support. This can be very significant where the insurgent organization is too rudimentary to support guerrilla warfare. In situations where the strength of the regime is the key reason for the use of terror, the insurgent movement is worse off than where organizational deficiencies are the problem. The movement is worse off because the government may be ameliorating the conditions that provide motivation and support for the insurgency and/or may be using force effectively to eliminate the insurgents. If organizational failings are the problem, the insurgents may rectify them and move toward guerrilla warfare.

Guerrilla warfare is the most important activity in the *strategic stalemate* phase. The earliest part of this stage is characterized by armed resistance carried out by small bands operating in rural areas where terrain is rugged and government control is weak. If the guerrillas face significant government opposition, they have the option of reverting to stage one. The most likely considerations in the decision-making calculus of the guerrillas are the vitality of the incumbent regime, its projected capability against guerrilla warfare, and external political-military factors.

The insurgent aim in the initial part of stage two is to isolate the people from the government. The organization established in phase one begins to supply small guerrilla units, and full- and part-time personnel play a more prominent role. During the early part of stage two there is still a lack of organization above the village level, and groups operate from shifting and remote bases. Military actions in early stage two are small hit-and-run attacks against convoys, military and economic installations, and isolated outposts. These scattered attacks are intended to goad the government into adopting a static defensive posture and dispersing its forces in order to protect many potential targets.[9]

If there is satisfactory progress during the early part of stage two, insurgents normally move into the second part of that stage and expand their organization in the regions they control. In addition, regional forces emerge, which, along with the full-time forces, enable the insurgents to join villages together into a political network that constitutes a major base area. At this point, the guerrillas step up the mobilization of the population by exploiting and satisfying (as best they can) popular aspirations. Meanwhile, there is usually a stress on ideology that is designed to supplant whatever type of legitimacy sustains the existing regime.[10]

During stage two the parallel hierarchy is more visible than during stage one. Besides resembling the state apparatus, it also includes auxiliary organizations controlled by revolutionary cells linked to the central political structure. Moreover, a government-in-exile may be created.[11] The organizational evolution in late stage two includes the establishment of arsenals, arms production facilities, and hospitals. The logistics operation encompasses activities that range from procurement of basic foodstuffs and war supplies to acquisition of material aid from external sources. Once base areas are set up, the delivery of supplies from nearby friendly states becomes less risky and more likely.

In the military realm, emphasis turns to the recruitment of full-time guerrillas, the establishment of an extensive reserve system, and the creation and training of regular army units. If voluntary recruits are insufficient, there may be forced abductions. Since the latter often make poor fighters, voluntary enlistments are stressed. Three operational levels often constitute the military organization in late stage two: regional, district, and local. The regional troops, the best-armed and -trained, form the strike forces that are the backbone of the movement. At the next level, full-time cadres lead district battalions, though subordinate companies are composed of part-time soldiers. The local forces are made up of both full- and part-time guerrillas, with the part-timers predominant. A central headquarters coordinates all three levels in pursuit of common military and political objectives.

Even though the parallel hierarchy and military organization may be relatively secure in late stage two, the guerrillas usually do not elect to fight positional battles or even defend their base areas, for they consider themselves to be in a position of strategic stalemate. Instead, the insurgents avoid large government sweeps and patrols in order to demonstrate the government's inability to destroy them and to contrast the regime's ephemeral authority with the guerrillas' permanency.[12]

While base areas are being constructed, the insurgents continue to establish bands of followers and send agents into contested or government controlled areas to implant new cells, networks, and groups there. The insurgents make a major effort to deceive the government, hoping its response will be tardy, insufficient, and tactically misdirected. Military actions in late stage two are basically large-scale guerrilla attacks carried out from secure base areas. In addition to operations designed to acquire additional supplies and to reduce areas of government control, armed propaganda teams are dispatched to further undermine the enemy. In the terminal period of this stage considerable attention is devoted to seizing and securing large areas and preparing the physical battlefield for mobile-conventional warfare. Thus, military considerations receive as much attention as political calculations when it comes to target selection.[13]

The third and final stage of the protracted popular warfare strategy, the *strategic offensive,* is, as noted, characterized by the transformation of guerrilla forces into regular, orthodox forces. Although regular units may engage in some positional warfare, primary emphasis is on mobile conventional operations, with small guerrilla bands supporting the main effort in an ancillary role. The principal military objective at this point is to destroy the government's main forces; the principal political aim is the displacement of the governing authorities. Because of the scale of military operations, high-level leadership skills (the command, control, and coordination of multiple operations by large units), effective communications, an efficiently functioning complex logistical system, and external assistance are usually necessary—unless, of course, government forces quickly disintegrate.[14]

It is important to note that although the Maoist strategy of protracted popular war theoretically consists of an orderly progression through three phases, victory can come at any point if the government suddenly loses its will. Where a loss of will does not occur and the conflict proceeds as Mao envisaged, the insurgent leadership faces the need to assess the relative positions of the two sides and to make judgments concerning whether or not the conflict has entered into a new phase. Because such judgments may be erroneous, leaders must be ready, if necessary, to revert to the actions and policies appropriate for a previous phase.[15] This element of flexibility increases the attractiveness of Mao's approach and no doubt also explains its adoption by insurgents in many Third World states, such as Algeria, Vietnam, Malaya, the Philippines, Thailand, Oman, Portuguese Guinea, and Mozambique.

It was probably inevitable that a number of variations on Mao's strategy would occur as it was adopted and implemented elsewhere. The Algerian insurgency against the French during the 1950s is a case in point. The goal of the Algerian insurgents, who were Arab nationalists and Muslims rather than Marxists, was to achieve independence from France by waging a protracted struggle that emphasized popular support and gradually escalating violence (i.e., guerrilla warfare followed by conventional operations). Their "oil spot" strategy was reminiscent of Mao's because it was based on the idea of gradually expanding political control in the countryside and surrounding the cities. Unlike the Chinese experience, the Algerians were never able to make the transition to the conventional warfare stage, because the French were able to rectify early military deficiencies and thereby defeat the insurgents militarily. But while the French won on the battlefield, the Algerians won the war. The reason for this paradox was that the Algerians were able to maintain widespread popular support and wear down French resolve through skillful propaganda efforts at home and abroad, to exploit violent excesses by the French (torture and terrorism), and to pose the prospect of a costly and interminable struggle.

In the final analysis, what the Algerian war showed was that victory is possible without the structured phasing and military progression associated with the implementation of Mao's strategy. The key to overcoming the deficiencies of what turned out to be more of an ad hoc approach (and military regression) was gaining and maintaining popular support through good organization and astute psychological warfare campaigns.[16]

Further variations from Mao's strategic thinking, which occurred in Algeria and elsewhere, are evident with respect to terrorism, activity in urban areas, the targeting of the economic infrastructure, and international policies. In contrast to Mao, who downplayed terrorism and concentrated almost exclusively on the rural areas, the Algerians, as well as such groups as the Vietcong in Vietnam, the New People's Army (NPA) in the Philippines, and Sendero Luminoso (SL) in Peru, concluded that greater violence in the cities and more extensive use of terrorism were necessary. Another twist added by the Algerians—and later by the SL, Farabundo Martí National Liberation Front (FMLN) in El Salvador (after 1985), and the Union for the Total Independence of Angola (UNITA), among others—is the objective of destroying the national economy through sabotage as a major way to weaken and discredit the government. Finally, the Algerians, the Vietnamese and a number of other groups have sought to undermine support for their adversaries through propaganda campaigns directed at popular opinion inside the borders of either the colonial power (France in the Algerian and Vietminh cases) or the major outside benefactor of the government (the United States in the Vietnam War).

Whatever the variations in specific cases, the protracted-popular-war strategy is a demanding one because of the need to obtain extensive popular support and to create a complex organizational apparatus, tasks that usually require considerable time and secure base areas for insurgents. The strategy calls for directly or indirectly engaging increasing numbers of people in a long-term conflict with the government in order to control the countryside and thereby isolate the urban centers and wear down the government's will to resist. Such an undertaking is vulnerable to determined government psychological, organizational, and military-police countermeasures at many points, as the British demonstrated in both Malaya and Kenya in the 1950s and Oman in the 1960s. Moreover, many groups currently following the strategy find it more difficult to rally popular support than the Chinese or Algerians did because they have a narrower base. The Chinese and Algerians transformed resentment of political, social, and economic discrimination by foreigners into a widespread surge of nationalism directed at imperial and colonial ruling authorities (the Japanese and the French), but many of today's insurgents represent smaller segments of the population (class, ethnic, racial, or religious groups) and face an indigenous government rather than a foreign one. Under such circumstances it is far more difficult to galvanize nationalist sentiments, even when an effort is made to depict governments as tools of neoimperialist foreign interests.

The successful application of the strategy by insurgents in today's world may also be impeded by unfavorable environmental factors and enhanced government capabilities. In China, Vietnam, and, to a lesser extent, Algeria, the insurgents were able to secure bases and then to consolidate and expand their organization and base of popular support in relative security because of favorable topographical and demographic patterns (i.e., large, well-populated countries with inaccessible areas). As we shall see later when further examining the environmental factor, several contemporary insurgent movements that subscribe to a strategy of protracted popular war operate in physical and human settings that are less than desirable. Another burden they must confront and neutralize is the enhanced firepower, mobility, and intelligence capabilities of government forces, which are the outgrowth of technological developments in the areas of transportation, weaponry, detection systems, and information processing.

Under current circumstances, the successful use of the strategy is more difficult because of the kinds of obstacles just enumerated. One consequence of this is a tendency on the part of many insurgents to place more emphasis on external assistance (moral, political, material, and/or sanctuary) to compensate for weaknesses with respect to one or more factors, especially the environment and government response. In fact, with few exceptions—notably the New People's Army in the Philippines and SL in Peru—most insurgent movements have cast aside the notion of following Mao's prescription for self-reliance.

THE MILITARY-FOCUS STRATEGY

The military-focus strategy is different from the strategy of protracted popular war because it gives primacy to military action and makes political action subordinate. Though fully aware of the value of popular support, the insurgents make no systematic, sustained effort to acquire it through extensive political organizing efforts in the rural areas. Instead, proponents of the military focus believe that popular support either is sufficient or will be a by-product of military victories. Moreover, widespread support may be unnecessary if the government's forces are defeated on the battlefield.

The American Civil War, during which the South adopted a military-focus strategy emphasizing the defensive in pursuit of its goal of secession, is a case where adequate support from the population existed when hostilities commenced. Since there were already political structures that extended down to the local level, the Confederacy did not have to worry about creating political institutions to gain support. Furthermore, its secessionist aim obviated any effort to gradually expand its control over areas in the North. Under such conditions, the South could afford to concentrate most of its energy and resources on military affairs. Although the Confederacy did mount four sizable invasions of the North (Lee's campaign in Maryland, an advance into Kentucky, the Gettysburg campaign, and a march to Washington's suburbs in 1864) and although there were advocates of an offensive strategy of carrying the war to the North shortly after the early success of Bull Run, the overall strategy of the South was to conduct a defensive conventional war in the South that would gradually wear down the North's will to continue by increasing the human and material costs the North would have to pay. But, throughout the war the main emphasis was on the military dimension of the conflict because, in contrast to insurgents who adopt a strategy of protracted popular war, there was no perceived need to mobilize and gradually expand popular support or to make prolonged guerrilla warfare and/or terrorist operations the fulcrum of the struggle.

The Biafran civil war (1967–1970) is a more recent case and was similar to the American Civil War in several ways. Although the human and

physical environment was different, the principal goal of the dominant ethnic group in eastern Nigeria, the Ibo, was to secede, and the strategy was
clearly one that emphasized military activity. With the exception of a belated effort to conduct guerrilla attacks, military operations were essentially
conventional, reflecting the Sandhurst training of the Ibo officers. Moreover, aside from a bold move to seize the midwestern region in the summer
and fall of 1967 that ended in failure, conventional military operations
(many of which were artillery and mortar duels) took place in the eastern
region. Like the South in the American Civil War, the main strategic objective of the Ibo was to rely on military successes in order to erode the federal
government's will to continue the conflict by increasing the human and material costs of the government and by creating political pressures through
the acquisition of international recognition. In the end, the strategy failed,
not only because the government was able to consolidate its position and
exploit its considerable relative advantage with respect to resources but also
because conventional operations and ideals were, in the view of Robert de
St. Jorre, totally unsuited to the terrain, the ability of the Biafran military,
and the superior firepower of the adversary.[17]

Not all insurgents who adhere to a military-focus strategy believe that
conventional military operations are a viable option. Where there is a sharp
asymmetrical balance of military force that favors the opposition, immediate
action is manifest in lesser forms of violence—that is, terrorism and/or guerrilla
warfare. The most notable example in recent times is the Cuban insurrection,
which came to be viewed as an alternative to the strategy of protracted popular
war and hence engendered an acrimonious debate between Chinese and Cuban
Communists, who were involved in supporting or sponsoring insurgencies in
the 1960s and 1970s.[18] Given its contemporary importance, the Cuban variation of the military-focus strategy deserves further comment.

Che Guevara, a much-publicized figure in insurgent folklore, opened
his book *Guerrilla Warfare* with the following comments:

> We consider that the Cuban Revolution contributed three fundamental les-
> sons to the conduct of revolutionary movements in America. They are: (1)
> Popular forces can win a war against the army. (2) It is not necessary to wait
> until all the conditions for making revolution exist; the insurrection can create
> them. (3) In underdeveloped America the countryside is the basic area for
> armed fighting.[19]

While one may debate the originality of the first and third points, the
second claim merits attention because Guevara seems to give more scrutiny
to the initial phase of insurgency that does Mao. John Pustay suggests that
one reason for this may be that Castro and Guevara had to start by recruiting at the grass-roots level, whereas Mao did not have to start from scratch.
In his words:

Castro, Guevara, and their eleven cadre men, on the other hand, were forced to form guerrilla insurgency units by drawing upon recruitment sources at the grass-roots level. They had to start essentially from nothing and build a revolutionary force to achieve victory. It is reasonable, therefore, for Guevara to discuss in detail the initiatory steps in creating a viable guerrilla force. Of priority is the assembly of revolutionary leaders and cadre guerrilla fighters in exile or in some isolated spot within an object country "around some respected leader fighting for the salvation of his people." Guevara then calls for elaborate advanced planning, for the advanced establishment of intelligence networks and arsenals, and above all for the continued maintenance of absolute secrecy about the potential insurgency until overt resistance is actually initiated. Thus Guevara fills in the details, overlooked by Mao and slightly covered by Giap [the Vietnamese Communist strategist], of the initiatory phases of the first general stage of Maoist insurgency warfare.[20]

Guevara's discussion of strategy contains a number of ideas found in Mao's thinking. In addition to the previously mentioned point about situating the conflict in the countryside, there is Guevara's stress on the importance of bases in inaccessible terrain, the need for popular support, and the requirement for civil organization after areas have been seized. Moreover, like Mao, he argued that complete victory will only be achieved when the guerrilla army is transformed into a regular army.[21] While it is tempting to interpret this as little more than an attempt by Guevara to reiterate Mao's strategy, a closer look at the Cuban case reveals noteworthy divergencies from the strategy of protracted popular war.

Guevara contended that insurgent leaders do not have to wait for the preconditions of insurgency to appear, because they can act to catalyze existing grievances required for positive action. Thirty to fifty men, he believes, are adequate to start an armed rebellion in Latin American countries, given their conditions of favorable terrain for operations, hunger for land, repeated attacks upon justice and the like.[22] In other words, Guevara suggested that the mere fact of taking up arms in situations where grievances exist will create suitable conditions for revolution. Guevara depicted the beginning of the insurrection as follows:

> At the outset there is a more or less homogenous group, with some arms, that devotes itself almost exclusively to hiding in the wildest and most inaccessible places, making little contact with the peasants. It strikes a fortunate blow and its fame grows. A few peasants, dispossessed of their land or engaged in a struggle to conserve it, and young idealists of other classes join the nucleus; it acquires greater audacity and starts to operate in inhabited places, making more contact with the people of the zone; it repeats attacks, always fleeing after making them; suddenly it engages in combat with some column or other and destroys its vanguard. Men continue to join it; it has increased in number, but its organization remains exactly the same; its caution diminishes, and it ventures into more populous zones.[23]

Like Lenin and Mao, Fidel Castro believed that an elite vanguard was a necessary condition for a successful insurrection; unlike Lenin and Mao, he did not believe the vanguard had to be a Marxist-Leninist party. Historical circumstances, according to Regis Debray, determine the form of the vanguard. Debray noted in his treatise on the Cuban insurrection, *Revolution in the Revolution?*:

> Fidel Castro says simply that there is no revolution without a vanguard; that this vanguard is not necessarily the Marxist-Leninist party; and that those who want to make the revolution have the right and the duty to constitute themselves a vanguard, independently of these parties.
>
> It takes courage to state the facts out loud when these facts contradict a tradition. There is, then, no metaphysical equation in vanguard = Marxist-Leninist party; there are merely dialectical conjunctions between a given function—that of the vanguard in history—and a given form of organization—that of the Marxist-Leninist party. These conjunctions arise out of prior history and depend on it. Parties exist here on earth and are subject to the rigors of terrestrial dialectics. If they have been born, they can die and be reborn in other forms. How does this rebirth come about? Under what form can the historic vanguard appear?[24]

During the Cuban revolution, Castro dealt with the question about the form of the vanguard by rejecting of the idea of subordinating the guerrilla force to the party. Instead, he placed primary emphasis on the guerrilla army as the nucleus of the party. Putting it another way, Debray argued that the guerrilla force is a political embryo from which the party can arise. While Mao stressed the leading role of the party and the need for substantial political preparation *before* the military struggle, Debray claimed the Cuban case made it clear that military priorities must take precedence over politics.

Debray contended it is an old obsession to believe revolutionary awareness and organization must and can, in every case, precede revolutionary action. Rather than wait for the emergence of an organization, it is necessary to proceed from what he called "the guerrilla foco" (focus), nucleus of the popular army. This foco is referred to as "the small motor" that sets "the big motor of the masses" in action and precipitates formation of a front as victories of the small motor increase.[25] Debray's belief in the widespread applicability of this strategy is obvious in this remark:

> The Latin American revolution and its vanguard, the Cuban revolution, have thus made a decisive contribution to international revolutionary experience and to Marxism-Leninism. *Under certain conditions, the political and the military are not separate, but form one organic whole, consisting of the people's army, whose nucleus is the guerrilla army. The vanguard party can exist in the form of the guerrilla foco itself. The guerrilla force is the party in embryo.* This is the staggering novelty introduced by the Cuban Revolution.[26]

For insurgents who see the Cuban experience as analogous to their own situation and believe Mao's strategy of protracted popular war is inappropriate in their environments, there is another way, the *military focus* emphasized in Cuba. In this approach the key ingredients are violence in the form of small to moderately sized guerrilla attacks, limited political organization, and limited popular support. Although it is not a strategic assumption stressed by Castro or examined sufficiently by Debray, a weak government is closely related to the Castroite version of the military-focus strategy. Indeed, it is questionable whether Castro could have achieved his aims if the Batista government had not been in a state of profound decay and the military weak and divided. As a matter of fact, in any of the types of insurgency that threaten either the political community or the political system, a reasonably strong government will undoubtedly take resolute steps to eradicate the insurgents. On the other hand, where preservationist or reformist insurgents are operating, the guerrilla focus might prove effective even in the face of a strong government, because government leaders might decide to reduce their losses by initiating policy changes that do not threaten the integrity of either the political community or the political system.

As is the case with the conspiratorial and protracted-popular-war strategies, the exhilaration of a historic victory (in Cuba) gave rise to claims that a military-focus strategy based on guerrilla warfare had widespread applicability, especially in the Latin American countries. In fact, Che Guevera's belief that the Cuban experience could be replicated in Bolivia led him to a fateful end in that country. Guevara's dismal failure, and the recognition that not all governments were as fragile as Batista's had been in Cuba, prompted insurgent intellectuals in Latin America to reassess strategic approaches, leading to the emergence of a new strategy of urban warfare in which terrorism is prominent.[27]

THE URBAN-WARFARE STRATEGY

Terrorist acts in support of political objectives are, as we know, hardly a new phenomenon. Although assassinations, kidnappings, and the slaughter of innocent people can be traced back to antiquity, our concern here is the systematic articulation that has occurred in recent times of an urban-centered strategy, in which terrorist attacks play the key role. The emergence of this strategy as an alternative to those discussed thus far is due not only to the resiliency and relative strengths of incumbent governments but also to increased urbanization in many parts of the world. In the modernized societies of Europe and North America, inaccessible rural areas where guerrillas may operate with impunity simply do not exist. Accordingly, insurgents who pursue political aims through violent acts have been compelled to locate in the cities and to operate on a small scale in order to survive. In less-developed countries, most especially in Latin America, the strategy of urban warfare has also been attractive. In some cases, such as Venezuela, Argentina, and Uruguay, the situation is similar to Europe and North America; that is, the population is essentially urban rather than rural.

In other situations, where there is an urban-rural mix, as in many other Latin American countries, the failures of insurgents to establish footholds in the countryside in the 1960s led insurgent leaders to reassess social, political, and economic changes in the hope of uncovering new government vulnerabilities that could be exploited. One such change was the increasing migration from the rural to urban areas, which, in most cases, was accompanied by the establishment of teeming slums filled with poor, psychologically disoriented people whose search for a better life had yielded little more than bitter disillusionment. Insurgent leaders saw such conditions as presenting significant opportunities for carrying out, and gaining support for, insurrectionary activities. In sum, the locus of potential for insurgencies had shifted to the cities. Moreover, the socioeconomic differentiation of the urban centers provided ample targets for sabotage and terrorism and the population density made unusable such government military assets as aircraft, artillery, mortars, and the like.

Although their ultimate goals may vary, insurgents engaged in urban violence all pursue the intermediate aim of eroding the government's will to resist. Like the protracted popular war and military-focus strategies, eventual mass support is considered important; but the process for achieving it is different. The essential strategy of the urban terrorist, according to Carlos Marighella, one of its foremost proponents, is to "turn political crisis into armed conflict by performing violent actions that will force those in power to transform the political situation of the country into a military situation. That will alienate the masses, who from then on will revolt against the army and police and thus blame them for this state of things."[28] To cause this transformation, urban insurgents engage in various actions, including armed propaganda; strikes and work interruptions; ambushes; assassinations; kidnappings; temporary occupation of schools, factories, and radio stations; assaults on fixed targets (e.g., banks, businesses, military camps, police stations, and prisons); and sabotage of economic assets. In addition, they usually want to infiltrate the police and military to foster a breakdown from within. The organization responsible for these actions is basically a small one with cells that have a "link man" in each.[29] The purpose of the cumulative acts of violence is to create havoc and insecurity, which will eventually produce a loss of confidence in the government.

For Latin American theorists like Marighella and Abraham Guillen, the actions in the cities is crucial but not decisive, because the struggle must eventually be transferred to the countryside. As Marighella saw it, the function of urban terrorists was to tie down the government forces in the cities, thus permitting the emergence and survival of rural guerrilla warfare, "which is destined to play the decisive role in the revolutionary war."[30] Accordingly, the major question is how effective urban warfare is in undermining the government and in gaining popular support, not whether urban warfare alone can be successful.[31] The perceived need to transfer the conflict to the rural areas stems from the belief that widespread popular support will be needed to defeat an adversary that controls the state apparatus and is unlikely to remain passive in the face of a challenge to the political community or the regime.

Initiating an insurgency by means of urban warfare and eventually transferring it to the countryside is, for the most part, a Latin American notion that not all urban insurgents subscribe to. Provisional IRA leaders believe that violence in the cities and abroad directed at British officials and military personnel, as well as unarmed civilians, will eventually wear down British will and lead to a withdrawal from Ulster. Likewise, organizations like Action Direct in France, the Red Brigades in Italy, the Fighting Communist Cells in Belgium, the Japanese Red Army, and Basque Homeland and Liberty (ETA) in Spain have pursued their goals (which in the case of all except ETA are somewhat ambiguous) through urban violence and have given little or no indication of plans to eventually carry out a rural struggle. In effect, this means that there are really two variations of the urban-warfare strategy, one of which calls for a move to the countryside, and one solely centered on the cities.

With the exception of South Yemen in 1967, the urban-warfare strategy has been ineffective.[32] Although the Tupamaros in Uruguay and the Monteneros in Argentina succeeded in provoking a heavily militarized government response, the brutal repression associated with it crushed the insurgent movements. As a result, insurgents in places like El Salvador, Guatemala, and Peru have returned to either the rural-based protracted-popular-war or military-focus strategies discussed earlier. Others, like the previously mentioned groups in Europe, continue to carry out urban terrorist actions, but appear to have little prospect of achieving their ultimate goals.[33]

Assessing Strategic Approaches

The aim of the preceding section was not to suggest that there are four perfectly distinct categories into which all past and present insurgent strategies can be precisely fitted. This does not mean, however, that differences between strategic approaches are indiscernible. We have suggested four strategic approaches that have guided and inspired many insurgent leaders. One reason the four approaches stand out is that their original proponents and adherents have claimed they have widespread, if not universal, applicability. Despite the fact that the ex post facto conceptual codifications of these strategies involve oversimplifications, idealization, selective history, and perhaps distortion with respect to what really transpired, it is nonetheless true that the strategies have been adopted by others.

The adoption of the strategic approaches is not always clear-cut, and this in turn leads to several important points. First, while in some cases the adopted strategies are emulated in a careful and specific way, in other cases they are loosely articulated and applied. For example, the adoption and implementation of the strategy of protracted popular war by the New People's Army in the Philippines and the Vietcong in Vietnam was effected in a programmatic way, with great attention to the political and military requisites associated with that strategy. In contrast, some Afghan and Palestinian groups that claim to be following the Maoist version of the strategy have been far less attentive to details, particularly with respect to stages and their sequencing. Thus, an important question for the researcher is how, and to what degree, groups diverge from the specifics of whatever strategy they have adopted. An examination of writings and pronouncements of insurgent leaders, as well as their plans and operational directives, should enable analysts to arrive at some answers that may help explain insurgent fortunes. Insurgent failures and shortcomings, for instance, might be traced to an incomplete understanding and application of the particular facets of the strategy they profess to be following.

The second consideration that the analyst should keep in mind is the reality that insurgent movements that are divided frequently have independent groups pursuing several strategies simultaneously. A case in point was the FMLN in El Salvador prior to 1985; the People's Revolutionary Army of Joaquín Villalobos was clearly following a military-focus strategy, while the Popular Liberation Forces, led by Leonel González, favored the protracted popular war. Another example is the Palestinian resistance: the Popular Democratic Front has followed a Maoist protracted-popular-war approach, while Fatah has subscribed to a less rigid approach akin to the Algerian protracted-popular-war experience, and the Popular Front for the Liberation of Palestine-General Command and the Abu Nidal organization have adopted the military-focus approach (principally terrorist actions).

The effects of such strategic dissonance are of no small consequence. For instance, precipitate violence (guerrilla or conventional attacks) in keeping with the military-focus strategy can undercut the strategic and tactical aims of groups following the protracted-popular-warfare strategy, because it risks galvanizing major government countermeasures. Since they perceive themselves to be in a weak position relative to the government during the earliest stage of insurrections, adherents of the protracted-popular-war strategy want the government to remain relatively inactive and complacent while they are gradually establishing their insurgent infrastructure. Cultivating inaction and complacency, however, is very difficult when other groups disagree with that strategy and carry out acts of violence against government forces. The key questions for the analyst are whether there is a lack of consensus on strategy, what the conflicting strategies are, what actions take place, and what the effects of the discordant behavior are.

Both the choice of a strategy and its effectiveness are related to the criteria used to evaluate the progress of insurgencies. Although the links between factors will be drawn at various points in subsequent chapters, it may be helpful to illustrate this general point before proceeding. Two factors that can have a major impact on the choice of a strategy are the environment and government response. For some groups that have chosen an urban-warfare strategy (e.g., the Provisional IRA and the Red Brigades in Italy), the choice has been dictated by the fact that the environment is largely urbanized rather than being a backward rural area with inaccessible regions and by the fact that the balance of coercive force decidedly favors the government.

None of this should lead to the assumption that all insurgents correctly assess the overall situation when choosing a strategic approach. To the contrary, in some cases insurgents badly misread the situation. Regardless of whether they chose a military-focus or protracted-popular-war strategy, Palestinian groups committed to the liberation of all Palestine in the late 1960s and early 1970s accurately assessed Israel's advantageous position, but deluded themselves when it came to the physical and human environment. As time passed, they came to recognize that acquiring mass popular support and setting up bases in both Israel and the occupied territories was difficult, if not impossible, because the area was relatively small, had little natural cover, and had a highly developed road and communications system. Furthermore, the population inside Israel was composed of a Jewish majority and a relatively tranquil Palestinian Arab sector. By the mid-1970s the recognition that the physical environment left much to be desired could be seen in references to the "jungles of the people," an oblique acknowledgment that real jungles did not exist. Moreover, it is probable that the 1974 decision by pragmatic elements of the PLO to concentrate on liberating the occupied West Bank and Gaza Strip rather than destroying Israel was influenced by a growing understanding that the physical and human environment inside Israel and the occupied areas was simply not conducive to any of their strategies.

Summary

Before making a systematic appraisal of the strengths and weaknesses of an insurgency, it is important to have as clear a picture as possible of the goals, forms of warfare, and strategy of the insurgents. With these firmly in mind, it is possible to set forth the things that insurgents should be doing to be successful. As far as strategies are concerned, four general approaches have been popular in recent and present times—the conspiratorial, protracted popular war, military focus, and urban warfare. Each places a different combination of requirements on insurgents. The conspiratorial approach emphasizes an elite small-scale organization and low-level violence;

protracted popular warfare stresses political primacy, mass organization, and gradually escalating violence; the military-focus approach emphasizes military primacy and concentrates on either guerrilla or conventional warfare; urban warfare involves small-scale organization and low to moderate terrorist or guerrilla attacks in urban centers, with some proponents envisaging an eventual transition to warfare in the rural areas. Insurgents may follow these approaches exactly or adopt them more loosely. In some cases, aspects of the strategy may be underplayed or overplayed or have new dimensions blended in. But even where this is done, the general strategy is recognizable. The key questions for the analyst are these: What approach is being followed, and what are the divergences and their implications? As for gauging the effectiveness of various strategies, it is essential to identify those factors that experts deem crucial for their success and then assess how the insurgency is progressing, if at all, with respect to each. That process will be the subject of subsequent chapters.

Notes

1.   John Shy and Thomas W. Collier, "Revolutionary War," in Peter Paret, ed., *Makers of Modern Strategy* (Princeton, N.J.: Princeton University Press, 1986), p. 829. Lenin's crucial assumption concerning a general governmental crisis is set forth in "Left-wing Communism—An Infantile Disorder," in Robert C. Tucker, ed., *The Lenin Anthology* (New York: W.W. Norton Co., Inc. 1975), p. 602. An example of the successful use of the conspiratorial strategy was the April 1978 coup in Afghanistan by the People's Democratic Party of Afghanistan. See Abdul Samad Ghaus, *The Fall of Afghanistan* (McLean, Va.: Pergamon-Brassey's, 1988), pp. 187–208. Those interested in a detailed analysis of coups, especially the tactical and operational aspects of strategy, should read Edward Luttwak, *Coup d'État* (New York: Alfred A. Knopf, 1969).

2.   "Left-Wing Communism," p. 572.

3.   *Ibid.*, pp. 550–618 contains a vigorous defense of united-front tactics.

4.   Robert H. McNeal, *The Bolshevik Tradition* (Englewood Cliffs., N.J.: Prentice-Hall, 1963), p. 45. For Lenin's major work on the question of seizing power and the role of the party, see his *What Is to Be Done*, S. V. Utechin and Patricia Utechin, trans. (London: Oxford University Press, 1963). Needless to state, volumes have been written about Lenin and the Bolshevik coup; for a brief summary account, see David Shub, *Lenin*, abridged ed. (New York: Mentor Books, 1950), especially pp. 76–139; and Alan Moorehead, *The Russian Revolution* (New York: Bantam Books, 1959), pp. 132–260. For a more detailed, systematic analysis of the Bolsheviks, see Bertram D. Wolfe, *Three Who Made a Revolution* (New York: Delta Books, 1948).

5.   See *Selected Military Writings of Mao Tse-tung* (Beijing: Foreign Language Press, 1967), pp. 92–98, on the characteristics of China's revolutionary war that made it different from the Russian experience. To better understand the evolution of Mao's thinking, it is useful to put it in its sociopolitical context. See, for instance,

Stuart Schram, *Mao Tse-tung* (Baltimore: Pelican Books, 1966), especially chaps. 5 and 6.

6.   *Selected Military Writings of Mao Tse-tung,* pp. 210–219, deals with the stages of a protracted armed struggle. For a succinct account of Mao's strategy, see Benjamin I. Schwartz, *Chinese Communism and the Rise of Mao* (Cambridge, Mass.: Harvard University Press, 1951), pp. 189–204; and John J. McCuen, *The Art of Counter-Revolutionary War* (Harrisburg, Pa.: Stackpole Books, n.d.), p. 31.

7.   *Selected Military Writings of Mao Tse-tung,* p. 228. On the first phase of protracted popular war, see McCuen, *The Art of Counter-Revolutionary War,* p. 31.

8.   John S. Pustay, *Counterinsurgency Warfare* (New York: Free Press, 1977), pp. 54–59.

9.   *Ibid.,* pp. 59–71; McCuen, *The Art of Counter-Revolutionary War,* p. 33.

10.   Pustay, *Counterinsurgency Warfare,* pp. 71–72; McCuen, *Counter-Revolutionary War,* p. 34. On types of legitimacy, see Charles F. Andrain, *Political Life and Social Change,* 2d ed. (Belmont, Calif.: Duxbury Press, 1974), pp. 153–157.

11.   Ted Robert Gurr, *Why Men Rebel* (Princeton, N.J.: Princeton University Press, 1970), pp. 294–295; Pustay, *Counterinsurgency Warfare,* pp. 36, 72; McCuen, *Counter-Revolutionary War,* pp. 34–35.

12.   Pustay, *Counterinsurgency Warfare,* pp. 72–74; McCuen, *The Art of Counter-Revolutionary War,* pp. 34, 36.

13.   Pustay, *Counterinsurgency Warfare,* pp. 75–76.

14.   *Ibid.,* pp. 76–78; McCuen, *The Art of Counter-Revolutionary War,* pp. 37–40.

15.   The notion of reversion to previous stages (i.e., from conventional to guerrilla war and then later from guerrilla to conventional) can be seen in Mao's discussion of strategic changes during the anti-Japanese War. See *Selected Military Writings of Mao Tse-tung,* pp. 277–279.

16.   On strategy in the Algerian War, see Joan Gillespie, *Algeria: Rebellion and Revolution* (London: Ernest Benn Limited, 1960), chap. 9; Edgar O'Ballance, *The Algerian Insurrection, 1954–1962* (Hamden, Conn.: Archon Books, 1967), pp. 42, 62–63, and especially 205–210; and Alf Andrew Heggoy, *Insurgency and Counterinsurgency in Algeria* (Bloomington, Ind.: Indiana University Press, 1972), chap. 5, particularly pp. 90–91 and 95–100.

17.   On Southern strategy during the American Civil War, see Clement Eaton, *A History of the Southern Confederacy* (New York: The Macmillan Company, 1958), pp. 124–125. For an account of the Biafran civil war, see John de St. Jorre, *The Nigerian Civil War* (Toronto: Hodder and Stoughton, 1972), pp. 125–231 and especially 273–282.

18.   For a succinct account of the differences between the Maoist and Debray schemes, see Arthur Jay Klinghoffer, "Mao or Che? Some Reflections on Communist Warfare," *Mizan* (March–April 1969): 94–99.

19.   Che Guevara, *Guerrilla Warfare* (New York: Vintage Books, 1961), p. 1.

20.   Pustay, *Counterinsurgency Warfare,* p. 112.

21.   Guevara, *Guerrilla Warfare,* pp. 3–12, 80–86.

22.   *Ibid.,* p. 112.

23.   *Ibid.,* p. 71; Brian Crozier, *The Study of Conflict* (London: Institute for the Study of Conflict, 1970), p. 7.

24.   Regis Debray, *Revolution in the Revolution?*, Bobbe Ortiz, trans. (New York: Monthly Review Press, 1967), pp. 20–21, 95–105, 98–99; Crozier, *The Study of Conflict*, p. 8.

25.   Debray, *Revolution in the Revolution?*, pp. 83–84.

26.   *Ibid.*, p. 106. Italics are from Debray. Despite Debray's claims, the idea of military action preceding popular support was already present in the literature on insurgency. It was one of several possibilities raised in "La guerre revolutionarie et ses donnes fundamentales," *Revue militaire d'information* (February–March 1957): 9–29.

27.   On the failure of Castroism in Latin America, see Douglas S. Blaufarb, *The Counter-insurgency Era* (New York: Free Press, 1977), pp. 280–286; John Pimlott, ed., *Guerrilla Warfare*, (New York: Bison Books, 1985), pp. 108–115.

28.   Carlos Marighella, "On Principles and Strategic Questions," *Les tempes modernes* (November 1969).

29.   Robert Moss, *Urban Guerrilla Warfare*, Adelphi Paper no. 79 (London: The International Institute for Strategic Studies, 1971), p. 3.

30.   Carlos Marighella, "Minimanual of the Urban Guerrillas," Appendix to Moss, *Urban Guerrilla Warfare*, p. 26.

31.   The rural-urban linkage within the framework of a protracted war of liberation is perhaps best illustrated in the writings of Abraham Guillen, one of the major revolutionary thinkers in Latin America; see his *Philosophy of the Urban Guerrilla*, Donald C. Hodges, ed. and trans. (New York: William Morrow, 1973), pp. 229–300. Although Guillen allows for the possibility of a Leninist type of takeover under certain conditions, the essential thrust of his argument concentrates on prolonged conflict. Guillen, it should be noted, focuses on Latin America. While he believes that armies of liberation must be created in each country, he contends that they must be part of a larger continental strategic command that can orchestrate the liberation of all Latin America.

32.   For a succinct, incisive critique of the urban terrorist approach, see Anthony Burton, *Revolutionary Violence* (New York: Crane, Russak, 1978), pp. 130–144; Walter Laqueur, *Guerrilla* (Boston: Little, Brown, 1976), pp. 403–404. The success in South Yemen is noted by Pimlott, p. 136. One might also make a case that Palestine in the 1940s and Cyprus in the 1950s were also examples of what, on balance, was an urban-warfare strategy. If one accepts this, the common denominator in the Yemen, Palestine, and Cyprus cases is a weakened imperial power desiring to cut its losses. In today's world those using an urban-warfare strategy face indigenous governments, none of which has succumbed.

33.   It is clear that terrorism may achieve short-term objectives such as extracting ransom, publicizing the movement, solidifying existing support, and provoking overreaction by the government. It is not clear that terrorism as the primary form of warfare can be strategically decisive. Where it has contributed to success, it has been one of several forms of warfare. While it is tempting to ascribe the British withdrawal from Palestine to dramatic terrorist actions by Jewish extremist groups like the Irgun and Stern Gang, this ignores the guerrilla warfare and small-scale conventional operations by the major Jewish military force, the Haganah, and its elite strike force, the Palmach.

IV The Environment

THE FIRST MAJOR CRITERION FOR EVALUATING AN INSUR-
gency is the environment. It has two general components. The first is the
physical aspect, which refers to the terrain, climate, and the transportation-
communications system. The second, the human dimension, focuses on demography, socioeconomic conditions, and the political culture and system.
Both physical and human aspects of the environment are important because
they provide opportunities for insurgents and place constraints on insurgent
strategies as well. In many cases, success or failure can be traced to the
way insurgent and government strategies, plans, and policies are related to
environmental characteristics.

The Physical Environment

TERRAIN

The physical setting plays a significant part in insurgent conflicts. To
begin with, it can have a major impact on the choice of a strategy. Countries
that are small and urbanized, for instance, are unsuitable for strategies that
call for substantial guerrilla warfare. It comes, therefore, as no surprise to
find that groups like the IRA in Northern Ireland have opted for an urban-
warfare strategy. Simply put, the reality is that any thought of adopting
either a protracted-popular-war or military-focus strategy would be a mistake because armed insurgent units could easily be detected and attacked
during the beginning stages of the conflict, except in those rare instances
where the government demonstrates little, if any, will to resist.

The physical environment plays a key role in those situations where
the government is assumed to enjoy political-military supremacy at the beginning of hostilities and insurgents adopt a protracted-popular-war or mili-

tary-focus strategy that emphasizes guerrilla warfare. Rugged terrain—vast mountains, jungles, swamps, forests, and the like—is usually related to successful guerrilla operations, because it hinders movement by government troops and provides inaccessible hideouts for the guerrillas' main bases. A. H. Shollom explained it thus:

> One of the main factors contributing to the development of a partisan movement was the presence of suitable terrain in which to operate. We include in such terrain: swamps, mountains and forests where mobility is limited to movement on foot and in light vehicles. The fact that the partisan operates in such terrain will be to his advantage, for in an environment of this nature, the regular forces lose the use of their vehicles and artillery as well as the ability to mass superior members. In essence, the terrain reduces the better equipped, better trained, and better armed regular force to a level where the partisan is its equal. It has been estimated that approximately 5,000 Communist partisans in Malaya were being hunted by 230,000 regular soldiers and police, a seemingly overwhelming majority, but the jungle is the equalizer. In this jungle it took 1,000 man-hours for each partisan killed. In open terrain the future of these partisans would be something less than secure.[1]

The triple-canopied jungles of Indochina, a tremendous asset to the forces of Ho Chi Minh in two wars, are another example of good terrain for guerrilla operations and bases. Until the introduction of large numbers of American troops in the mid-1960s, heavily jungled areas such as the U Minh forest south of Saigon and War Zone D to the north were well nigh impregnable.

Unlike areas with heavy foliage, open spaces (e.g., deserts) are normally unfavorable for guerrillas; air surveillance and attack make insurgents susceptible to detection and destruction. In Arthur Campbell's words:

> Open plains are obstacles to guerrillas because they have to concede mastery of the air to their opponents. Before the onset of air power, Lawrence and his Arabs were able to retreat at will into the Arabian deserts, but the FLN in Algeria, opposed by a powerful French air force, were denied access to the vast reaches of the Sahara. . . .[2]

A more recent illustration can be seen in the differing approaches Egypt and the PLO adopted to combat Israel following the June 1967 war. Not long after the cease-fire, Mao sent President Gamal Abdel Nasser of Egypt a military plan of action inspired by China's experience; it called for breaking the Egyptian army into guerrilla units to fight the Israelis in the occupied Sinai Peninsula. Nasser rejected this course, pointing out that because the Sinai had a sparse population, was arid, and allowed visibility of thirty to forty miles, guerrilla forces would stand no chance. Unlike Egypt, the PLO believed there was merit in Mao's thinking. Accordingly, it mounted a guerrilla campaign against Israeli military outposts and settlements in the West Bank from 1968 to 1970. The West Bank is small and has little vegetation; even a few people can be seen for miles, so the Palestinians could neither move in large numbers nor set up permanent or semipermanent bases without being detected and attacked by the Israeli Defense Force. As a result, Palestinian guerrilla raids originated from across the borders of Lebanon and especially Jordan. And given the paucity of vegetation in Jordan (except for a limited area along the Jordan River), guerrilla bases across the borders also proved vulnerable to detection and attack, especially from the air.[3] It is worth noting, however, that where effective air power like Israel's is lacking, vast expanses of desert may be exploited successfully by insurgents intimately familiar with the terrain (e.g., the activity of the Polisario guerrillas in the Western Sahara from 1977 to 1984).[4]

Even when the terrain is favorable for guerrilla warfare, its effects may be limited by size and proximity. Small areas can be cordoned off, isolated, turned into free-fire zones, and penetrated. By contrast, where areas having good terrain are extensive and guerrillas take advantage of this by expanding their operations, the government will find it more difficult to maintain and defend its civilian administration, to supervise the populace, and to concentrate troops and firepower.[5] This is precisely the predicament the Soviets confronted in Afghanistan, where the sheer size of the country would have required an enormous commitment of resources to pacify the countryside. Considerations such as these led Mao to believe that a vast countryside is a sine qua non of successful protracted war.[6]

As for *proximity*, it is preferable to have areas with good terrain reasonably close to one another in order to facilitate planning, command, control, and communications and to gradually establish and integrate a logistical structure to support intensified hostilities. Conversely, widely separated areas make it extremely difficult, if not impossible, for insurgents to contemplate sustained large-scale guerrilla or mobile conventional operations. Such a situation would seem to exist in the Philippines, where there are plenty of jungle areas conducive to guerrilla warfare. But, since the Philippines is an archipelago, and the operational areas of the insurgents are thus separated from one another, the New People's Army's military operations have been localized. Whether the NPA can move beyond decentralized local operations and adopt and implement a coordinated nationwide strategy involving large-scale military operations remains doubtful.

One important benefit that favorable topography bestows on insurgents (which merits closer attention at this point) is the seclusion of base areas. Bases are necessary for guerrilla warfare, particularly in the earliest phases, when, as Che Guevara pointed out, the essential task of the guerrilla fighter is to avoid being eliminated by taking up positions out of reach of the enemy.[7] Maintaining a strong base of operations as the war progresses is no less important. In his *Selected Military Writings*, Mao wrote of the crucial role of bases:

> Without such strategic bases, there will be nothing to depend on in carrying out any of our strategic tasks or achieving the aim of the war. It is a character-

istic of guerrilla warfare behind the enemy lines that it is fought without a rear, for the guerrilla forces are severed from the country's general rear. But guerrilla warfare could not last long or grow without base areas. The base areas, indeed, are its rear.

History knows many peasant wars of the roving rebel type, but none of them ever succeeded. In the present age of advanced communications and technology, it would be all the more groundless to imagine one can win victory by fighting in the manner of the roving rebels. However, this roving rebel idea still exists among many impoverished peasants, and in the minds of guerrilla commanders it becomes the view that base areas are neither necessary nor important. Therefore, ridding the minds of the guerrilla commanders of this idea is a prerequisite for deciding on a policy of establishing base areas. . . . Only when this ideology is thoroughly overcome and the policy of establishing base areas is initiated and applied will there be conditions favourable for the maintenance of guerrilla warfare over a long period.[8]

Concealed permanent base areas allow the insurgents to plan, train, rest, recuperate, and marshal equipment and to organize the people in relative security. A case in point is the network of bases set up by one of Afghanistan's most notable guerrilla leaders, Ahmed Shah Massoud, in the mountains overlooking the Panjshir Valley. The positive contribution of these bases to Massoud's successful guerrilla attacks is clear from reports by observers and several major Soviet campaigns in the valley that failed to locate and dislodge his forces. Likewise, Jonas Savimbi's forces in southern Angola have expanded operations and proved to be a tenacious foe of the government because, among other things, they have a solid and secure basing structure.

The absence of permanent bases inside a country means that insurgent units cannot generate a steadily increasing level of guerrilla warfare. The experience of the Polisario guerrillas in the Western Sahara is instructive here. While the Polisario has been able to establish temporary facilities in certain areas and to carry out periodic and sometimes quite successful raids, the overall capability of the insurgents remains limited. All things considered, Polisario's fighters resemble what Mao called "roving bands" because they have no permanent bases inside the Western Sahara.

One final note with regard to bases is that whether bases are permanent or semipermanent, there is a natural temptation to defend them against major government assaults. Such a course invites disaster when the insurgents are not ready to confront the government in set-piece battles. An example is the attempt and subsequent costly failure of the guerrillas to defend their Grammos and Vitsi bases during the Greek civil war.[9] What this obviously suggests is that by throwing prudence to the winds, guerrillas in such circumstances simply go from a bad to a worse situation.

The specific issue of bases underscores the more general connection between insurgent success and topography. This does not imply that favorable topography is necessary in all insurgencies, for there are exceptions, such as the Jewish and Cypriot revolts against the British and Lenin's seizure of power in Russia. In these cases, topography played no significant role; the insurgents succeeded because they had popular support and the government was weak and wavering. When, as in most cases, governments evince a strong commitment and are able to prevent a deterioration of morale in the military and police forces, topographical features and base areas become vital for insurgents who emphasize rural guerrilla warfare.

For insurgents who opt for urban warfare, base areas and topography are not major concerns. Urban areas, however, have not been decisive in situations where governments demonstrate a reasonable commitment to the struggle. Although the complex and functionally interdependent nature of large urban centers yields tempting targets and provides concealment for terrorists, groups that have relied almost exclusively on terrorism as a form of warfare (notably the Baader-Meinhof group in Germany, the Japanese Red Army, the Basque ETA in Spain, the IRA, the Red Brigades in Italy, the Tupamaros in Uruguay, and the Monteneros in Argentina) have not come close to achieving their long-term aims and, in most cases, have been dealt severe losses. The reasons for this have been noted by Gurr, who pointed out that police and military forces are usually concentrated in cities and that unless the insurgents include most of the urban population and have the sympathy of the security forces, a rare set of conditions, they are easily dispersed.[10] Hence, while cities may provide opportunities for terrorists whose operations are ancillary to rural warfare (e.g., Afghanistan), they have not, by themselves, proven to be areas where decisive strategic successes can be achieved against committed governments with adequate resources.

CLIMATE

In writings on insurgency, the effect of climate has not received anywhere near the attention that terrain has received. Perhaps this is because climate can help or hinder both sides depending on the strategic and tactical circumstances. When insurgents are conducting small guerrilla attacks, heavy rain or snow makes it difficult for governments to exploit their advantages with respect to equipment and transportation both on the ground and in the air. While guerrillas can move on foot, government forces tend to rely on aircraft, armored personnel carriers, jeeps, trucks, and tanks for transportation. Since the maintenance and movement of machines are impeded by bad weather and resulting mud, snowdrifts, and the like, the guerrilla has a relative advantage, in part because lulls in government operations are common during periods of bad weather. In Oman, for example, the activity of the Sultan's Armed Forces in Dhofar province dropped off noticeably during the rainy season, and in Afghanistan, Soviet military activity decreased during the winter months. Although guerrilla attacks also tend to be reduced, insurgents can use bad weather to regroup and reorganize in relative security.

When the fighting in an insurgency escalates to the mobile-conven-· tional level, the greater transportation and logistical needs of both sides are hampered by bad weather. Whether the insurgents or the government can benefit varies. It depends on short-term calculations about enemy troop dispositions and the ability to overcome adverse weather. As the 1954 battle of Dien Bien Phu in the first Indochina war and various attacks on U.S. Special Forces camps in the second Indochina war showed, bad weather can be used to tactical advantage. In both cases, assaults were timed to coincide with heavy cloud cover that prevented or interfered significantly with government efforts to provide close air support and to resupply beleaguered garrisons. Despite these situations, however, over the long term climate does not appear to be factor that favors either side in any critical way.[11]

THE TRANSPORTATION-COMMUNICATIONS INFRASTRUCTURE

One aspect of the physical environment that can have considerable bearing on the fortunes of an insurgency is the state of the transportation-communications systems, especially in large countries experiencing rural guerrilla warfare. Under those circumstances, the responsibility of government forces to provide security for many areas (i.e., cities, towns, military installations, and so forth) puts great strain on manpower and resources. Government strategies usually emphasize mobile-reaction units to compensate for shortcomings associated with the need to provide sufficient static defenses throughout the country. If transportation and communications systems are highly developed, the missions of mobile-reaction teams can be carried out more easily and expeditiously. Conversely, poor roads, rail networks, and river transport systems and inadequate communications make mobility difficult and therefore favor the insurgents.[12] Gurr has these comments on this point:

> Guerrilla war is common in underdeveloped countries because of poor transportation and communication networks and the isolation of rural areas, which facilitate guerrilla incursions. Free access to rural people enables guerrillas to propagandize, control, and secure support from them. The relatively dense road and rail networks of the Congo helped make it possible for United Nations and Congolese forces to suppress a number of regional rebellions between 1961 and 1966; the lack of comparable facilities has contributed to the inability of the Sudanese army to control the Anya-nya rebellion in the southern Sudan. The insulation of the American colonies from Britain by 2,000 miles of ocean facilitated a successful revolt; a comparable geographic separation has been of little value to rebels in Portuguese Angola and Mozambique. The Castro guerrillas were able to sustain themselves in the Sierra Maestra against a much larger army that lacked surface or aerial mobility;

Spanish-American dissidents in the more rugged terrain of northern New Mexico had no such chance, in June 1967, against police helicopter patrols.[13]

The Human Environment

DEMOGRAPHIC DISTRIBUTION

Although students of insurgency have devoted substantial attention to the physical attributes of the environment, the human dimension is equally important. Of primary interest here are demography, social structure, economics, and the political culture and system. Demography, for instance, can have a major impact on the course of events. Where the population is small and concentrated, it is easier for the government to control the people and sever its links with the guerrillas. When most of the people live in cities, the situation does not appear as favorable to insurgent movements as when the population is concentrated in rural areas, although some contemporary insurgent strategists believe otherwise. As suggested earlier, if a society is highly urbanized, the government can control and monitor the people more easily and minimize the role and effects of rural guerrilla bases. But if the government is weak and the insurgents have a significant degree of international support, it is possible for the insurgents to achieve their aims. Again, an example is Palestine in 1947–1948, when Jewish attacks combined with external moral, political, and material support for the Zionists to force the British government, weakened by World War II and beset with economic problems, to retreat. When the authorities demonstrate both the resolution and the competence to combat the insurgent threat and thus compel the insurgents to opt for protracted warfare, an urban environment, although conducive to terrorist activities, hardly suffices; an underdeveloped rural society is more promising.

SOCIAL STRUCTURE

To better understand insurgencies, we need to go beyond the basic demographic attributes of a population and inquire about the impact of its social structure. Societies may be divided vertically by race, ethnicity, and religion, or horizontally by class or caste. While vertical cleavages are self-explanatory, a few remarks about class and caste are in order before proceeding. Although the criteria for distinguishing social classes vary somewhat and remain the subject of academic debate, we view classes as differing according to wealth (and the various benefits derived therefrom) and occupation. Both wealth and occupation confer status. Castes are extremely rigid groups divided by economic and occupational differences and explicit privileges, all of which are legitimized by theological or philosophical ideas. While there is mobility between classes (at least theoretically) membership in castes is static. Since caste systems are rare, we will focus once again on classes when we consider economic factors.

Societal cleavages along racial, ethnic, and religious lines are frequently among the root causes of insurgency and can be either helpful or detrimental to the progression of an insurrection. Where one group enjoys disproportionate political and economic power and benefits relative to other groups, insurgents often find an opportunity to gain support from the disadvantaged groups. If the relatively deprived group constitutes a majority of the population, the possibilities of gaining support are naturally greater. Colonial governments are especially vulnerable, as the French found out in Algeria and Vietnam. The same is true of minority-based governments, such as Ian Smith's in white-ruled Rhodesia (now Zimbabwe), which exclude the majority from political participation and practice economic discrimination. Even if disadvantaged groups do not constitute a majority, they can still provide the foundation for a serious insurrection if they are sizable: witness the Kikuyu in Kenya in the 1950s, Ovimbundu tribesmen in Angola, the Kurds in Iraq and Iran, and the Eritreans in Ethiopia.

It should not be inferred from the above comments that all situations in which minorities experience political and economic deprivation are advantageous for insurgent movements. In circumstances in which the disadvantaged groups are small minorities, governments may galvanize support against them by emphasizing ancient antagonisms and the threats that the minorities pose to the privileges of the majority. When this transpires, insurgents (such as those in northern and northeastern Thailand or the Moros in the southern Philippines) find it very difficult, if not impossible, to attract wide popular support, because their identification with minorities undercuts their appeal to the majority. The reliance on minorities for support is especially precarious for insurgents when such groups can be isolated by topographical features. A striking example is the case in Oman, where support for the Popular Front for the Liberation of Oman came primarily from the *jebali* (mountain people) of Dhofar province. With the coastal area to the east and an inhospitable desert (the Rub al-Khali) to the west, the government was able to separate the guerrillas from the rest of the country by constructing military interdiction barriers across the insurgents' north-south lines of transportation. Insurgents who confront conditions such as these (as we shall see in later chapters) compound their problems if they pursue far-reaching goals that threaten either the political community or system. If they are less ambitious and seek only reforms, they may have some success.

Two final points should be made about societal divisions and insurgencies. The first is that rival groups may have a deleterious impact on an insurgent movement, the government, or both. Where more than one disadvantaged group is incorporated into insurgent ranks, the size and capability of the movement may increase. Sometimes, however, it creates problems with respect to cohesion. In Afghanistan, for instance, all ethnic and religious groups are engaged in the struggle against the Soviets and the Afghan government. At the same time, however, the ancient animosities between groups, most notably Hazara, Tajik, Uzbek, and Baluchi resentment of the Pathans, have been a source of disunity, fragmented political-military strategies, and internecine strife. Such rivalries also present the government with opportunities to infiltrate insurgent ranks and play one group off against another. But, as the Afghan case also shows, the government can suffer the same malady: witness the endemic strife inside the People's Democratic Party of Afghanistan, which has been caused in no small part by the different ethnic composition of its Khalq and Parchamite wings (the former is Pathan-based; the latter is composed largely of Tajiks and other minorities).

The second point about societal groups relates to their internal structure of authority. The essential question is how conducive the structure is to organization and discipline. Three general structural configurations of power provide a useful frame of reference: hierarchical, pyramidal, and segmentary. Hierarchical power structures have clearly delineated lines of authority from top to bottom (e.g., the Roman Catholic church). Pyramidal structures may have an authority figure who is first among equals, but there are multiple centers of more or less equal power (e.g., the Shiite grand ayatollahs in Iran). Segmentary structures are marked by a diffusion of power to local groups that act autonomously (e.g., *jebali* tribes in Oman). While all power configurations can accommodate conspiratorial and urban-warfare strategies, segmentary structures are not as favorable for military-focus and especially protracted-popular-war strategies because they obstruct the organizational development associated with those strategies. Disunity, in particular, is often the natural by-product of insurgencies waged by groups with segmented structures. By way of illustration, many observers believe that Ahmed Shah Massoud's ability to create a sophisticated organization in the Panjshir Valley in Afghanistan has been facilitated by the fact that the Tajiks are not a tribally oriented people. In contrast, similar organization among the Pathans has been impeded by their segmentary society.

One thing this brief discussion of societal factors should make clear is that it would be a great mistake to focus simply on the more familiar economic and political dimensions of the human environment of insurgencies. Although the relationships between societal divisions and the fortunes of insurgent movements are various and complex, they cannot be passed over lightly, because they may provide key explanations of insurgent success or failures. As later chapters will show, popular support, organization, unity, and government response can be affected in very important ways by societal factors. In many cases, their impact is an outgrowth of their interplay with economic factors.

ECONOMIC FACTORS

As even a cursory look at insurrections makes clear, in most cases economic factors of one sort or another play a key part in explaining the outbreak of political violence. Accordingly, it is necessary to assess trends related to familiar economic measurements, such as gross national product, growth rates, inflation, employment, productivity, and income distribution. While both stagnation and sudden downturns in the economy after a period of growth have been associated with insurgencies, it may also be the case that violence occurs during periods of prosperity and growth. In light of this, it is necessary to relate economic indicators to the expectations of various groups within the society to find out whether social groups and/or classes have come to believe that they are victims of institutionalized discrimination related to socioeconomic benefits (i.e., income, jobs, education, housing, health services, and so on).

Numerous past and current cases provide ample evidence that economic inequities that create a perception of relative deprivation are a major cause of insurrectionary violence. In some situations, such as in El Salvador, Nicaragua under the Somoza regime, and the Philippines, where the peasant and working class are denied a fair share of the wealth by small ruling elite and capitalist classes, economic considerations are the primary motive; in many other cases they are interwoven with, and reinforce, other grievances. During the nationalist anti-Japanese conflict in China, for instance, the economic plight of the peasantry was consciously and successfully exploited by Mao. Likewise, the FLN in Algeria made flagrant economic discrimination by the settlers an integral part of its overall nationalist appeal.

Many current conflicts that seem on the surface to be based on communal rivalries turn out, upon closer inspection, to have significant economic dimensions. For example, no serious commentator would deny that the Provisional IRA's ability to take advantage of Catholic-Protestant differences in Northern Ireland is related to actual and perceived economic discrimination against the Catholics. Nor could the actions against the Maronite Christian political and economic establishment in Lebanon by the Shiites in Hezbollah and other groups be explained without taking into account the long-standing relative impoverishment of the Shiite community.

Institutionalized economic discrimination is often a main (if not the main) underlying cause of insurgency, as demonstrated by the preceding examples and a plethora of others, such as the insurrections involving the Kurds in Iran, Turkey, and Iraq; blacks in southern Sudan; and Marxists in Thailand, Oman, and Malaya. What also needs to be pointed out is that some groups in relatively advantageous economic circumstances may also resort to illegal political violence to prevent a loss of their privileged status. To some degree, this is one motive behind the actions of Protestant conservative groups in Northern Ireland and right-wing organizations in some Latin American countries. Suggestions have also been made that the minority-based Tamil insurgents in Sri Lanka have played upon the Tamil community's fears that mandating Sinhalese as the official language (in lieu of English) would mean that the Tamils would lose some of the disproportionate share of coveted civil service positions they have come to hold by virtue of their superior educational achievements.

In calling attention to the pervasive importance of economic factors in insurgent conflicts, I do not wish to imply their primacy in all cases. In the Afghan insurgency, for instance, economic factors have been inconsequential. The Afghan conflict has been fueled by ethnic (at the outset), religious, and nationalist factors, as well as resistance to the loss of power by local tribal chiefs and mullahs, a necessary outcome of Marxist centralizing efforts and reforms. While it is true that land, marriage, and educational reforms had economic implications, the real threat perceived by the insurgents was not the economic impact per se but rather the loss of local political influence they entailed.

The exceptions notwithstanding, economic factors frequently are crucial to understanding an insurgency. Therefore, it behooves the analyst to ask whether, and in what way, they account for the development of the insurgency. The questions of whether economic or social conditions and trends give rise to insurgent activity is closely related to the existing political culture and system and the nexus between the two. An examination of the political setting furthers our understanding of why some people and societal groups are more inclined than others to create, join, and otherwise support insurgent movements.

POLITICAL CULTURE

Political culture refers to the salient and enduring attitudes or orientations of people toward aspects of politics that are observable. More specifically, it encompasses their knowledge, feeling, and judgments about aspects of politics. Although studies of political culture cover a vast range of orientations toward politics, we shall limit our attention to those with noteworthy implications for insurgency.

In their pioneering cross-national study of political culture, *The Civic Culture*, Gabriel A. Almond and Sidney Verba developed three concepts—parochials, subjects, and participants—to characterize the differences between people in terms of their awareness of the political process and their feelings and judgments about their ability to influence it.[14] These differences help us further understand the opportunities insurgent leaders have to mobilize support from societal groups.

Parochials are those citizens who have little or no awareness of the political system at the national level and no perception of their ability to influence it. They are generally illiterate, live at a subsistence level, and are located in isolated areas. Although relatively deprived and neglected, they eschew involvement in political activity, including insurgencies. The rural

Indian population of Guatemala during the insurrection in the 1960s is an example. Despite their poverty and insurgent overtures, the Indians remained passive and indifferent, thus preventing the insurgent movement from developing a much-needed base of mass support among them. Groups like the Guatemalan Indians do not provide much in the way of support for insurgents unless governments intrude significantly into their areas and affairs. They simply prefer to be left alone.

Subjects are those who have become part of the political system and are aware of its impact on their lives but who are not active in shaping policy. Normally, subjects are not inclined to join insurgent movements, as the conservative orientations of slum dwellers in many countries, especially Latin America, have shown. This does not mean that adverse treatment and discrimination by the government will be tolerated ad infinitum. Skillful propaganda and organizing by insurgent cadres can change orientations by creating a new awareness. But since such a process may take years, governments have the time and opportunity to respond. The magnitude of change in popular attitudes will obviously be affected by the nature of the government's response. Where the response is poor, erstwhile loyal subjects may become alienated from the system, authorities, and policies.[15] Once that happens, they may support insurgent movements in order to effect changes in policies they consider illegitimate. Although this may also entail support for a change of regime and/or authorities, subjects are not motivated to become active participants in day-to-day political processes. What they want is better judicial, economic, and social treatment. If this is achieved by astute government reforms, they may defect from the insurgency and revert to their generally passive roles. Not surprisingly, the rank-and-file members of many insurgent organizations in the Third World fall within this category.

Participants are generally educated citizens who are not only aware of national political institutions and policies but are also cognizant of the policy process and wish to actively engage in it. They are confident they can have an effective impact on national events and policies. With such an orientation, they provide the best potential for recruitment by insurgents if their desire to participate is blocked. It should come as no surprise to find that the educated strata of societies provide most of the leaders of insurgent movements.

Besides these three basic orientations, other attitudes rooted in more-general societal values and norms may be politically relevant to insurgencies. Given the vast range of social values and norms in the world, I would go beyond my purposes here if I tried to identify and classify all of them. Instead, I will suggest a few possibilities that are important for analysts to be aware of, with the caveat that the consideration and assessment of others may be necessary on a case-by-case basis.

In this context, attitudes and orientations involving acceptance of authority, interpersonal and intergroup trust, and tolerance of violence and foreigners can be quite important with respect to the other major factors used to analyze insurgencies. Resistance to the imposition of authority beyond immediate social groups (e.g., tribes) and low interpersonal and intergroup trust may be more important reasons for the divisiveness that plagues so many insurgent movements than any temporary ideological, strategic, and tactical disputes. Such an attitude toward authority may also undermine government efforts, no matter how benign, to organize and gain support from the people. Where there is a low tolerance for violence, insurgent recruitment will suffer and violent acts, particularly terrorist ones, will probably be repugnant, if not counterproductive. If there is a high tolerance for violence, however, the potential for the existence and growth of insurgencies is greater. Finally, the attitude toward foreigners may be important. This is especially so when the foreigners have been the object of historical rivalries and hatreds. In such cases, foreign involvement can undermine whichever side they are supporting.

The situation in Afghanistan demonstrates how important deeply rooted socio-political orientations are in providing a better understanding of the flow of events in an insurgency. The tenacity of the guerrillas in the face of the vastly superior resources of their adversary can be attributed, in large part, to the attitudes of the various ethno-religious groups, particularly the Pathans. Age-old resistance to authority in defense of tribal autonomy and individualism have created stiff opposition to the extension of central government authority and a high tolerance for violence; and the emphasis on vengeance (*badal*) in the *Pushtunwali,* or code of conduct, has contributed to an upsurge of support for the guerrillas in the wake of indiscriminate attacks by government and Soviet forces. Moreover, historical animosities toward the Soviets have exacerbated this tendency, producing a clear target for popular wrath. These trends are further reinforced by Islamic religious values and norms, such as those promising eternal rewards for martyrs who fall defending Islam against nonbelievers (infidels). On the negative side of the ledger are attitudes indicative of low intergroup trust, which have militated against cooperation and unity among insurgent groups. What all this suggests is that any analysis of the strengths and weaknesses of the two sides in Afghanistan that ignores the country's political culture would be seriously deficient. Hence, an effort to understand political culture is generally worthwhile; in doing so, students of insurgency need to rely on the expertise of regional and country specialists, particularly anthropologists and sociologists.

THE POLITICAL SYSTEM

To obtain a profile of the political system, one can consult the same area experts, along with political scientists specializing in the country. Since the political community will have been dealt with in the stage of analysis that has already examined societal groups and their interplay, the focus at this point should be on the system, on authorities, and on general policies and their relationship to the political culture. As noted in chapter 2, there are a number of useful and readily available classification schemes in the literature on comparative politics that delineate basic differences between political systems. Some of the schemes are quite detailed, others more general.[16] Regardless of which one the analyst chooses, there are basic questions that need to be answered.

With respect to the political system, one must ascertain the dominant values and structures involved in the political process and whether they are congruent with the political culture. In addition, one must look at subcultures (groups with orientations toward politics that deviate in various ways from overall orientations). For example, consider a traditional autocracy where, as shown in chapter 2, the values tend to be elitist and ascriptive and structures are limited and controlled. What this means is that final decision-making authority at the national level is the exclusive domain of a select group deemed to have the right to rule by virtue of heredity (e.g., members of royal families in places like Morocco, Saudi Arabia, Persian Gulf sheikdoms, and Ethiopia under Haile Selassie). While other groups such as the military, clergy, landowners, and businessmen have influence, their role is supportive of existing arrangements from which they benefit. To the extent that political structures beyond the decision and support elites (e.g., parties, interest groups, and the media) are allowed to exist, their activity is controlled and carefully circumscribed. Any independent and organized opposition is prohibited, and general participation is discouraged. More often than not, religious values and norms play a key part in legitimizing a traditional autocracy.

While a number of traditional autocracies are remarkably stable, they are nonetheless vulnerable to global socioeconomic forces (the so-called process of social mobilization), such as increased media exposure, education, and geographic mobility. Such forces often heighten people's awareness of politics. This in turn can reduce parochialism and lead to demands for government services and even participation. Such changes in the political culture can be a source of trouble for traditional autocracies, particularly those with limited resources. Increased socioeconomic demands arising from former parochial groups that have made the transition to being subjects (e.g., many Indians in Guatemala in the 1980s) and demands from existing groups with subject orientations place great stress on leaders to alter the distribution of benefits. The central political question at this point is whether the decision-makers and key supporting elites are willing to share the wealth or are intransigent. For traditional autocracies like Saudi Arabia and Kuwait, excess petrodollars made it much easier to cope with such demands. For others who are less fortunate the problem may become acute because economic stagnation or regression means that a transfer of resources is the only option, and this usually meets with resistance on the part of privileged elites who stand to lose part of their wealth if this occurs.[17]

Demands for participation create even greater dilemmas for traditional autocracies because, as we have seen, the political values and structural makeup of such systems do not allow for broadened participation. It is precisely this situation that creates an incongruence between the political culture and the political system. In some cases, leaders (e.g., King Hassan of Morocco) may buy time by establishing constitutional monarchies that permit selected oppositional parties and interest groups (e.g., unions) to function in a limited and controlled way. The long-term viability of such arrangements, however, remains questionable because the numbers of people with participatory orientations may increase. Failure by leaders to open channels to unfettered participation may then lead to insurgent activity.

It is worth restressing how important it is to have an understanding of the political culture and the political system and how they are related to one another because the emergence—and degree of intensity—of insurgencies may be caused by political shortcomings. While social or economic factors may be primary causes of insurrections, situations may be exacerbated or ameliorated by the decisions and policies of political leaders. For example, even symbolic participation may win support for governments, at least for a time. Examining the political system and culture helps us determine not only why political responses are either wise or foolish but also the potential for future responsiveness. As we shall see in chapter 8 on government response, many things can be done to mitigate, diminish, or eliminate insurgencies. But, whether they are likely or feasible courses of action relates closely to the calculations of political elites, whose range of choices is affected by values, ideologies, and the internal power structure (i.e., the system).

Summary

A careful analysis of the physical and human dimensions of the environment is a good starting point for an analysis of an insurgency. An assessment of topography and transportation-communications systems can reveal a good deal about the potential or actual effectiveness of the forms of violence used by insurgents, particularly guerrilla warfare, whereas a careful look at demography, social groups, the economy, and the political culture and political system will shed light on the causes underlying insurgencies. Of course, no matter how favorable the physical milieu may be and no matter how bad social, economic, and political conditions may be, a serious insurgent threat will not emerge unless there are determined leaders who have the requisite skills to exploit potential opportunities and to organize at least some popular support. What that consists of, and how it is acquired, is the subject to which we now turn.

Notes

1.   A. H. Shollom, "Nowhere Yet Everywhere," in Franklin Mark Osanka, ed., *Modern Guerrilla Warfare*, (New York: The Free Press of Glencoe, 1962), p. 19. Numerous other authors have called attention to the importance of rugged terrain in an insurgency. See, for instance, Virgil Ney, "Guerrilla Warfare and Modern Strategy," *ibid.*, p. 28; Brooks McClure, "Russia's Hidden Army," *ibid.*, pp. 87–91; Roger Trinquier, *Modern Warfare* (New York: Frederick A. Praeger, 1964), pp. 16–17; and Otto Heilbrunn, *Partisan Warfare* (New York: Frederick A. Praeger, 1962), pp. 39, 160.

2.   Arthur Campbell, *Guerrillas* (New York: The John Day Company, 1968), p. 283.

3.   On the Mao-Nasser exchange of views, see Muhammad Haykal, *The Cairo Documents* (Garden City, N.Y.: Doubleday, 1973), p. 312. The effect of the terrain on Palestinian operations is summarized in Bard E. O'Neill, *Armed Struggle in Palestine* (Boulder, Colo.: Westview Press, 1978), p. 103.

4.   Numerous observers have noted the ability of the Polisario insurgents to conduct guerrilla attacks in the desert. See, for instance, *New York Times*, March 15, 1977; *International Herald Tribune*, May 1977; *Washington Post* May 29–30, 1977; *Los Angeles Times*, November 15, 1977; and *The Age* (Melbourne), August 3, 1978.

5.   C. E. S. Dudley, "Subversive Warfare—Five Military Factors," *Army Quarterly and Defence Journal* (U.K.; July 1968):209.

6.   Mao Tse-tung, "On Protracted War," in *Selected Military Writings of Mao Tse-tung* (Beijing: Foreign Language Press, 1963), pp. 200–201.

7.   Che Guevara, *Guerrilla Warfare* (New York: Vintage Books, 1961), p. 9. On the importance of bases, see Heilbrunn, *Partisan Warfare*, p. 45; McClure, "Russia's Hidden Army," p. 90; Boyd T. Bashore, "Duel Strategy for Limited War," in Osanka, ed., *Modern Guerrilla Warfare*, p. 197; Anthony Crockett, "Action in Malaya," *ibid.*, p. 312; George B. Jordan, "Objectives and Methods of Communist Guerrilla Warfare," *ibid.*, p. 406; and John J. McCuen, *The Art of Counter-Revolutionary War* (Harrisburg, Pa.: Stackpole Books, n.d.), p. 69.

8.   Mao Tse-tung, "Strategy in Guerrilla War Against Japan," *Selected Military Writings*, pp. 165–166.

9.   Heilbrunn, *Partisan Warfare*, p. 46, and Edward R. Wainhouse, "Guerrilla Warfare in Greece, 1946–1949: A Case Study," in Osanka, ed., *Modern Guerrilla Warfare*, p. 226.

10.   Robert Ted Gurr, *Why Men Rebel* (Princeton, N.J.: Princeton University Press, 1970), p. 266; Campbell, *Guerrillas*, p. 283.

11.   Ney, "Guerrilla Warfare and Modern Strategy," pp. 28–30, cites climate as a consideration in his discussion of environment, but does not explain its relationship to guerrilla fortunes; Shollom, "Nowhere Yet Everywhere," p. 18, calls attention to logistical needs caused by severe weather; Bernard B. Fall, "Indochina: The

Seven Year Dilemma," in Osanka, ed., *Modern Guerrilla Warfare*, p. 258, cites the Vietnamese tactic of hitting the French when the weather was inclement to deny the latter effective air support.

12.   Campbell, *Guerrillas*, pp. 252–253; Gene Z. Hanrahan, "The Chinese Red Army and Guerrilla Warfare," in Osanka, ed., *Modern Guerrilla Warfare*, p. 159.

13.   Gurr, *Why Men Rebel*, pp. 263–264.

14.   Gabriel A. Almond and Sidney Verba, *The Civic Culture* (Princeton, N.J.: Princeton University Press, 1963). A more succinct treatment of political culture that provides the basis for our coverage of the subject is Gabriel A. Almond and G. Bingham Powell, Jr., *Comparative Politics*, 2d ed. (Boston: Little, Brown, 1978), chap. 2.

15.   A recent report of cautious, conservative peasants gradually giving assistance to insurgents as a result of the latter's exploitation of socioeconomic problems may be found in *Christian Science Monitor*, April 14, 1987. A year later, James LeMoyne observed that much of the support for the rightist Nationalist Republican Alliance during National Assembly elections had come from peasants and slum dwellers. See *New York Times*, March 24, 1988.

16.   For typologies of political systems, see Almond and Powell, *Comparative Politics*, pp. 71–76; David E. Apter, *The Politics of Modernization* (Chicago: University of Chicago Press, 1965), pp. 28–42, 357–421; and Charles F. Andrain, *Political Life and Social Change*, 2d ed. (Belmont, Calif.: Duxbury Press, 1974), pp. 188–292.

17.   The problem of reconciling the interests of key elites with necessary reforms is discussed in D. Michael Shafer, *Deadly Paradigms* (Princeton, N.J.: Princeton University Press, 1988), pp. 120–122.

V   Popular Support

In most circumstances insurgent leaders know they would risk destruction by confronting government forces in direct conventional engagements. Instead, they opt to erode the strength of the government through the use of terrorism or guerrilla warfare, not only to increase the human and material cost to the government but also to demonstrate its failure to maintain effective control and provide protection for the people. Eventually, according to the insurgent's logic, the authorities will grow weary of the struggle and seek to prevent further losses by either capitulating or negotiating a settlement favorable to the insurgents.

The recourse to terrorism and guerrilla warfare reflects the inferiority of insurgent movements vis-à-vis governments, which are initially in an advantageous position because they control the administrative apparatus of the state and, most important, the army and police. To offset the superior resources of the government, many insurgent leaders stress the critical strategic role of popular support. In the words of Mao Tse-tung, "The richest source of power to wage war lies in the masses of the people." Echoing this sentiment, Bernard Fall suggested that the evidence amassed on the guerrilla battlefields on three continents over three decades indicates that civilian support is the essential element of successful guerrilla operations.[1] That popular support has become a cornerstone of insurgent thinking in this century can be seen in its constant reiteration in one form or another in written and spoken commentaries of countless insurgent leaders. The importance of popular support in insurgent conflicts can also be seen in the attention that it receives in counterinsurgency literature and thinking. It is acknowledged explicitly in government campaigns to "win the hearts and minds of the people" and implicitly in the rule of thumb that governments need a favorable ten-to-one ratio of military forces to subdue guerrillas. The unspoken assumption underlying such a ratio is that despite their inferiority in numbers and resources, insurgents are hard to subdue and control because of their hit-and-run tactics, dispersal, frequent ability to exploit advantageous terrain, and ability to gain support from segments of the population.

As important as popular support is, it is treated in rather general terms by most analysts and practitioners. Although precise calculations of popular support are impossible, given the absence of careful and systematic survey research in countries where insurgencies are taking place (because of prohibitions by one or both sides and security considerations), estimates can be made. These can be based on such sources as documents and statements by the parties to the conflict, observations by journalists and others who are able to visit insurgent and/or government areas, accounts of defectors, and the behavior of both sides toward the people. Government analysts have the added advantage of highly classified data from agents, interception of electronic communications, and the like. Since information from any single source can be distorted or completely erroneous, corroboration from several sources is necessary. In the case of Afghanistan, for instance, widespread support for the insurgents has been established by inadvertent statements by the Russians and Afghan authorities, reports by journalists from all parts of the world who have visited guerrilla zones, the deliberate Soviet policy of destroying villages and crops to drive the people away from guerrilla areas, and information supplied by Russian defectors.

To better understand the role of popular support in an insurgency, available data need to be structured, interpreted, and related to other aspects of insurgency. To facilitate this undertaking, the notion of popular support will be discussed in terms of (1) its two types (active and passive), (2) the role of the intellectuals and the masses, and (3) the various techniques that insurgents use to gain support. As we proceed, we will link the various aspects of popular support to other relevant factors of the analytical framework.

Types of Popular Support

PASSIVE

Passive support includes individuals who quietly sympathize with the insurgents but are unwilling to provide material assistance. Although at first glance passive supporters may seem inconsequential, that is not the case; at a minimum, they are not apt to betray or otherwise impede the insurgents, and this is important because a key aspect of counterinsurgency strategy for government units combating elusive terrorists and guerrillas is the acquisition of information from the people. Thus, passive support is a valuable commodity for insurgents.

ACTIVE

The most important kind of support the people can render to the insurgents is, of course, active. *Active support* encompasses those who are willing to make sacrifices and risk personal harm either by joining the movement or by providing the insurgents with intelligence information, concealment, shelter, hiding places for arms and equipment, medical assistance, guides, and liaison agents. It also includes people who, in some cases, carry out acts of civil disobedience or protest that may result in severe punishment by the government. The vital part active support plays is summarized aptly by the Vietminh manual on guerrilla warfare:

> Without the "popular antennae" we would be without information; without the protection of the people we could neither keep our secrets nor execute quick movement; without the people the guerrillas could neither attack the enemy nor replenish their forces and, in consequence, they could not accomplish their mission with ardour and speed. . . .
>
> The population helps us to fight the enemy by giving us information, suggesting ruses and plans, helping us to overcome difficulties due to lack of arms, and providing us with guides. It also supplies liaison agents, hides and protects us, assists our actions near posts, feeds us and looks after our wounded. . . . Cooperating with guerrillas, it has participated in sabotage acts, in diversionary actions, in encircling the enemy, and in applying the scorched earth policy. . . . On several occasions and in cooperation with guerrillas, it has taken part in combat.[2]

The importance the Vietminh ascribed to active popular support was consistent with their adherence to a protracted-popular-war strategy in which, we saw in chapter 3, popular support is the most vital element. This does not mean active popular support is irrelevant when it comes to other strategies. For insurgents following the military-focus approach, substantial support is either assumed to exist or will be acquired as a consequence of military success; for those following conspiratorial and urban-warfare approaches, extensive mobilization of active support is considered unnecessary. But even here, active support does have a role. Conspirators, it will be recalled, benefit from a context of generalized discontent and seek to energize selectetd segments of the population at particular points in time. Even proponents of urban warfare, whose operations and organization are small-scale, need at least some active support to survive. Moreover, those urban-warfare strategists who envisage a transition to rural warfare believe that increased active support will eventually become necessary. The fact that at least some degree of active popular support is important in all insurgencies is evident from accounts of many past cases—for instance, the Boer War in South Africa, Greece, the Philippines, Malaya, Indochina, Algeria, Cuba, Cyprus, Kenya, China, and Sarawak.[3]

A striking contemporary example of the contribution of both passive and active popular support for an insurgent movement is Afghanistan, where poorly trained and severely divided rebels with uneven leadership and external support fought Soviet and Afghan government forces to a stalemate, even though their enemies were superior in terms of men and equipment. Almost every observer who has visited the area points to two factors: a physical environment with many features conducive to guerrilla warfare and, more important, support for the insurgents from the vast majority of the people. The critical role of popular support was also acknowledged by the Soviets, occasionally in words, but very clearly in a deliberate strategy of neutralizing the populace through indiscriminate attacks and forcible displacement of people from the most active guerrilla zones.

On the other side of the balance sheet are examples of insurgent failures that in part were due to an inability to obtain at least a modicum of popular support. Che Guevara's ill-fated movement in Bolivia and the insurgency in Guatemala in the 1960s are cases in point. In both instances, efforts to entice backing from poverty-stricken peasants did not succeed and the resulting stagnation of the insurgent groups rendered them vulnerable to government campaigns to isolate and cripple them.

THE INTELLECTUALS AND THE MASSES

Populations from which insurgents seek support are not homogeneous. Instead, as indicated earlier, they are divided by some or all of the following factors: education levels, socioeconomic classes, race, ethnicity, and religion. These distinctions are important to bear in mind when analyzing popular support.

Educational levels are especially significant and provide the basis for dividing the insurgents into two general categories, the intelligentsia and the masses, each of which plays a different role. In developed countries, the terms *intelligentsia* and *intellectual class* are usually associated with leading thinkers who normally, but not exclusively, have completed graduate training at the university level. In Third World countries it is broadened to include those with at least some undergraduate or equivalent training.

Intellectuals are particularly crucial with respect to active popular support because they constitute the principal source for recruitment to both high- and middle-level leadership positions (i.e., commanders of guerrilla units and terrorist networks and political cadres).[4] The part that intellectuals play in catalyzing insurrections has been noted by Ted Robert Gurr, who points out that their desertion from the government has repeatedly been a harbinger of revolution.[5]

The existence of intellectual leadership is necessary for insurgent success, because it provides strategic vision, organizational know-how, and technical competence. Conversely, insurgent movements without leadership from the intellectuals, such as peasant uprisings, are, in the words of David A. Wilson, "notoriously ineffective."[6] Although support from the intellectuals is vital for insurgent success, the picture with respect to mass support is

more complicated, for, as noted in chapters 2 and 3, conspiratorial insurrections stress small, cohesive, elite groups. But, aside from coups, successful
conspiratorial insurgencies require at least selective support from the mass
population, especially if their goals call for changes in the political system or
withdrawal from the political community, both of which are apt to generate
considerable government resistance.

The acquisition of popular support from both intellectuals and the
masses is affected by the social composition of the political community. In
our discussion of the human environment, it was suggested that if distinct
cleavages along racial, ethnic, religious, or class lines exist and coincide with
economic and political disparities, there is fertile ground for obtaining at
least some popular support for an insurgency. The larger the groups that
feel relatively deprived, the greater the possibilities for mobilizing mass support and sustaining a widespread insurgency (e.g., the black population in
Rhodesia at the time of the Ian Smith government, the Eritrean insurrection
in Ethiopia, and the UNITA insurgency in Angola, which draws its strength
from the largest tribal group, the Ovimbundu). The smaller the disadvantaged groups, the smaller also the potential, since they can be more easily
dealt with by encapsulating them and perhaps even exiling or exterminating
them. At this juncture, an earlier point bears repeating: insurgencies based
on minority groups stand a much better chance of accomplishing their aims
if they are reformists, rather than secessionists, traditionalists, pluralists,
egalitarians, or anarchists, because reformists generally do not require much
support that cuts across group lines.

Techniques for Gaining Popular Support

While a review of the sociological composition of a political community will greatly increase understanding of the potential for popular support
for an insurgency, the actual level of support depends on the organizational
skills and techniques of insurgent leaders. The question of organization is
treated in the next chapter, so our comments here will be confined to methods or techniques used to gain support.

In the most promising of all insurgent environments, community support and security are "safeguarded best when the native population identifies itself spontaneously with the fortunes of the guerrilla movement."[7] But,
since spontaneity is rare, insurgent movements actively proselytize the people. Insurgents generally employ one or several of the following methods to
gain the desired support and recruits:

1. charismatic attraction
2. esoteric appeals
3. exoteric appeals

4. terrorism
5. provocation of government repression
6. demonstrations of potency
7. coercion

All except the last of these methods are aimed, in one way or another, at convincing the people to render support because the insurgents' goal is just and achievable.

CHARISMATIC ATTRACTION

In certain cases, assertive individuals emerge as the clearly identifiable leaders of insurgent movements. When such men are either perceived to have supernatural qualities or manifest impressive speaking skills and a dynamic, forceful personality, they frequently are able to motivate others to join their cause through their example and persuasiveness. This is especially true in political communities where a tradition of heroic leadership is highly valued (e.g., many Middle Eastern and African states). While the process of "great men" inspiring sizable numbers to follow them may unfold in an unpremeditated and natural way, in some instances the insurgent movement may deliberately exaggerate the prowess and attributes of its leader in order to attract adherents. In these cases, the individual leader becomes the principal reason why some people support insurgent movements. The phenomenon of charismatic attraction has been exemplified by Mao Tse-tung, Fidel Castro, Lenin, and, more recently, Jonas Savimbi in Angola, to name but a few. In the absence of survey data, it is impossible to specify exactly how many people joined their causes because of charismatic attraction, as opposed to other factors, but many observers of the insurgencies led by these men have indicated that the force of their personality was important. In view of this, the analyst must be alert to the possible importance of charisma in the specific case under investigation.[8]

ESOTERIC APPEALS

A second way to obtain popular support that is frequently associated with charismatic leadership is to emphasize esoteric appeals, which are directed primarily at the intellectual stratum. Esoteric appeals seek to clarify environmental conditions by putting them in a theoretical context that has neat, orderly interpretations and explanations for all perceived social, economic, and political "realities." The theoretical contexts may be ideological or theological in nature. While both ideology and theology claim to provide the truth about man's destiny, their basis for doing so differs fundamentally. Ideologists are secular in their approach; they claim to limit their analyses to the observable, concrete world. They further claim that their formulations about mankind's behavior constitute scientific or lawlike explanations about the past, present, and future. A classic example is Marxism-Leninism, which depicts history as progressing through a series of class struggles, the last of which will result in an inevitable victory of the proletariat (working class) over the capitalist class. This will eventually lead to a utopian future where exploitation and alienation will be absent forever after. Of the powerful attraction of political ideologies like Marxism-Leninism in the political arena, Gabriel Almond wrote:

> An ideology imputes a particular structure to political action. It defines who or what the main initiators of action are, whether they be individuals, status groups, classes, nations, magical forces, or deities. It attributes specific roles to these actors, describes their relationships with one another, and defines the arena in which actions occur.[9]

Marxist revolutionaries, for example, have found that Lenin's thesis on the exploitative nature of imperialism has been especially persuasive in Third World countries because it provides a coherent, logical, and comprehensive explanation of the poverty, illiteracy, and oppression that often characterizes the local political, economic, and social environment. Furthermore, by pointing a finger at indigenous feudal or capitalist classes and their links with foreign imperialist elements, it provides an identifiable target for the frustrations of the intellectuals, many of whom are either unemployed or underemployed.[10]

Theology is similar to secular ideology because it also lays claim to the truth about man's past and future. It differs from ideology in that it asserts that truth reposes in sacred revelations by a supreme being and comes to lay persons through the interpretations of those revelations by a privileged class of men (learned religious leaders). Although associated with the spiritual rather than material realm, the metaphysical belief systems articulated by religious thinkers usually possess a logical consistency that is compelling, especially to those in search of higher meaning. In recent and current times, the role of theology in inspiring active popular support has been exemplified dramatically by the sacrifices of the Sikhs in India and Islamic insurgents in the southern Philippines, Afghanistan, Syria, Lebanon, and Iran. While some believe that "liberation theology" in Latin America has also inspired active popular support, its overall impact remains unclear, particularly since the church officially opposes violence.

While the belief systems underlying esoteric appeals are directed primarily at the intellectuals, other aspects of ideology and theology are important in gaining and maintaining support from both the intellectuals and the masses. Where people are frustrated by perceived deprivations, they need their discontent focused on a villain if they are to be energized to carry out or support violence. One of the functions of ideology and theology, the explicit identification of friend and foe, meets this need. Identifying the source of frustration and grievances is important because, as Gurr notes, "discontented people act aggressively only when they become aware of the supposed source of frustration, or something or someone with whom they associate frustration."[11] In Marxist thought, poverty, repression, alienation, and the like are the natural result of rule by members of feudal or capitalist classes who exploit workers and peasants. For Islamic insurgent thinkers, the source of trouble is a ruling group that has either deserted the holy path of Islam by establishing a secular state or by allowing conspicuous deviations from prescribed Islamic behavior; in other words, discontent and deprivation are blamed squarely on the sinful or lax beliefs and behavior of specific ruling authorities and, at times, the political system.

The attraction of esoteric appeals based on ideology or religion is even greater where foreign countries either impose their authority directly (imperialism), exert tremendous influence through international economic networks (neo-imperialism), or intervene in support of local authorities, because the outside power—along with the local authorities—can be depicted as the source of deprivations, in order to evoke nationalist feelings. This is, of course, exactly what happens in the context of Marxist-Leninist theories that accent the intimate connection between international imperialism and indigenous capitalist or feudal ruling classes. Linking foreign and domestic forces of exploitation to create a clear target for popular wrath can also be seen in the cosmology of Islamic extremists, who portray the West, and particularly the United States ("the Great Satan"), as the source of evil and disintegrative moral and social changes that have led Islamic countries to humiliation and to a loss of their collective souls.[12]

Aside from this essentially nationalist variation, the general effectiveness of esoteric appeals as a method for gaining popular support should not be overemphasized. While some intellectuals may be attracted by the belief systems, in the Marxist cases that Almond examined ideology was rarely perceived by persons at the time they joined political movements.[13] Where ideology may be important is in determining which insurgent groups people join (i.e., choosing one group instead of another because it is more intellectually compelling). Theology seems to be more important than ideology as a means of recruitment because those who join insurgencies led by religious leaders already have some familiarity with the basic beliefs and behavioral norms of the faith. Even here, the decision to engage in, or support, violence does not spring from beliefs alone, for, as Gurr pointed out, men's susceptibility to beliefs that rationalize violence is a function of their discontent.[14] Discontent presupposes that there are existing concrete grievances.

EXOTERIC APPEALS

Exoteric appeals focus on the concrete grievances of both the intelligentsia and the masses. In the case of the intellectuals, unemployment or underemployment can result in not only inadequate material necessities but also psychological dissatisfaction (i.e., lack of recognition, status, and self-worth). Exoteric appeals are essential for the acquisition of popular support from the masses. Using Communist groups to illustrate this point, Almond noted:

> The masses are only capable of registering their grievances; they cannot grasp the shape and form of the historical process in which those grievances are merely incidents. Hence, at the level of mass appeals, the Communist movement portrays itself in ways which are adapted to specific social and political settings. Persons attracted to these external representations may later be systematically exposed to the esoteric or internal doctrine in the training schools and in the higher echelons of the movement.[15]

The adaptation to specific social and political settings involves the identification of existing grievances. Since specific grievances, such as conspicuous corruption, repression by local officials, and insufficient land, food, jobs, health services, schools, and so forth, vary from case to case, both analysts and parties to the conflict must exercise care in determining exactly what the problems are. Astute insurgent leaders, most notably Mao, have stressed the need to first go among the people and find out what their grievances are in order to formulate propaganda appeals that will fall on receptive ears. Mao summarized this process in the following words:

> In all practical work of our Party, correct leadership can only be developed on the principle of "from the masses to the masses." This means summing up (e.g., coordinating and systematizing after careful study) the views of the masses (i.e., views scattered and unsystematic), then taking the resulting ideas back to the masses, explaining and popularizing them until the masses embrace the ideas as their own, stand up for them and translate them into action by way of testing their correctness. Then it is necessary once more to sum up the views of the masses, and once again take the resulting ideas back to the masses so that the masses give them their whole-hearted support.[16]

As sensible as Mao's prescription may seem, it is frequently ignored by both insurgents and government leaders, who presume a priori that they understand the people's mind. A misreading of the content, extent, and intensity of popular grievances can have costly and sometimes fatal consequences. Two contemporary examples, one involving an insurgent group, the other a government, illustrate this point. In Oman, the PFLO rightly identified government neglect as a source of discontent among tribesmen in Dhofar province, but wrongly assumed that the tribesmen wanted—or would accept—reforms in the areas of property ownership, religion, and traditional authority patterns. When PFLO leaders tried to solidify and expand support by implementing a program consisting of communal property, the elimination of Islamic influences, and centralized control in "liberated zones," they met stiff resistance from tribesmen, who highly valued private ownership, individualism, and tribal autonomy. When the PFLO reacted to the resistance with harsh repression, defections from the rank and file ensued and the insurgency became more vulnerable to government reforms that were directed at popular demands for better administration and social services.

As for government misconstruing exoteric grievances, it would be hard to find a better example than the urbanized Marxists who seized power in Afghanistan in April 1978 and proceeded to promulgate land, educational, and marriage reforms that they mistakenly assumed would meet with popular approval. Instead, they found spreading opposition among tribal and religious leaders, as well as rank-and-file Afghans, who perceived themselves as losers under the new arrangement. Ironically, the government's reforms proved to be the major impetus behind the insurrection in its early phase (1978–1979). Hence, what at first appeared to be popular measures designed to address exoteric grievances actually became the source of exoteric grievances that fueled an insurrection. The lesson is clear: assumptions about popular grievances that do not have a solid empirical basis can be quite erroneous, since the source of exoteric grievances is the people, not what elites, however well disposed, presume.

TERRORISM

Where esoteric and exoteric appeals do not yield expected support (because they are defective or because of effective government action and/or environmental disadvantages), the insurgents may turn to terrorism.[17] In this context, the purpose of terrorist acts is to obtain popular support by demonstrating the government's weaknesses in the face of insurgent initiatives.[18] Whether the insurgents will be successful in this undertaking depends in large part on two factors: the target of terror and the length of terrorist campaigns.

If individuals or groups disliked by the people are the target, terrorism may lead oppressed and exploited people to identify with the insurgents. By manipulating resentment (based on grievances) and using selective terror against hated individuals and groups, the insurgents may well be able to increase popular support. Such was the case in Algeria, where colonial officials and the Muslim sympathizers were targeted, and again in the Cypriot insurrection against the British.[19] However, prolonging and intensifying terrorism may be counterproductive for two reasons. First, it can disrupt traditional life-styles, making life increasingly miserable for the general population; second, failure to replace terrorism with more-effective military operations can create the impression that the insurgents have lost the initiative and that their chances of success are remote. Even worse, as terrorism continues there is a danger that it will become indiscriminate. If this occurs, insurgents can end up alienating potential domestic and international supporters. In the fall of 1951, for instance, the insurgents of the Malayan Communist Party realized that intimidation was not gaining popular support, so they issued a directive prohibiting attacks on innocent people. More recently, our case studies suggest the IRA in Ulster and the Red Brigades in

Italy have suffered both defections and decreased popular support because of their indiscriminate actions. The precariousness and uncertainty surrounding indiscriminate terrorism was clearly evident during the rocket attacks by insurgents against the Afghan capital of Kabul in the summer of 1988. Although one observer indicated that the solidarity between the people and the *mujahidin* led some to ascribe the attacks to the government side (specifically, to the Russians), the leader of the Jamiat-i-Islami (the Society of Islam) forces was concerned that the ultimate impact would be counterproductive. Hence, he ordered his fighters to ensure that the rocket attacks focus on military and government targets, not civilian areas.[20]

As for transnational terrorism, there is little to suggest that it is a significant means of acquiring popular support. If anything, the decision to engage in transnational terrorism generally is associated with a marginal capability to operate inside the country, questionable or shaky domestic support, and a desperate need to demonstrate that the insurgent movement is neither defunct nor impotent. As dramatic and newsworthy as transnational terrorist acts like bombings and skyjackings may be, there is no evidence that any groups that have carried them out since the late 1960s gained any appreciable degree of popular support because of such actions. In fact, one of the reasons some of the most infamous groups, such as the Popular Front for the Liberation of Palestine and Black September, terminated such acts is because they tarnished the image of the Arabs. That the PLO understood the negative perceptions of transnational terrorism both internationally and within parts of the Palestinian community could be seen in the inconsistent statements by their public relations spokesmen and other officials, which vacillated between bragging and taking responsibility for such acts, and disavowing them altogether.[21]

PROVOCATION OF GOVERNMENT REPRESSION

A fifth means that the insurgent utilizes in winning popular support is "catalyzing and intensifying counterterror which further alienates the enemy from the local population."[22] In other words, the insurgents try to provoke arbitrary and indiscriminate government reprisals against the population, calculating that this will increase resentment and win the insurrectionary forces more support. The success of such an insurgent ploy is affected by the nature of the government response and by the social groups involved. Excessive violence by military and police units and government-sponsored vigilantes (death squads) is generally recognized as a factor accounting for increased support for insurgents in many cases, such as Bangladesh in 1971 and El Salvador in the late 1970s and early 1980s. Even where ruthless methods by the government restore law and order in the short term, the long-term effect may be, as Richard Clutterbuck has indicated, to sow the seeds of further insurgency.[23] A good example is Guatemala, where indiscriminate violence by right-wing death squads helped quell an insurrection in the late 1970s, but created resentments that led to renewed insurgent activity by the early 1980s.

The importance of social heterogeneity as a factor in examining popular support is less clear in the context of harsh government repression. Jerry Silverman and Peter Jackson have argued that group solidarity between the insurgents and the people may lead the population to forgive violent excesses by insurgents, but not those of government forces that are drawn from rival racial, ethnic, or religious groups.[24] That insurgent leaders believe ruthless violence against the people by governments controlled by rival groups can be instrumental in obtaining support is obvious in their propaganda and information campaigns, which seek to dramatize "massacres," "slaughters," and the like and to associate them with the different social composition of the ruling authorities.

Efforts to exploit intergroup differences, distrust, and dislike in this way have had mixed results. On the one hand, there have been numerous reports of indiscriminate government crackdowns and violence leading to increased popular support for insurgents (e.g., the upswing in support for Tamil insurgents in Sri Lanka in the late summer of 1984 after uncontrolled attacks by Sinhalese army units), while on the other hand, there are instances in which such behavior has actually led to animosity directed at the insurgents. In Vietnam, for example, the Vietcong ploy of provoking American air attacks against villages by firing at aircraft from nearby areas sometimes led local Vietnamese to blame the guerrillas. Similarly, in southern Lebanon, there were cases in 1969 in which Israeli attacks in Shiite Muslim areas in retaliation for PLO raids led the Shiites to petition the government in Beirut to remove the Palestinians, who are fellow Arabs.

While a definitive answer as to why these and other differential reactions occurred requires more careful and systematic inquiry, a few propositions may be useful. To begin with, indiscriminate violence by government forces seems to provide the greatest impetus for supporting insurgencies among uncommitted persons who have lost close friends or (especially) relatives because of such violence, as well as among those who were already contemplating supporting the insurgents because of other grievances. The inclination to render support to insurgents seems particularly strong on the part of those who have lost friends, relatives, parents, and so forth to government violence and in cultures where vengeance is customary and expected. In Afghanistan, for instance, the code of conduct known as the *Pushtunwali* stresses, besides other things, blood vengeance *(badal)*. Where loss of life is concerned, it is desirable to kill a member of the offender's group. Accordingly, it is hardly surprising that visitors to guerrilla areas in Afghanistan report that *badal* is a key factor galvanizing support for the resistance because of the Soviets' indiscriminate violence. In the words of one Afghan guerrilla, "Every time a Russian helicopter gunship strafes a village, every man in it will not rest until he has drawn Russian blood." On

another occasion, Abdul Haq, one of the leading field commanders, explained the tenacious resistance to the Russians with one word—"re-
venge."[25] In contrast to the Afghan situation are cultures in which, despite
government violence, people simply wish to be left alone by both sides.
According to many knowledgeable observers, this was probably true with
respect to most of the peasants in Vietnam and in the rural areas of El
Salvador today.

DEMONSTRATIONS OF POTENCY

The sixth technique insurgents may rely on to obtain support, demonstrations of potency, has two dimensions: meeting the needs of the people
through an administrative apparatus (shadow government) that provides
social services (e.g., schools, health clinics), and gaining the military initiative. The first aspect demonstrates not only the insurgents' presence but
also the corresponding government failure to deal with shadow government
political cadres. Besides governing, guerrilla political operators normally
seek to meet some of the people's basic needs and cooperate with them in
such mundane affairs as harvesting crops and building schools. Of this,
Andrew Molner and his associates wrote:

> The agent, much like a ward or precinct politician, surveys the needs, likes
> and dislikes of the people in his district. He may keep individual records on
> all who live in his area of responsibility. He may find jobs for the unemployed,
> arrange housing for those who do not have shelter, or assist farmers with their
> crops.
>
> In rural areas and small villages, where the close personal contacts
> among the villagers make it difficult to organize secret cells, a special tech-
> nique is used. An insurgent force marches into and takes over a village. They
> assist the farmers in the fields in this way to develop close contacts in spite of
> having come uninvited.[26]

Quite often the extension of such aid to people will be the first step in
involving them with the insurgent movement, either actively or passively.
This would seem to be especially true where the government has been delin-
quent in meeting the people's needs.

The second means of demonstrating potency, gaining the military initiative, is designed in part to create the impression that the insurgency has
momentum and will succeed. A number of writers have stressed the importance of initiative to insurgents, for in addition to winning adherents for
the movement, it boosts and sustains morale within insurgent organizations. "Units that are active and successful in the accomplishment of as-
signed missions build up a high esprit de corps and attract followers; success
is contagious." Put another way, "No guerrilla movement in the field can
afford to remain inactive for long; by so doing, it loses its morale and sense
of purpose."[27]

In his quest to gain the initiative, the insurgent has at his disposal a flexible arsenal—ambushes, sabotage, kidnapping, assassinations, mass attacks, and so on. In order to maximize the effectiveness of such diverse methods, however, insurgents must have coordinated strategy, which in turn requires cohesion. Although the question of cohesion will be discussed in the next chapter, a few comments about its relationship to popular support are necessary at this point. Insurgent movements with competing centers of loyalty will not only raise command and control problems that undercut military operations and initiative but also lead some potential supporters to believe the resistance is in a state of confusion. The corresponding image of weakness may dissuade many from joining. Moreover, violent conflict between insurgent groups will undoubtedly sap the movement's overall strength, divert it from the main enemy, and deny it a positive public image. The spectacle of various guerrilla organizations criticizing each other in order to enhance their stature is bound to be bewildering to those being recruited.

Military initiative will require continuous victories. Since guerrillas are usually weak at the start of hostilities, these may be small successes. But such tactical self-sacrifices at the beginning may be necessary for eventual victory.[28] Local victories in guerrilla war, however, are heavily dependent on popular support; hence, initiative and popular support are interdependent.

Initiative requires freedom of action. As Mao wrote, "Freedom of action is the very life of an army and once this freedom is lost, an army faces defeat or annihilation."[29] Although freedom of action is normally associated with operations in the target country, there are times when it is related to sanctuaries outside the country. These sanctuaries, which involve external support, are of great importance if during the incipient stages of the conflict the resistance movement has difficulty operating within the target country's borders. In such circumstances the attitude of contiguous states will assume a major role in the conflict, for in a sense the territory of such states constitutes the insurgent's last fallback position. But, one should not conclude from this that guerrillas can indefinitely operate from outside the target state. At some point, they must establish a popular base within the target country. Douglas Hyde has called attention to the fact that guerrillas from Sarawak found that operating from bases across the border in Indonesia had a deleterious effect on the insurgent movement because it prevented direct and continuous contacts between leaders and the guerrillas in Sarawak. As a result, the insurgents had to make an effort to set up bases in Sarawak itself.[30]

A final aspect of initiative that deserves mention is what Hyde has called the dramatic gesture. This tactic, which may involve guerrilla, conventional, or terrorist acts, is employed by the insurgents to convince world and domestic opinion that they are not just rabble but are active and fighting for a worthwhile goal.[31] The problem with dramatic gestures, of course, is that not only do they frequently indicate other techniques for gaining popular support have failed but their effect will be short lived if they are not followed up by skillful use of the other techniques. Moreover, terrorist acts may have the effect of alienating the people if they are repugnant, a case in point being the negative reaction in 1978 of both the general population and even some insurgents when the Red Brigades murdered Aldo Moro, the former Italian prime minister.[32]

COERCION

Despite their best efforts, insurgents may still find major segments of the population unresponsive. When this happens, there is a great temptation to turn to the final technique for gaining support, coercion. This is the least effective because of the resentment it causes and the weak commitment of those who are directly victimized. The situation in insurgent-controlled areas of El Salvador during 1984 amply demonstrates this point. Frustrated by a lack of support, the insurgents pressured peasants to collectivize plots of land to feed the rebel forces, to send their children to insurgent-run schools, to form labor gangs to repair roads and carry wounded guerrillas, and to join military units as fighters. Young men who did not respond favorably were abducted and compelled to join. The bitterness that resulted from this was obvious to visiting journalists and was acknowledged by insurgent cadres. One leader of the Popular Liberation Forces said, "We do not renounce our right to recruit from the population, but we realize that our image has been damaged by the recruitment. It is better to build the consciousness of the people to induce them to join us."[33]

The negative impact of coercion on attempts to gain popular support raises the larger question of insurgent rectitude in dealing with the population. Simply put, painstaking efforts to acquire support by relying on various combinations of techniques other than coercion can be undermined by actions that victimize the population. Mao recognized this and clearly articulated it in a code of conduct for dealing with the people. In what he referred to as "Eight Points of Attention," he admonished his military forces thus:

1. Speak politely.
2. Pay fairly for what you buy.
3. Return everything you borrow.
4. Pay for anything you damage.
5. Do not hit or swear at people.
6. Do not damage crops.
7. Do not take liberties with women.
8. Do not ill-treat captives.[34]

As we have seen in chapter 3, some contemporary insurgents who subscribe to the protracted-popular-war strategy have deviated from Mao's admonitions. They incorporate economic sabotage and terrorism into their strategic approach (e.g., the NPA in the Philippines, the SL in Peru, and the FMLN in El Salvador). In all these cases such actions have weakened the government's capability, but they have also led to popular resentment and thus undercut the insurgents' quest for active support.[35] The long-term impact of economic sabotage and terrorism remains to be seen. If the three governments under attack do not rectify their own deficiencies and begin to address socioeconomic problems seriously, the insurgents may succeed, despite their excesses. But if the governments do begin to turn things around, such insurgent excesses may prove to have been a fatal mistake.

Summary

Of all the factors influencing the progression of insurgencies, popular support probably receives the most attention in the literature and oratory of the participants. This is to be expected, in view of its critical role in offsetting government strengths. Because acquiring popular support, especially active support, is not an easy task, it requires considerable effort on the part of the insurgents. Their success or failure will be affected by the choices they make from among the seven methods for inducing support and the skill and wisdom they show in applying the methods. Whether those choices and the quality of their effort will prove beneficial is, in turn, dependent on the judgments and assessments they make vis-à-vis the other elements of the larger strategic equation. This is especially true for the analysis of such variables as the environment, organization, cohesion, external support, and the government response, because the situations with respect to each of these will reveal various opportunities and obstacles. Attention to the broader strategic perspective also permits sounder judgments about how much popular support is needed. Where that need is viewed as considerable, a strong organizational effort is called for, and that is the point to which we now turn.

Notes

1.   Bernard B. Fall, *The Two Viet-Nams*, 2d ed., rev. (New York: Frederick A. Praeger, 1967), p. 345. The quote from Mao may be found in *Selected Military Writings of Mao Tse-tung* (Beijing: Foreign Language Press, 1967), p. 260.
2.   Cited in Otto Heilbrunn, *Partisan Warfare* (New York: Frederick A. Praeger, 1962), p. 87. The Vietminh directives quoted by Professor Heilbrunn were first published by the État-Major de la Force Publique in Leopoldville in *Bulletine Militaire* (June and August 1955) under the title "Guerrilla selon l'ecole Communists."
3.   See, for example, John J. McCuen, *The Art of Counter-Revolutionary War*

(Harrisburg, Pa.: Stackpole Books, n.d.), pp. 30, 53, 55–56; Arthur Campbell, *Guerrillas* (New York: John Day Company, 1968), pp. 4, 279–281; Julian Paget, *Counter-Insurgency Campaigning* (New York: Walker & Co., 1967), pp. 22–23, 27–28; Virgil Ney, "Guerrilla Warfare and Modern Strategy," in Franklin Mark Osanka, ed. *Modern Guerrilla Warfare* (New York: The Free Press of Glencoe, 1962), pp. 31–34; Douglas Hyde, *The Roots of Guerrilla Warfare* (Chester Springs, Pa.: Dufour Editions, 1968), pp. 53, 55, 104–108, 122–123, 131–132; Roger Trinquier, *Modern Warfare* (New York: Frederick A. Praeger, 1964), pp. 8, 55; Peter Paret and John W. Shy, *Guerrillas in the 1960's*, rev. ed. (New York: Frederick A. Praeger, 1962), pp. 45–51; Heilbrunn, *Partisan Warfare*, pp. 16, 34, 36, 86–87.

4.   For an analysis of the role and traits of the intelligentsia in the Thord World, see Harry J. Benda, "Non-Western Intelligentsias as Political Elites," in John H. Kautsky, ed., *Political Change in Underdeveloped Countries* (New York: John Wiley and Sons, 1967), pp. 235–251. On their role in insurgencies, see David A. Wilson, *Nation Building and Revolutionary War* (Santa Monica, Calif.: The Rand Corporation, 1962), p. 7; Gil Carl Alory, *The Involvement of Peasants in Internal Wars*, Research Monograph no. 24 (Princeton, N.J.: Center for International Studies, Princeton University, 1966), pp. 16–19.

5.   Ted Robert Gurr, *Why Men Rebel* (Princeton, N.J.: Princeton University Press, 1970), p. 337.

6.   Wilson, *Nation Building and Revolutionary War*, p. 7; Alroy, *The Involvement of Peasants in Internal Wars*, pp. 16–19.

7.   Ney, "Guerrilla Warfare," p. 34.

8.   Suggestive analyses of the psychological foundations of the leader-follower relationship may be found in Bruce Mazlish, *The Revolutionary Ascetic* (New York: Basic Books, 1976), especially pp. 22–43; E. Victor Wolfenstein, *The Revolutionary Personality* (Princeton, N.J.: Princeton University Press, 1967), pp. 174–239. Both Mazlish and Wolfenstein limit their focus to revolutionary leaders. For a more general and historical examination of the leader that distinguishes between eventful and event-making man, see Sidney Hook, *The Hero in History* (Boston: Beacon Press, 1943), pp. 151–183.

9.   Gabriel A. Almond, *The Appeals of Communism* (Princeton, N.J.: Princeton University Press, 1954), p. 62. On the basic distinction between esoteric and exoteric appeals, see Almond, pp. 65–66; and Morris Watnick, "The Appeal of Communism to the Underdeveloped Peoples," in Kautsky, ed., *Political Change in Underdeveloped Countries*. The same dichotomy is implicit in Peter Van Ness, *Revolution and Chinese Foreign Policy* (Berkeley: University of California Press, 1970), pp. 118–119; and Gurr, *Why Men Rebel*, p. 195. The functions of ideology have been discussed by many scholars, among whom David Apter stands out. As Apter maintains, an ideology imparts a sense of solidarity and self-esteem to followers; see his *The Politics of Modernization* (Chicago: University of Chicago Press, 1965), pp. 354–370.

10.   V.I. Lenin, *Imperialism: The Highest Stage of Capitalism* (New York: International Publishers, 1969), pp. 1–128. Other aspects of Leninist thought, such as the leading role of the intellectuals within the revolutionary party, enhance its attractiveness for many intellectuals. See John H. Kautsky, *Communism and the Politics of Development* (New York: John Wiley and Sons, 1968), p. 77. Van Ness, *Revolution and Chinese Foreign Policy*, p. 118, notes one effect of the Chinese revolutionary

model was to provide revolutionary cadres with a theoretical plan or practical ideology for making a revolution.

11.   Gurr, *Why Men Rebel*, p. 119.

12.   Thomas H. Greene has argued that "an ideology that appeals to national identity is the most powerful symbolic means of mobilizing revolutionary support." See his *Comparative Revolutionary Movements* (Englewood Cliffs, N.J.: Prentice-Hall, 1974), p. 52. Also see Carl Leiden and Karl Schmitt, *The Politics of Violence* (Englewood Cliffs, N.J.: Prentice-Hall, 1968), pp. 107–108.

13.   Almond, *Appeals of Communism*, p. 65. The failure of the masses who support insurgencies to perceive the larger ideological aims of leadership elites is a major conclusion of Haim Gerber, *Islam, Guerrilla War and Revolution* (Boulder, Colo.: Lynne Rienner, 1988).

14.   Gurr, *Why Men Rebel*, p. 208.

15.   Almond, *Appeals of Communism*, p. 66.

16.   Mao Tse-tung, "On Methods of Leadership," in *Selected Works*, vol. 4 (New York: International Publishers, 1958), p. 113, quoted by McCuen, *The Art of Counter-Revolutionary War*, pp. 55–56.

17.   McCuen, *The Art of Counter-Revolutionary War*, p. 32, and Paget, *Counter-Insurgency Campaigning*, p. 28, see terror as a response to government action; Gurr, *Why Men Rebel*, p. 236, views terror as systematically related to the balance of coercive control and believes it is likely when the dissidents are very weak relative to the regime.

18.   The impact of terrorism has led some scholars and practitioners to contend that terror is the most powerful weapon for establishing community support. Roger Trinquier, for example, calls it the principal weapon of modern warfare (revolutionary warfare) and suggests that by making people feel insecure, it leads them to lose confidence in the government and to be drawn to the guerrillas for protection; see his *Modern Warfare*, pp. 16–17. It has been argued that the Chinese Communists' ability to get popular support without large-scale terror is atypical, because most insurgents start without the degree of popular backing that Mao had and therefore must resort to terror. See, for example, Brian Crozier, *The Study of Conflict* (London: The Institute for the Study of Conflict, 1970), p. 7.

19.   Alf Andrew Heggoy, *Insurgency and Counterinsurgency in Algeria* (Bloomington, Ind.: Indiana University Press, 1972), p. 114; Jerry M. Silverman and Peter M. Jackson, "Terror in Insurgency Warfare," *Military Review* (October 1970):62–64; Paget, *Counter-Insurgency Campaigning*, p. 65.

20.   Silverman and Jackson, "Terror in Insurgency Warfare," pp. 64–67; McCuen, *The Art of Counter-Revolutionary War*, p. 33. The Malayan case is noted by Richard L. Clutterbuck, *The Long, Long War* (New York: Frederick A. Praeger, 1966), p. 63. Paget, *Counter-insurgency Campaigning*, pp. 29, 93, points out that the Mau Mau in Kenya retained a degree of popular support until they alienated the population with the massacre of Kikuyu tribesmen in the village of Lari in March 1953. Ironically, the Kikuyu were the main base of support for the Mau Mau. Heilbrunn, *Partisan Warfare*, p. 89, points out that the Vietminh were concerned about the effects of terror on the people and therefore argued that, although sabotage was important, it should serve the interests of the people by not interfering with the lifestyle and production of the region. On the Afghan rocket attacks, see *Washington Times*, August 1 and 24, 1988.

21.   Until the Jordanian civil war of 1970, Fatah, the largest and most important organization in the PLO, saw little to be gained from transnational terrorism. After 1970, Fatah secretly backed the operations of Black September. By the end of 1973, Fatah had pulled back from transnational terrorism. Since that time, it has been critical of transnational terrorism and ambivalent about terrorism inside Israel and the occupied territories. My own discussions with Palestinians over the past fifteen years revealed considerable disenchantment with, and criticism of, transnational terrorist attacks.

22.   J.K. Zawodny, "Unconventional Warfare," in Henry A. Kissinger, ed., *Problems of National Strategy* (New York: Frederick A. Praeger, 1965), pp. 340–341. Peter Braestrup, "Partisan Tactics—Algerian Style," in Osanka, ed., *Modern Guerrilla Warfare,* p. 393, argued that such was the case with the French in Algeria; see also Fall, *The Two Viet-Nams,* pp. 348–352.

23.   Clutterbuck, *The Long, Long War,* pp. 178–179. On the effects of death-squad activity in El Salvador, see T. David Mason and Dale R. Krane, "The Political Economy of Death Squads: Toward a Theory of the Impact of State-Sanctioned Terror," *International Studies Quarterly* (1989):175–198.

24.   Silverman and Jackson, "Terror in Insurgency Warfare," p. 67; *Washington Times,* August 24, 1988.

25.   See *New York Times,* March 22, 1982; *Washington Times,* October 25, 1988.

26.   Andrew R. Molner, James M. Tinker, and John D. LeNoir, *Human Factors Considerations of Underground in Insurgencies* (Washington, D.C.: American University, Center for Research in Social Systems, 1966), p. 109; also see Vo Nguyen Giap, *People's War, People's Army* (New York: Bantam Books, 1968), p. 50.

27.   George B. Jordan, "Objectives and Methods of Communist Guerrilla Warfare," in Osanka, ed., *Modern Guerrilla Warfare,* pp. 404, 409; Paget, *Counter-Insurgency Campaigning,* p. 22. Other writers also stress the importance of initiative in guerrilla warfare; see, for instance, McCuen, *The Art of Counter-Revolutionary War,* pp. 20, 35; Hyde, *The Roots of Guerrilla Warfare,* p. 123; Campbell, *Guerrillas,* p. 26; Heilbrunn, *Partisan Warfare,* pp. 60–61, 67–68. Trinquier, *Modern Warfare,* p. 52, argues somewhat differently in that he believes the goal of guerrilla warfare is the creation of insecurity rather than local success. In this formulation he appears to overlook the fact that the two are compatible because local success can create insecurity as well as achieving other guerrilla aims, such as obtaining popular support and boosting insurgent morale.

28.   Edward L. Katzenbach, Jr., and Gene Z. Hanrahan, "The Revolutionary Strategy of Mao Tse-tung," in Osanka, ed., *Modern Guerrilla Warfare,* pp. 144–145.

29.   Mao Tse-tung, "On Protracted War," in *Selected Works,* vol. 2 (London: n.p., 1954), p. 211ff., quoted in Heilbrunn, *Partisan Warfare,* p. 56.

30.   Hyde, *The Roots of Guerrilla Warfare,* pp. 86–88. He also cited his conversations with Huk leaders in the Philippines who said the government's ability to sever the leaders from the rest of the movement was a key reason for their downfall.

31.   *Ibid.,* pp. 36–37, 43.

32.   While the Aldo Moro assassination is generally viewed as the most impressive operation of the Red Brigades, it was also a turning point. The operation caused a rift in the Brigades, alienated the public, and provided an impetus to improved counterterrorist policies. According to one former Brigade member, it also led less-competent and more-unsavory elements to enter the organization. See *New York Times,* January 29, 1982; *Christian Science Monitor,* May 11, 1982, and March 27, 1987; and *Washington Post,* June 1, 1983.

33.   Quoted in *Christian Science Monitor,* August 28, 1984, and August 27, 1984.
34.   *Selected Military Writings of Mao Tse-tung* (Beijing: Foreign Language Press, 1967), p. 343.
35.   *New York Times,* March 24 and June 5, 1988; *Washington Post,* May 20 and July 26, 1988; *Christian Science Monitor,* June 17, 1988.

VI Organization and Unity

THE ABILITY OF INSURGENT MOVEMENTS TO COMPENSATE for the material superiority of their opponents by acquiring popular and external support is closely related to their organizational skills. Indeed, when analysts and observers emphasize the point that insurgency is more a political phenomenon than a military one, they usually have in mind the great amount of time and effort insurgents devote to organization, either on the elite level, if it is selective, or the mass level, if it is mobilizational. When examining an insurgent organization, three structural dimensions—scope, complexity, and cohesion—and two functions—instrumental services and channels for expressive protest—are of primary interest.[1] The two functions will be discussed in the context of complexity because of their close relationship to the complexity factor.

Scope

Scope refers to the numbers and kinds of people across the political spectrum who either play key roles in the movement (political cadres, terrorists, guerrillas, and regular soldiers) or provide active support. As might be expected in light of the clandestine nature of much insurgent activity, most attempts to tabulate insurgent numbers are rough estimates. Because of this and the variations among insurgencies with respect to goals, strategies, forms of warfare, environmental conditions, external support, and government responses, there are no precise numerical thresholds that correlate with success or failure. Consequently, upward or downward trends need to be assessed in terms of the overall situation. Noticeable single-direction increases or decreases in insurgent numbers over the course of several months or longer can suggest the trends of an insurgency. Particularly important are continuing defections from insurgent ranks, since they are usually a harbinger of hard times, if not failure. It was not happenstance that the setbacks and containment of the PFLO in Oman in the mid-1970s followed steadily increasing desertions during the early 1970s.[2] Nor was it surprising to see the diminishing effectiveness of the Thai Communist insurgents after significant defections among Thai intellectuals following a return to civilian rule and an amnesty program in 1982. Many of the defectors had at one time bolstered the insurgency after fleeing repression by a military government.[3]

Complexity

PARALLEL HIERARCHIES

Whatever the scope of the insurgency, the effective use of people will depend on the skill of insurgent leaders in identifying, integrating, and coordinating the different tasks and roles essential for success in combat operations, training, logistics, communications, transportation, and the medical, financial, informational, diplomatic, and supervisory areas. The complexity of the organizations designed to perform these functions reflects insurgent strategies.

Insurgents who subscribe to conspiratorial and urban-warfare strategies stress small closely knit and secretive organizations with minimal complexity; those who adopt military-focus or protracted-popular-war strategies require more-sophisticated organizational structures because they normally anticipate a long struggle that will involve support for substantial military activity. Some insurgents who follow a military-focus strategy may do so because they do not have to be concerned with creating political structures, because they already exist. During the American Civil War, for example, the Confederacy simply used existing state and local government structures to perform various functions in support of the war. But not all insurgents who opt for a military-focus strategy inherit organizational structures. Although they may emphasize fighting rather than waiting for political structures to take shape, the insurgents cannot, as Guevara and Debray have both pointed out, ignore organization altogether. Indeed, structural development is necessary in order to take advantage of military success and further escalate the struggle.[4] Those who follow a protracted-popular-war strategy not only share this view but go a step further by stressing party primacy and assiduous political organizing prior to hostilities. The complex organizations that emerge are commonly referred to as parallel hierarchies or shadow governments in the literature on insurgencies.[5]

The parallel hierarchy can take several forms. One is the use of existing government political-administrative institutions through the infiltration of insurgent agents. If infiltration is widespread, the insurgents are able not only to obtain information about government plans and impending actions but also to expand their influence by exercising de facto control over parts of the population. Moreover, if the ruling authorities begin to lose their grip on power and confront a crisis, the infiltrators stand ready to take the reins of government.

A more familiar form of parallel hierarchy, one that goes beyond infiltration, is the creation of political structures or institutions to administer, organize, and rule the population in areas controlled by the insurgents ("liberated zones"). They also challenge the government in contested areas by establishing small, secretive cells that will carefully proceed with tasks of assessing the insurrectionary potential of the people and recruiting followers and supporters. Should the insurgents fail to establish cells, more-sophisticated organizational development will not occur.[6]

While the details of shadow governments vary at the central level, each typically consists of a small executive committee made up of the top leaders; departments responsible for governmental functions such as finances, diplomacy, information, and the like; and a large assembly of representatives from the broader ranks of the movement. The larger assemblies meet infrequently and usually confine their activity to ratifying and applauding policies already decided upon at the higher levels. Communist insurgent movements with politburos, central committees, administrative offices, and popular congresses are typical examples; in fact, they are often emulated in whole or in part by non-Communist insurgents, albeit with varying degrees of success.

In his insightful and informative portrait of the Algerian nationalists, Alf Andrew Heggoy pointed out that organizational methods were borrowed from both the Communist Party and the French colonial administration and pragmatically adapted to local needs. However, during the early years of the conflict, the functioning of the organization was anything but smooth, largely because military officers in charge of local commands tended to act as independent warlords and to ignore orders from the central political leadership, which was based outside the country in Egypt and Libya. Despite the problems between the exterior and interior commands, effective political leadership was nevertheless provided by the political assistants in the local commands, who were responsible for propaganda, financial affairs, and establishment of the political-administrative cells that were to gradually undermine and replace the authority of the French administration. Heggoy concluded that the essential reason the insurrection succeeded was because the shadow government represented the rebellion directly to the rural peasantry.[7]

A more recent example of non-Communists adopting Marxist-Leninist organizational ideas is the UNITA insurgency in Angola. Even though external assistance from South Africa and elsewhere has no doubt been very important to UNITA (especially in offsetting generous Soviet and Cuban aid to the government), the political controversy over such aid has obscured the contribution of UNITA's organization to its survival and successes. Visitors to UNITA areas in the southeast consistently paint a picture of a smoothly functioning central governing apparatus that extends its authority to the village level and manages to provide basic services. UNITA's government has various ministries (e.g., health, information, natural resources, and so forth) and a radio station (Voice of the Resistance of the Black Cockerel) that broadcasts in several languages. UNITA's ministries also manage more than nine hundred primary and secondary schools and the export of diamonds, ivory, timber, and other resources.[8]

The Algerian and UNITA examples raise a very important point worth underscoring: creating central structures that perform various governmental functions is necessary but not sufficient for acquiring and expanding popular support. To mobilize and increase support, the organization must be extended to lower levels and various sectors of a society. To do this, regional and local administrative structures must be established. Villages or small towns in liberated areas will thus have a leader (chief, commissar, etc.) and officials in charge of various functions (health, education, law enforcement, tax collection, and so on) who receive directions from the central apparatus. To further the mobilization of support, insurgents may also establish auxiliary organizations or "fronts" based on various segments of the population, such as youth, peasants, workers, women, fishermen, and artists.[9] The role of auxiliary organizations in winning adherents is exemplified by the insurgency in the Philippines in the late 1940s and early 1950s, when many people joined the Huks through front organizations, often without even knowing party aims.[10] The ability to extend organizational structures such as these was also instrumental in creating nationwide popular support in Algeria. In Angola, by contrast, the shadow government has been limited to the southeast and thus UNITA's support is basically confined to that area.

In acknowledging the tremendous impact of Communist organizational formats on insurgent leaders, I do not mean to suggest they are the only basis for parallel hierarchies. Religious groups with hierarchical or pyramidal structures are, by their very nature, complex and hence can be used for planning, coordinating, and executing political and military activities. Where the religious groups are a minority, good organization will enhance their ability to consolidate support and use whatever resources are available to them. Yet, while this may enable them to cause serious problems for the government, their nationwide potential is low. Such is not the case with large religious groups, especially those that constitute a majority of the population. Although, strictly speaking, it was not an insurgency (because of the emphasis on nonviolence), the political uprising against the shah demonstrated the efficacy of religious organizational structures; the extensive Shiite network of mosques throughout the country was used adroitly by

Ayatollah Khomeini and his followers to galvanize and direct opposition to the shah. In the final analysis, organization proved to be crucial in the success of the Iranian revolution.[11]

Of course, most insurgencies against governments as powerful as the shah's do not succeed without recourse to greater and more prolonged violence. Consequently, their leaders find it necessary to devote considerable attention to establishing a sophisticated military apparatus. In highly developed insurgent movements, guerrillas are usually divided into full- and part-time units, operating on central, regional, and local levels. The full-time guerrillas operate from secure bases and carry out attacks against government military units and installations on a continuous basis and will constitute the core of regular military formations if the movement progresses to mobile-conventional warfare. For the most part, full-time guerrillas operate in specific areas, examples being the Q761, 762, and 763 Vietcong regiments in the areas north, east, and west of Saigon during the 1960s in the Vietnam War. Part-time or local guerrillas, meanwhile, stay in their communities and provide a number of invaluable services, such as collecting intelligence, harassing the enemy, storing supplies, and providing a coercive arm to protect the political organizers. In addition, the local guerrillas can attach themselves to main-force units for specific operations, either as combatants or as scouts and guides.

Organized full- and part-time guerrilla units are only part of the story, for military successes also depend on the performance of an array of combat support tasks—command, control and communications, planning, training, medical care, finance, logistics, and so forth. The performance of such tasks becomes vitally important when insurgents are engaging in orthodox, conventional operations. Accordingly, organizational development must accompany the escalation of violence. The nexus between organization and the transition to mobile-conventional warfare was summarized aptly in the following comments by Mao:

> In order to ensure the development of guerrilla hostilities into mobile warfare of an orthodox nature, both the quantity and quality of guerrilla troops must be improved. Primarily, more men must join the armies; then the quality of equipment and standards of training must be improved. Political training must be emphasized and our organization, the technique of handling our weapons, our tactics—all must be improved. Our internal discipline must be strengthened. The soldiers must be educated politically. There must be a gradual *change from guerrilla formations to orthodox regimental organization. The necessary bureaus and staffs, both political and military, must be provided.* At the same time, attention must be paid to the *creation of suitable supply, medical, and hygiene units.* The standards of equipment must be raised and types of weapons increased. Communication equipment must not be forgotten. *Orthodox standards of discipline must be established.*[12]

Few better examples of Mao's admonition about the crucial need for ade-

quate organizational development when making the transition from guerrilla to conventional warfare could be found than the battle of Jalalabad in
early 1989 following the Soviet exodus from Afghanistan. In that episode,
disappointing setbacks and high casualty rates were attributed to, among
other things, insufficiences of certain types of equipment for conventional
warfare, poor training, a lack of discipline, and deficiencies in coordination
and command unity.[13]

FUNCTIONAL ASPECTS OF PARALLEL HIERARCHIES

By increasing the complexity of their organization, the insurgents will
be better able to demonstrate potency by performing the instrumental and
expressive functions that attract new followers. As Gurr has noted, the most
immediate reason for a disgruntled individual to join an organization is to
increase options open to him for attaining the things he values or desires.
Participation can provide psychosocial satisfactions, such as companion-
ship, self-definition, and reinforcement of shared beliefs, as long as members follow the normative prescriptions for conduct in the organization.
An illustration of the psychological aspect inherent in Gurr's argument is
provided by Professor Jerrold M. Post, who has pointed out that German
youths who entered insurgent organizations were alienated loners who entered adult years with a low sense of self-esteem because of failures at school
or work and/or because they came from broken or unstable families. By
joining an insurgent organization, they acquired a sense of belonging after
a life of rejection, and the organization became the family they did not have.
Furthermore, membership can also benefit from the fact that in stable, effective organizations members can achieve security from external interference.
Finally, if the organization has the resources, it can enhance the material
welfare of its members. Although external support to the insurgents and
their control of base areas facilitates the accommodation of material needs,
many dissident organizations lack the capability to meet psychosocial needs
for status, communality, and ideational coherence. Where these needs go
unfilled and there is a general lack of progress and organizational conflict,
division and desertion become more likely.

We should not conclude that a general lack of progress will doom the
insurgent movement because significant numbers of members of dissident
groups may be intensely hostile to the government and intrinsically value
opposition to it. Providing ways to express this hostility can thus be an
important function performed by insurgent organizations. About this, Gurr
wrote:

> Members of dissident organizations are therefore most likely to want means
> that satisfy both instrumental and expressive functions. The failure of instru-
> mental means should not necessarily be expected to weaken the organization.
> Lack of success in obtaining demanded values is more likely to intensify than
> to reduce dissident opposition, because initial hostility not only persists, it is

intensified by the effort expended in what was thought to be value-enhancing action. . . . The fact that external groups—the regime or political competitors—are responsible for not responding to the demands makes it likely that hostility will continue to be focused on them, not on the dissident leaders who specified the unsuccessful mode of action. Expressive protest also is intrinsically satisfying, hence reinforcing for the discontented, even in the absence of other value gains.[14]

COMPLEXITY AND SUCCESS OR FAILURE

As noted above, the progress of insurgent movements facing resolute governments is closely tied to their organizational achievements. Although environmental conditions may be conducive to active support for insurgents, whether such support materializes through the use of the various techniques discussed in chapter 5 depends on the creation and extension of a complex political-military apparatus. In China, Vietnam, and Algeria, the ability to mobilize support through a complex organization was a major factor enabling insurgents to defeat a strong adversary. Without an extensive apparatus, the insurgents would probably have met the same fate as the Monteneros in Argentina, the Tupamaros in Uruguay, Red Brigades in Italy, the Red Army of Japan, and other groups that have relied on small-scale cellular structures and eschewed complexity, because the strength of the government and the nature of the environment posed too many dangers.

The importance of complexity may also be illustrated by the cases in which insurgents have considered it important, but have failed, in one way or another, to bring it to full fruition. The Afghan resistance illustrates this point. On the one hand, the insurgents were able to sustain what could best be described as a low-to-moderate level of guerrilla warfare against superior Soviet forces because the vast majority of the people opposed both the Russians and the government; on the other hand, full exploitation of popular sympathies was undercut by uneven organization. Where there were regional shadow governments, like the one established by Ahmed Massoud in the Panjshir Valley and throughout the northeast, training, logistics, and intelligence functions were performed efficiently and operational coordination was more extensive and effective. No small wonder that Massoud was able to withstand several major Russian search-and-destroy operations and then return his guerrillas to the battlefield. While Massoud's regional shadow government, together with a few others in places like Wardak province, the Hazarajat, and Nuristan, were instrumental in *mujahidin* successes, in areas where insurgents did not benefit from a complex political apparatus observers reported that insurgent training left much to be desired, coordination and planning was rudimentary, and activity was small-scale.

Taken as a whole, the Afghan resistance was not well organized, because despite the pretensions of the political parties based in Pakistan, there was no centralized political apparatus to give a common sense of direction, integrate plans and strategy, standardize training, collect and disseminate intelligence, and provide a balanced and rationalized flow of materials. As a result, guerrilla activity leveled off and the full potential of the resistance, which enjoyed either passive and active support from an estimated 90 percent of the people, was never realized.[15] Fortunately for the *mujahidin*, the Afghan government was inept and disunified, and Russian counterinsurgency policies were poorly conceived and implemented. In the final analysis, the Russians' decision to withdraw in 1988 is best explained by their own blunders, environmental factors, external support, and, perhaps most important, a changed Soviet leadership with new and different priorities. To attribute that withdrawal to the organizational accomplishments of the Afghans would be an exaggeration, if not a clear mistake.

Much like the Afghan resistance, the PLO has had its greatest strength in places where parallel hierarchies exist. During the high point of Palestinian guerrilla activity in 1969–1970, active support came primarily from refugee camps in Lebanon and Jordan that were under the political control of resistance organizations. In the area the resistance considered most vital, the West Bank, active support was meager, in spite of general antipathy toward the Israelis, largely because there was no functioning parallel hierarchy. When a similar situation emerged in Jordan after the expulsion of the insurgents in the fall of 1970 and spring of 1971, Palestinian violence was reduced to transnational terrorism and an occasional guerrilla attack. With the Palestinians' military effectiveness at such a low point, observers puzzled at the seeming paradox of the PLO's success in the diplomatic arena as the 1970s unfolded. While this success could be partially attributed to perceived moderation on the part of Fatah and some other groups, one should not overlook the fact that the PLO had a central apparatus that included an efficient political department in charge of foreign affairs, which was led by the astute Farouk Qadummi. Without this central apparatus, the PLO would have been reduced to impotence, a point it came perilously close to reaching by 1985 as a result of the Israeli invasion of Lebanon in 1982, the ejection of the PLO from that country, and its subsequent dispersal throughout the Arab world.[16]

Likewise, the absence of central political structures would have prevented the PLO from taking political advantage of the uprising *(intifada)* in the Gaza Strip and the West Bank that began in 1987. These accomplishments notwithstanding, it is clear to all but the most biased observers that "armed struggle"—within the framework of a protracted-popular-war strategy—was a failure. Although both the physical environment and effective Israeli countermeasures militated against the strategy's success, the PLO's own organizational drawbacks also played a major role. Besides deficiencies related to complexity, especially the failure to implant a shadow government in the occupied areas, another organizational shortcoming was responsible, namely, endemic disunity—something that has plagued many other insurgent movements.

Cohesion

The pressure or absence of cohesion or unity among insurgents can have a profound effect on the developments and outcomes of insurgencies. One analyst puts it thus:

> The problem of unity is a particularly acute one for guerrilla forces. Technological powers, in possession of regular armed forces which boast long traditions of discipline and loyalty, rarely, if ever, experience open conflict within their military establishments; unity of command in wartime is no problem for them. But guerrilla movements, especially those in technologically less advanced societies, invariably are rent by factionalism.[17]

There are few, if any, experts on, and practitioners of, insurgency who have not stressed the importance of unity within insurgent ranks. John J. McCuen, for example, has contended that unifying the effort is the basic principle behind effective strategy, planning, tactics, and organization. "This has been so ever since 1902 when Lenin's *What Is to Be Done?* made revolution into a science."[18] Although the conduct of operations and responsibility may be delegated to local leaders, a general headquarters that exercises authoritative control over policy, discipline, ethics, and ideology is indispensable.[19]

The absence of unity undermines authoritative control and can create a host of problems for insurgents, not the least of which is a lack of a sense of direction. Regis Debray has noted:

> The lack of a single command puts the revolutionary forces in the situation of an artillery gunner who has not been told in which direction to fire, of a line of attack without a principal direction of attack: the attackers are lost on the field, they shoot at random, and die in vain. The amount and strength of firepower mean nothing without a plan, without assigning a fire or cross fire. The absence of a centralized executive leadership—a political-military leadership—leads to such waste, such useless slaughter.[20]

Moreover, as Mao pointed out in *The Strategy of Partisan Warfare*, "Without centralized strategic command the partisans can inflict little damage on their adversaries, as without this, they can break down into roaming, armed bands, and then find no more support by the population."[21]

Although unity is usually important for insurgent movements, its absence has not always resulted in failure, since other factors may offset the problems disunity creates. Where the governing authorities lose the will to persevere, as the French did in Algeria; see their advantage being undercut by widespread popular support for the insurgents, as happened in Angola in the 1960s; or face severe long-term geographic and demographic asymmetries in favor of the guerrillas, as was the case in Rhodesia, disunity need not preclude eventual success by insurgents. But if offsetting conditions such as these do not exist and if the government is strong, insurgents court disaster by fighting among themselves and failing to coordinate their efforts. This being the case, it is important to take a closer and more specific look at the effects of disunity.

THE EFFECTS OF DISUNITY

The disunity of insurgents can have many adverse consequences. First of all, it can undercut both political and military organizational efforts. The Vietminh guerrillas operating in the Mekong Delta in Vietnam during the war with the French provide an example of the consequences of disunity. Their internecine conflict, rooted in different religious and political outlooks, hindered their organizational efforts and precluded the establishment of a cohesive political network. As a result, insurgent activity was confined to terror and low-level guerrilla operations. This situation was in stark contrast to that in the Red River Delta in the north, where the unity of the revolutionary forces made it possible for the insurgents to gain momentum and even to make the transition to mobile-conventional warfare.[22]

A second and more specific result of disunity can be conflicting political and military policies, especially during the execution phase. Typically, this involves either inadvertent or deliberate military actions that undercut political endeavors. A case in point would be an attack by one insurgent group that occurs while negotiations are impending or taking place between the government and the top leadership of the insurgent movement or a designated intermediary. For instance, terrorist attacks against civilians—both Jews and non-Jews—by hard-line groups such as the Abu Nidal Organization and the Popular Front for the Liberation of Palestine-General Command have usually had as their principal aim the prevention of any dialogue that could lead to a compromise. By blowing up school buses, bombing synagogues, and attacking airliners, terminals, and ships, the hard-line groups have sought (with frequent success) to undermine whatever chances there were for negotiations by inflaming tensions and provoking Israeli retaliation.[23]

A third negative result of disunity is deficiencies in combat support. As the Afghan guerrillas discovered, where insurgent groups insist on autonomy and distrust one another, intelligence collection, analysis, and dissemination are fragmented and unsatisfactory; the flow of logistical supplies is generally unbalanced; training is inadequate and unstandardized, and systematic communications are lacking.[24]

A fourth disadvantage is the inability to plan, orchestrate, and integrate multiple military operations. When this happens, the potential for sizable campaigns, involving attacks in many areas, is seriously eroded, if not precluded altogether. Again, the experience of Afghan guerrillas (especially as Jalalabad in 1989) illustrates the point.

The fifth deleterious effect of disunity is the diversion of personnel and matériel from attacks against the main enemy to attacks against opponents inside the insurgent movement. Internecine violence involving losses of personnel and matériel has plagued most Palestinian and Afghan factions at one time or another, the Eritrean Liberation Front and the Popular Front for the Liberation of Eritrea, rival Kurdish groups in Iraq, and the Popular Movement for the Liberation of Angola (MPLA) and the National Union for the Total Independence of Angola (UNITA) in Angola during the anti-Portuguese war. Even more astounding and very costly is intergroup fighting while on the battlefield against government forces. Although this may seem hard to believe, it has occurred. During one of the major Soviet campaigns against Massoud's guerrillas in the Panjshir Valley, for example, rival insurgents belonging to Gulbuddin Hekmatyar's Hezb-i-Islami (Party of Islam) actually attacked Massoud's forces. Their aim was to wrest control of areas from Massoud because of his affiliation with a rival insurgent organization, Jamiat-i-Islami (Society of Islam).[25]

A sixth outcome of disunity, one that can be very damaging, is the undermining of external support. The reluctance of outside states to commit themselves to fragmented insurgents can be seen in Afghanistan where the Islamic Conference Organization made it quite clear that greater largesse depended on the unification of the various groups.[26] When insurgent movements contain groups that pose threats to actual or potential external supporters, the problem is even greater. A classic example was the Jordan-PLO relationship in 1969–1970. Since guerrilla bases in Jordan had become essential for the Palestinians following their organizational failures in the West Bank, the pragmatic elements of the PLO favored, and worked for, a modus vivendi with King Hussein only to see their efforts undermined by the Marxist PFLP and PDF, which carried out acts of sabotage as part of a campaign to overthrow the "feudal" regime. When the king moved forcefully against the PFLP, following a multiple skyjacking in 1970, the pragmatists felt compelled to join the fighting on the side of their Palestinian brothers. Once the dust had settled, the PLO found that it had been badly beaten, had suffered substantial human and matériel losses, and had been expelled from its self-proclaimed "pillar base" in Jordan. Unquestionably, disunity in PLO ranks had played a key part in provoking this disastrous turn of events.[27]

The chronic disunity of the PLO also illustrates the seventh problem to be discussed in this context—outside interference. When insurgent leaders are engaged in conflicts among themselves, they open the doors to undesirable involvement by both their adversaries and states supporting the insurgent movement. The lack of discipline and unity, and competition for recruits among insurgent factions often give governments opportunities to infiltrate the groups and sow the seeds of greater dissension. In a conversation with the French writer Alain Chevalerias, a captured Khad (secret police) agent indicated that one of the purposes of infiltrating Afghan insurgent groups was to exacerbate differences between factions. The ability of Israel's security agencies (Mossad and Shin Bet) to do precisely this has long been recognized by those who follow Palestinian affairs.[28] Even more obvious has been the multifaceted, shifting alliances of the Arab states with different PLO groups. These alliances also contributed to fighting among the Palestinians both in the Middle East and abroad because of the provision of weapons, intelligence, planning assistance, and, in some cases, actual military support, as in Syria's periodic use of the Palestine Liberation Army (PLA) brigade in Syria, its own Palestinian guerrilla organization Saiqa, and various other Palestinian factions, such as Abu Musa's Fatah-Revolutionary Council, against Fatah and other pragmatic groups.[29]

An eighth troublesome effect of disunity sometimes occurs when insurgents provide information about their rivals to the government in the hope that the authorities will apprehend or attack them. While the PLO again has been guilty of this, even the venerable Ho Chi Minh was reputed to have done the same in the early, formative stages of his resistance to the French.[30] As perfidious as such behavior may be, it may not always have a negative impact on the insurgency as a whole. In fact, over the long term it may contribute to cohesion if rival factions are eliminated. Whether the effects of betraying rivals are good or bad will depend largely on the size and social composition of the victimized groups and the credibility of the explanations given for such acts. Where betrayed groups or individuals are from small factions, and especially when they are from minority groups, the damage is likely to be smaller than when the victims are from large, more important groups. The rationale for betrayal is also important; hence, the betrayer will frequently characterize those who are betrayed as traitors, government agents, spies, or the like. For the analyst, the key questions are whether betrayal is occurring and, if so, what its impact is.

As the foregoing discussion makes clear, disunity can be a source of many difficulties for an insurgent movement. Accordingly, where disunity is obvious, a careful analysis of its specific effects is imperative, since it may reveal some of the major explanations for the course of events in an insurgency.

The Causes of Disunity

Since most insurgent leaders recognize the deleterious impact that disunity can have on their fortunes, they normally adopt organizational, coercive, and other policies designed to prevent or quickly end it. But, such efforts are often futile if the causes of disunity are ignored or misunderstood.

Our studies of insurgent movements suggest seven causes of disunity—social, political-cultural, personal, teleological, theoretical, strategic,
and tactical. Social and cultural causes of disunity are, as we saw in chapter
4, rooted in the environment. Social factors include group cleavages based
on race, ethnicity, religion, and sometimes regionalism. Where these exist,
and particularly where they are cumulative, it is very hard to create and
unify insurgent movements composed of multiple groups. The lack of cohesion in the Afghan insurgent movement is in part a reflection of historical
animosities and rivalries among ethnic and, in the case of the Hazara (who
are Shiites), religious groups. The resentment of the largest group, the Pathans, by the smaller groups is the most salient. Hence, it is not surprising
to find that most guerrilla units inside Afghanistan are composed of members of a single group. The same situation existed in the Rhodesian insurgency, where the Zimbabwe African People's Union (ZAPU) was drawn
from the dominant Mashona ethnic group while the membership of the
rival Zimbabwe African National Union (ZANU) was based on the Mata-
bele peoples. Likewise, in the Angolan insurrection against Portugal the tri-
partite division of the insurgents was based on ethnicity, with the Ovimbundu supporting UNITA, the Bakongo backing the Front for the National
Liberation of Angola (FNLA), and the coastal peoples sustaining the
MPLA. In Rhodesia and Angola, the strife between and among groups precluded unity, and even when the insurgencies succeeded because of other
factors, the newly independent states were quickly engulfed by renewed
hostilities involving the rival groups. Many forecast a similar future for Afghanistan.

The political culture of a country may also be a source of fissiparous
tendencies in an insurgent movement. This is especially so where there is
low interpersonal and intergroup trust combined with aversion to centralized authority. In chapter 4, we noted divisiveness as another element in the
Afghan case. It is also prevalent among Kurdish seccessionists and in Arab
insurgent movements like the Muslim Brotherhood in Syria and the Palestinian resistance, which are marked by splits. Although other factors often
play a role in such divisiveness, what is often overlooked is the suspicion,
conflict, secrecy, and conspiracy that have characterized authority relationships in the Arab world for centuries.[31] That they should be prevalent in
insurgent movements like the PLO comes as no surprise to students of the
area; it would be surprising if they were not.

Personal ambitiousness—that is, a straightforward struggle for control of an insurgency among individual leaders—can also cause disunity,
particularly when resources are dispersed and no single group is strong
enough to eliminate its rivals. With the passage of time, the leaders of various groups become more convinced that they, rather than their rivals,
should become first among equals, if not the only authority figure. The
bitterness and hatred that come to characterize such rivalries are recogniz-

able to all analyst of politics. The questions with reference to an insurgent movement are whether such a situation has emerged and how it contributes to disunity.

Disunity may also be caused by teleological, theoretical, or strategic differences. Although often intertwined, the three are distinct. Teleological differences—that is, discord over the ultimate political goal that insurgents ought to be pursuing—can be profoundly unsettling, as the admixture of reactionary and moderate traditionalists and egalitarians in the Afghan resistance has shown.

Where deep divisions over goals exist, it is frequently an outgrowth of theoretical disagreements, which, as we saw in discussing esoteric appeals in chapter 5, involve ideology and theology. The problem is that different ideological and theological assumptions about man and society can yield quite different prescriptions with respect to required actions, potential friends and enemies, and desired outcomes. While a combination of cultural, personal, and strategic differences clearly contributed to the previously noted disunity that led to the 1970 civil war in Jordan, it would be an oversight to ignore the part that theoretical divisions played. Put briefly, the Marxist ideology of the PFLP and PDF led the two groups to conceptualize the conflict with Israel in class terms. As they saw it, there was an unholy alliance of international imperialism, Zionism, and what they referred to as "Arab reaction," by which they meant Arab states with leaders who were considered either feudal-traditionalist or petit bourgeois. Since they assumed that the class interests of such leaders benefited from the status quo, the PFLP and PDF concluded that those leaders and their regimes would have to be overthrown before the conflict with Israel could be pursued successfully.[32] Seen in this light, the sabotage and violence against the Hashemite monarchy in Jordan in 1970 was logical. The problem was, it ran counter to the non-Marxists' (e.g., Fatah) desire to cooperate with, and retain, Jordan's support.

Insurgent disunity may also be caused by conflict over which strategies to adopt in the conflict, a subject treated in detail in chapter 3. As we saw previously, there are many possible strategies available to insurgents. An example is the contrast between the protracted-popular-war and military-focus strategies. The protracted-popular-war strategy emphasizes careful political preparation and the consolidation of a strong political organization (normally a party) before initiating hostilities; the military focus strategy calls for the commencement of violence and worrying about political consolidation later. Where strategies diverge as much as these, their simultaneous adoption by different groups results in quite different and often contradictory activity. A group committed to clandestine organizational activity during the earliest stage of the protracted-popular-war strategy, for example, can find its efforts undercut by the premature violence of groups following the military-focus strategy because such violence may awaken the government and lead it to crack down on those insurgents who are keeping a low profile and engaging in political undertakings.

Discord over strategy may also center on more specific issues, such as the forms of violence considered advisable at various points in time. Decisions about whether to carry out acts of terrorism, for instance, have often been a source of disunity. In Palestine during the 1940s, the Jewish resistance underwent considerable internal conflict because the principal group, the Haganah, opposed the terrorist acts by two extremist groups, the Irgun and the Stern Gang. Likewise, one of the ingredients in the split between the Provisionals and the Officials in the current IRA is the latter's disdain for the Provisionals' terrorist violence.[33]

Other strategic questions that can engender disputes among insurgents are whether to expand the arena of conflict to other states, whether to engage in negotiations with the government, and whether to seek support from other countries. Deciding which of these, if any, is pertinent requires careful inquiry.

As the above commentary suggests, there are many possible sources of disunity. While each may be quite damaging, insurgent movements afflicted by several at the same time usually find themselves in an even greater predicament. Although insurgents generally acknowledge the problem and the need to address it, effective remedies are hard to come by.

THE QUEST FOR UNITY

Unity rests on a combination of effective socialization, organizational schemes, and sanctions. Socialization involves inculcating loyalty and a common sense of purpose through propaganda and political education programs. Where social and political cultural factors pose a potential threat to cohesion, insurgents will normally emphasize one or more of the following: the need to close ranks against the common enemy; an ideology or theology that transcends group differences and distrust; and the equitable and mutual benefits to be derived from success.

Organizational schemes are also important in establishing cohesion, and here there are several possibilities. In one scheme, the politicians are in charge. This often happens in Communist movements, but there are two variants. One may be a chain of command that derives from the Politburo through the central executive committee, which exercises control over state, district, and branch committees. These, in turn, will control the military units within their jurisdiction. The other possibility is separate chains of command for the military and the civilian organizations. The latter was the case in the Greek civil war, where the stationary civil administration (parallel hierarchy) ran the liberated base areas while the guerrilla bands, under separate command, moved from sector to sector.

In the second scheme, the political and military exist independent of one another. Such was the situation in the World War II Italian resistance;

military resistance was in the hands of the Corps of Volunteers for Liberation, while civil resistance and local administration were handled by the Central Committee of Liberation. Currently, the relationship between the civilian Democratic Revolutionary Front (FDR) and the military Farabundo Martí National Liberation Front (FMLN) in El Salvador exemplifies this format.

The third organizational type is one in which the military element takes charge. An example would be the Irgun, which operated in Palestine during the British mandate.[34] A more recent approximation of the third scheme is the Cuban model, as described by Regis Debray.[35]

Recognizing and correcting organizational deficiencies are, of course, two quite different things. The FMLN in El Salvador, not without considerable prodding from Cuba, has for several years indicated an awareness of the need to effectively integrate not only its five military groups but also the activities of the civilian FDR. To accomplish this aim, a 1985 strategic assessment indicated the need to create a Marxist-Leninist party to provide leadership for a prolonged war that would put more emphasis on popular support and less on military actions.[36] By the end of 1989, the new party had not appeared. Moreover, problems stemming from a lack of cohesion continued, symbolized by the absurdity of the FDR actively competing in the March 1989 election while the FMLN was vigorously subverting it.

Where socialization and organizational formats fail to curb factionalism, obedience may be imposed by insurgent security forces, assuming, of course, that they are loyal and effective. The recourse to coercion may succeed if recalcitrant individuals and groups are relatively small and impotent. But, if dissident groups are sizable and have enough resources to threaten prolonged and costly fighting, larger main-line groups often avoid using coercion to ensure unity. The fact that the majority group in the PLO, led by Fatah, has been unwilling to crack down on smaller groups like the PFLP and PDF has been due, at least in part, to the reality that Fatah did not have the military ability to deal them swift and decisive blows. To have used sustained force against such groups would have resulted in bitter inter-Palestinian strife, which also might well have involved outside states intervening on one or both sides.

The reluctance to use force against rival factions and groups can dissipate quickly once a particular group sees that it has gained preponderant strength. In Sri Lanka, the Tamil Tigers emerged as the most important insurgent group by eliminating or silencing their opponents through brutal force and intimidation. Likewise, the Eritrean Popular Liberation Front eventually eliminated the Eritrean Liberation Front as a serious rival in the 1980s—but only after two decades of internal strife that many observers feel was the main factor preventing the Eritreans from fully exploiting severe government weaknesses in the 1970s.

The issue of disunity in an insurgent movement may not be amenable to forceful resolution of the type just mentioned. The fact is that once different groups emerge and gain autonomy and strength, they are difficult to discipline. In order to mitigate the effects of group rivalries and to foster a modicum of cooperation, insurgent leaders may create a unified command for a particular operation, agree on a division of labor among various groups, or establish a unified command. Otto Heilbrunn recalled this, for example:

> In Greece a unified command was established for one particular operation, while the non-Communist forces in Czechoslovakia decided on a proper division of labour, one movement specializing in sabotage, the second in collecting intelligence and transmitting it to London, and the third engaging in propaganda. In Albania, the Royalists first cooperated with the Communists and then with the Centre, and in Belgium only the extreme Left groups united, while in France, Italy, Holland, and temporarily in Greece, all groups put themselves under a unified command; the Communists, however, always retained their separate identity.[37]

Of the three possibilities, the idea of a unified command appears to be the most promising, since it is the one most conducive to giving the insurgents a sense of strategic direction and best suited for dealing with the various factors that divide the movement in the first place. For a unified command to be successful, however, the rival organizations must agree to subordinate their parochial interests to the overall interests of the movement, as defined by the unified command. If the unified command's decisions are to be considered authoritative and legitimate, the rival groups must reach a consensus on the mechanics of the decision-making process and on methods for invoking sanctions against deviationists. Consensus on such matters, of course, again raises the question of who will wield dominant power and who will invoke sanctions. Since groups are generally unwilling to make major concessions on these vital matters, the effectiveness of unified commands tends to be marginal, and their durability, limited. This has been the case with various Palestinian efforts along these lines (i.e., the Palestine Armed Struggle Command, the Central Committee of the Palestinian Resistance, the Unified Command of the Palestinian Resistance, and, more recently, the PLO Executive Committee).[38]

Summary

No analysis of an insurgency will be complete or meaningful without an assessment of the scope, complexity, and cohesion of the insurgent movement. A careful look at the structures and workings of insurgent political and military organizations can reveal a good deal about the progress of an insurrection and the type and magnitude of the threat confronting the government. Several questions are very important in this regard. What organizational requirements are associated with the strategy and forms of violence adopted by the insurgents, and are those requirements being met? In particular, if a sophisticated parallel hierarchy is considered necessary, has it emerged? Where is it located? How extensive is it? Does it provide effective command, control, and coordination? Is the insurgent movement unified? If not, what are the causes and effects of disunity? As one proceeds to answer such questions, relationships between organization and the other evaluative criteria should be readily apparent, notably those involving the acquisition of internal and external support. The various aspects of external support are the subject of the next chapter.

Notes

1.   See Ted Robert Gurr, *Why Men Rebel* (Princeton, N.J.: Princeton University Press, 1970), pp. 274–316, for an expanded discussion of the structural and functional aspects of organizations.

2.   The *New York Times,* February 7, 1975, reported that defections had reached 1,037 by 1975.

3.   William R. Heaton, "People's War in Thailand," in George Edward Thibault, ed., *The Art and Practice of Military Strategy* (Washington, D.C.: National Defense University, 1984), pp. 854, 856–857.

4.   Che Guevara, *Guerrilla Warfare* (New York: Vintage Books, 1961), pp. 71–73.

5.   The importance of parallel hierarchies has been noted by a number of specialists on insurgency. See, for example, Bernard B. Fall, *The Two Viet-Nams,* 2d ed. (New York: Frederick A. Praeger, 1967), pp. 130–138; John J. McCuen, *The Art of Counter-Revolutionary War* (Harrisburg, Pa.: Stackpole Books, n.d.), pp. 31, 33–35; Richard L. Clutterbuck, *The Long, Long War* (New York: Frederick A. Praeger, 1966), pp. 22, 56, 87–88; Julian Paget, *Counter-Insurgency Campaigning* (New York: Walker & Co., 1967), pp. 20–21; Douglas Hyde, *The Roots of Guerrilla Warfare* (Chester Springs, Pa.: Dufour Editions, 1968), pp. 92, 126; and Roger Trinquier, *Modern Warfare* (New York: Frederick A. Praeger, 1966), pp. 30, 70.

6.   On cellular development, see Edward R. Wainhouse, "Guerrilla Warfare in Greece, 1946–1948: A Case Study," in Franklin Mark Osanka, ed., *Modern Guerrilla Warfare* (New York: The Free Press of Glencoe, 1962), p. 223; McCuen, *The Art of Counter-Revolutionary War,* pp. 31–35; Hyde, *The Roots of Guerrilla Warfare,* pp. 67–69; and Paget, *Counter-Insurgency Campaigning,* p. 24.

7.   See Alf Andrew Heggoy, *Insurgency and Couterinsurgency in Algeria* (Bloomington, Ind.: Indiana University Press, 1972), pp. 107–129, on the details of the FLN organization.

8.   The UNITA organization is composed of a political bureau, central committee, political commissions, and peasant organizations. The political bureau is chaired and chosen by Savimbi. See *Washington Post,* August 13, 1977, and *Christian Science Monitor,* August 28, 1988.

9.   The commentary on auxiliary organizations, like that on parallel hierarchies,

is extensive. See, for example, Fall, *The Two Viet-Nams,* p. 134; McCuen, *The Art of Counter-Revolutionary War,* pp. 34–35; Hyde, *The Roots of Guerrilla Warfare,* p. 34. An especially good source for the treatment of the role of auxiliary organizations is Douglas Pike, *Viet Cong* (Cambridge, Mass.: MIT Press, 1966), chaps. 6 and 10.

10. Thomas C. Tirona, "The Philippine Anti-Communist Campaign," in Osanka, ed., *Modern Guerrilla Warfare,* p. 204; see also Hyde, *The Roots of Guerrilla Warfare,* pp. 90–91.

11. Jerrold Green, "Countermobilization as a Revolutionary Form," *Comparative Politics* (January 1984):153–168; James A. Bill, "Iran and the Crisis of '78," *Foreign Affairs* (Winter 1978–1979):332–333.

12. Mao Tse-tung, *On Guerrilla Warfare,* Samuel B. Griffith, trans. (New York: Frederick A. Praeger, 1962), p. 113. On the question of military differentiation, see Pike, *Viet Cong,* chap. 13; Virgil Ney, "Guerrilla Warfare and Modern Strategy," in Osanka, ed., *Modern Guerrilla Warfare,* pp. 35–36; Anthony Crockett, "Action in Malaya," *ibid.,* p. 310; Brooks McClure, "Russia's Hidden Army," *ibid.,* p. 89; James E. Dougherty, "The Guerrilla War in Malaya," *ibid.,* p. 302.

13. On Jalalabad, see *Hong Kong AFP* (April 17, 1989), reprinted in *Foreign Broadcast Information Service/Near East and South Asia* (hereafter *FBIS/NESA*), (April 18, 1989), p. 45; *New York Times,* April 13, 1989; *Washington Times,* March 22, 1989.

14. Gurr, *Why Men Rebel,* p. 304 (quote), 297–301; Jerrold M. Post, "Inside the Mind of a Terrorist," *Washington Post,* August 28, 1988, "Outlook" section.

15. The *Christian Science Monitor* on September 23 and 25, 1981, contains articles by Edward Giradet on the Massoud organization. On the Hazara parallel hierarchy, see Christer Lundgren's article in *Gnistan* (Stockholm; April 10, 1981), in *Joint Publications Research Service, Near East/North Asia* (hereafter *JPRS/NENA*), no. 78416 (July 9, 1981):22; *Economist* (May 23, 1981); *L'Unité* (Paris; December 18, 1981), in *JPRS/NENA,* no. 79951 (January 27, 1982):27; *Le Monde* (Paris), May 26, 1980; and *New York Times,* March 20, 1979, and March 2, 1980.

16. On the organizational complexity of the PLO, see Bard E. O'Neill, *Armed Struggle in Palestine* (Boulder, Colo.: Westview Press, 1978), pp. 153–156; and Cheryl A. Rubenberg, "The Civilian Infrastructure of the Palestine Liberation Organization," *Journal of Palestine Studies* (Spring 1983):54–78.

17. Ney, "Guerrilla Warfare and Modern Strategy," p. 30.

18. McCuen, *The Art of Counter-Revolutionary War,* p. 69.

19. George B. Jordan, "Objectives and Methods of Communist Guerrilla Warfare," in Osanka, ed., *Modern Guerrilla Warfare,* pp. 403, 407; and McClure, "Russia's Hidden Army," pp. 88–89, have stressed the importance of central control to the Russian partisan movement. Hyde, *The Roots of Guerrilla Warfare,* p. 65, notes that one of the Teo Yong Jin's first acts in Sarawak was to unify disparate groups.

20. Regis Debray, *Revolution in the Revolution?,* Bobbe Ortiz, trans. (New York: Monthly Review Press, 1967), pp. 73–74.

21. Cited in Jordan, "Objectives and Methods of Communist Guerrilla Warfare," p. 403.

22. McCuen, *The Art of Counter-Revolutionary War,* p. 198.

23. For example, the PFLP-GC's seizure of an apartment house in the northern Israeli town of Qiryat Shemona in the spring of 1974 was, according to a PFLP-GC

spokesman, aimed at blocking an Arab-Israeli settlement; see *New York Times,* April 13, 1974.

24.   The consequences of disunity are reported in *Washington Post,* February 26, 1980; *New York Times,* December 17, 1981, and January 12, 1981; *Christian Science Monitor,* September 28, 1981; *U.S. News and World Report* (January 18, 1980):38–39; *Le Matin* (Paris; September 28, 1981), in *JPRS/NENA,* no. 79364 (November 3, 1981):15; London BBC Service (March 10, 1982), in *FBIS/SA* (March 11, 1982):63; and *Guardian* (London; March 2, 1982).

25.   Internecine violence between Afghan groups has been noted by many sources. See, for example, *Washington Post,* July 12, 1981; *Christian Science Monitor,* August 4 and September 28, 1981; *Baltimore Sun,* September 3, 1981; *Hong Kong AFP* (July 31, 1980), in *FBIS/SA* (August 1, 1980):C2; and *Die Zeit* (Hamburg; September 25, 1981), in *JPRS/NENA* (October 30, 1981):3.

26.   On the Islamic Conference Organization's linkage of unity with external assistance, see *Washington Post,* February 26, 1980, and *New York Times.* March 2, 1980, Section IV.

27.   The role of Palestine disunity in the costly civil war in Jordan in 1970 is discussed in O'Neill, *Armed Struggle in Palestine,* pp. 165–166.

28.   On Afghanistan, see Alain Chevalerias, "Afghanistan, the Improbable Evacuation," *Le Spectacle du monde* (February 1988):42–44. Israel's penetration of the PLO and its efforts to instigate internal strife among Palestinians has been discussed with the author on several occasions during research trips to the Middle East. However, given the obvious sensitivity of this matter, the officials requested that they not be formally cited.

29.   Besides Saiqa and the PLA units stationed in Syria, the Syrians also had close ties with the PFLP-GC and Abu Nidal's Black June group, both of which carried out acts of violence against rivals from time to time. No doubt the most dramatic instances of Syrian-backed groups fighting against Fatah and others took place in 1976 during the Lebanese civil war when Syria intervened on behalf of the Christians! From 1983 to 1988 Damascus also backed rebellious Fatah members in several bloody conflicts with Arafat's loyalists.

30.   Bernard B. Fall, *The Two Viet-Nams,* 2d ed., rev. (New York: Frederick A. Praeger, 1967), pp. 93–94; John McAlister, Jr., *Vietnam: The Origins of Revolution* (New York: Alfred A. Knopf, 1969), pp. 83–84.

31.   On political style and characteristics in the Arab world, see James A. Bill and Carl Leiden, *The Middle East: Politics and Power* (Boston: Allyn and Bacon, 1974), chap. 3.

32.   The role of Marxist ideology and the problems it created for the PLO in Jordan is discussed in O'Neill, *Armed Struggle in Palestine,* pp. 129–130, 134–144, 165.

33.   Christopher Sykes, *Crossroads to Israel* (Bloomington, Ind.: Indiana University Press, 1973), p. 305, notes the Haganah's critical view of the Irgun and Stern Gang. On the Official-Provisional IRA discord over the issue of violent tactics, see Don Mansfield, "The Irish Republican Army and Northern Ireland," in Bard E. O'Neill, William R. Heaton, and Donald J. Alberts, eds., *Insurgency in the Modern World* (Boulder, Colo.: Westview Press), pp. 58–64.

34.   Otto Heilbrunn, *Partisan Warfare* (New York: Frederick A. Praeger, 1962), p. 39. On pp. 26–27, Heilbrunn offers three other possibilities, but since they are

relevant to partisans engaged in direct or de facto support of the army, they are not discussed in the text.

35.   Debray, *Revolution in the Revolution?*, pp. 95–116. Debray argues that the popular liberation army must command in Latin American insurgencies; further, the army will spawn the party during the struggle.

36.   *Washington Post*, November 9, 1985, and *New York Times*, December 22, 1985.

37.   Heilbrunn, *Partisan Warfare*, p. 30.

38.   A detailed review of Palestinian disunity and various organizational structures created in an attempt to overcome it may be found in O'Neill, *Armed Struggle in Palestine*, pp. 125–153.

VII   External Support

Up to this point, i have emphasized the part that popular support for insurgents plays in offsetting the strengths of governments and the importance of solid organization for acquiring and utilizing such support. I have also noted that the extent and contributions of popular support vary considerably from case to case, depending on a number of factors, including the strategies and political skills of insurgent leaders. Yet, as significant as popular support may be in providing assistance to insurgents, it rarely can provide all of the resources necessary for the accomplishment of insurgents' ultimate goals.

Unless governments are utterly incompetent, devoid of political will, and lacking resources, insurgent organizations normally must obtain outside assistance if they are to succeed. Even when substantial popular support for the insurgents is forthcoming, the ability to effectively combat government military forces usually requires various kinds of outside help, largely because beleaguered governments are themselves beneficiaries of external assistance, which in some cases compensates for their lack of popularity.[1] Although the viability of governments in Angola, Afghanistan, Kampuchea, and El Salvador in the mid-1980s would have been very dubious if it were not for external assistance from the Cubans, Soviets, Vietnamese, and Americans, respectively, aid to those governments enabled them to carry out reasonably sustained counterinsurgency military operations. This, in turn, compelled the insurgents to obtain material assets to successfully meet the government challenge and gain the initiative.

If external support is often necessary when insurgents enjoy popular support, it is even more crucial when they do not. Facing a long struggle against government forces with superior arsenals, insurgents must turn to sympathetic nations, other insurgent movements, private institutions in other states, and international organizations in order to increase their politi-

111

cal and military capabilities. Fortunately for them, several facets of the contemporary international system create favorable opportunities.

The Global Context

Among the features of the post–World War II international system
that facilitate the acquisition of external support, six are particularly noteworthy: East-West competition, the Sino-Soviet dispute, regional rivalries,
the worldwide proliferation of armaments, the activities of private groups,
and vast improvements in transportation and communications. Probably
the greatest impetus to external support for insurgent movements has been
the continuous rivalry between the major Communist powers and the West
since the late 1940s.[2] In an era when nuclear weapons have made direct
military engagements between the two sides extremely hazardous, the Soviets and Chinese have served state interests and ideological aims by supporting wars of national liberation against governments friendly to the West.
Although the United States and its allies have generally found themselves
backing governments, in more recent times they have turned the tables
somewhat by aiding a number of insurrections against Marxist or partially
Marxist regimes in places like Angola, Afghanistan, Nicaragua, and Kampuchea.

Assistance to insurgent groups has also been motivated by the Sino-
Soviet dispute, especially since the termination of the Cultural Revolution
in China and the death of Mao brought to power leaders who were equally,
if not more, committed to containing Soviet power. One outcome has been
Chinese support for insurgents opposed to Soviet-backed regimes (e.g., in
Afghanistan and Kampuchea). Both the East-West and Sino-Soviet rivalries
have thus multiplied the opportunities for insurgent groups to obtain external support of various kinds.

Another development favorable to insurgent groups has been the tendency of regional states to undermine rival neighbors by providing assistance to dissidents. In Africa, for instance, South Africa has backed insurgents in Angola and Mozambique, while the latter two states have aided the
South-West African People's Organization (SWAPO) and African National
Congress (ANC) in their campaigns against South Africa. In North Africa
and the Middle East, similar circumstances mark Sudanese-Ethiopian, Liby-
an-Sudanese, Egyptian-Libyan, Syrian-Jordanian, Syrian-Iraqi, and especially Iraqi-Iranian rivalries. Once again, the general effect is to increase the
overall potential for external support to insurgents.[3]

While states are clearly the most important source of external support,
the inputs of private, nongovernmental groups and organizations, as well
as other insurgent movements, should not be discounted by analysts, for in
many instances they provide not only political and moral support but also

money, equipment, training, and other kinds of tangible assistance. The Afghan guerrillas, for example, have received help from nongovernmental groups in France, which have provided doctors and radio operators and transmitters, and others in the United States, which have collected funds, publicized the plight of the resistance, and petitioned the U.S. government to increase its aid.[4] Likewise, the Irish Republican Army has received important aid from the Northern Irish Aid Society in the United States, and the Contras in Nicaragua benefited from assistance provided by private groups, especially following the congressional suspension of aid in 1984–1985.[5] Assistance from other insurgent groups, particularly in the area of training, has also become more prevalent than in the past, as the PLO's links with many groups demonstrates.[6] Although the aid from both private groups and other insurgent movements may not be decisive strategically, it can be quite important in helping sustain the political activities and low-level terrorism or guerrilla warfare operations of insurgent groups that find themselves in a very weak position.

The unprecedented production of military weaponry and equipment in today's world has also made the acquisition of external support easier. Not only do major and regional powers have a greater capacity to provide assistance but also a flourishing private arms industry can and has been tapped by insurgents.

The final factor facilitating the provision and acquisition of external support is the global transportation and communications revolution. All kinds of material supplies can be moved farther and faster because of quantitative and qualitative improvements in surface, water, and air transportation. Whereas in a previous era potential donors halfway across the world were of little use to insurgents, today distant suppliers, such as the United States and the Soviet Union, can play a major role because effective and expeditious transportation is available.

Also very important, but often underemphasized or taken for granted, is the impact that the phenomenal progress in communications has had on the provision of moral, political, and material support. Through radio, television, and printed page, outside supporters are able to mount extensive propaganda campaigns on behalf of insurgent groups and to reach for wider audiences. And, by providing communications equipment, external sources have been able not only to upgrade the command and control of insurgent forces in the field but also to facilitate political and organizational tasks. Reports of National Resistance Front (RENAMO) insurgents using word processors in their jungle base areas inside Mozambique exemplify the point.

As the preceding comments suggest, insurgent movements seem to have much greater opportunities for gaining external support than at any previous time in history because of a combination of international and technological factors. Whether they take advantage of the opportunities depends on their organizational capability. Nowadays many, if not most, insurgent movements have representatives in foreign countries whose main purpose is to obtain support from private and governmental sources. In some cases, insurgent organizations (like the PLO and, to a lesser extent, UNITA) have a rather extensive de facto diplomatic corps to carry out this mission. How well the mission is performed is related to the quality of the insurgent organization, since many general and specific tasks need to be accomplished. In general terms, acquiring external support involves political lobbying and negotiations about what will be provided, how it will be provided, and the terms of transferral. Specific organizational tasks include provision of policy guidance and coordination, as well as funding for basic needs (food, shelter, travel, transportation) of representatives and public relations requirements (typewriters, facsimile machines, videotapes, and so forth). The point here is simple yet important: external support doesn't just happen; it must be pursued through serious organizational efforts. Accordingly, well-organized insurgencies are in a better position to acquire external support than poorly organized ones. The exact nature of that support merits closer attention.

Types of External Support

To state simply that an insurgent movement enjoys support from particular states or nonstate actors does not tell us much, because the kinds of resources made available can differ considerably. Consequently, we must subdivide external support into four basic types: moral, political, material, and sanctuary.

Moral Support

Moral support consists of private and, more important, public statements that indicate sympathy for insurgents in very general terms. The content of such statements may reflect one or several themes. First, and most common, is an emphasis on grievances, which justify and explain the insurgents' recourse to violence; attacking governments for denying political rights and for repression, as well as for the social and economic deprivations they permit, are familiar themes. Another is to praise the courage and persistence of insurgents in the face of seemingly insurmountable odds. Third, the reputation of the insurgents may be burnished by suggesting similarities between them and heroic groups of the past. Fourth, the righteousness of an insurgent movement may be extolled by linking it to larger global forces seeking to end various exploitations and abuses by governments. Typifying this theme is Marxist governments' penchant for associating insurgent groups with such sublime collectivities as "the progressive forces," "the anti-imperialist front," "freedom-loving peoples of the world," and so on.

Yet, as helpful, comforting, and encouraging as moral support may be to insurgent movements, its contribution is marginal without political support.

POLITICAL SUPPORT

Political support for insurgents goes a step further than moral support; it is marked by explicit and active backing for the ultimate goals of insurgents in the diplomatic arena. Although moral and political support are often given simultaneously, this is not always the case, as two situations involving superpowers make clear. The first is Soviet support for the PLO. On the one hand, the Soviets have given consistent moral backing to the Palestinians by condemning Israeli "repressive measures" and commending the "liberating, just character" of the "patriotic partisans" and their "legitimate nationalist and anti-imperialist struggle." On the other hand, Moscow has emphatically dissociated itself from the PLO's goal of eliminating the state of Israel. In a Budapest press conference on November 11, 1968, for instance, Foreign Minister Andrei Gromyko stated that "the Soviet Union, while deploring Israel's views on the Middle East crisis, acknowledges Israel's rights as an independent state," a point that contradicted the ultimate aim of the PLO at that time.[7] This distinction between moral and political support has been reiterated numerous times, much to the chagrin of Palestinian leaders who have come to recognize the limits of what they can expect from the Soviets.

The second situation involves the ambiguity that surrounded American support for the Contras in Nicaragua. Although some Contra leaders were originally led to believe that the United States endorsed their goal of displacing or significantly moderating the Sandinista regime in Managua, American officials, responding to congressional objections, subsequently indicated that the real purpose of U.S. support was to interfere with Sandinista support for the guerrillas in El Salvador. Thus, while American leaders and spokesmen gave moral backing to the Contras by praising them as "freedom fighters" and the like, they disclaimed support for the overthrow of the Nicaraguan government. Not surprisingly, this distinction was not lost on the Contras.[8] Since American aid was essential for the survival of the Contras, Washington's influence on the course of events was significant. Unfortunately, the lack of clarity concerning what goals the United States really backed was reflected in strategic thinking, which was incomplete and poorly developed. For the first several years, the insurgency consisted mainly of cross-border guerrilla attacks from sanctuaries in Honduras and, to a lesser extent, Costa Rica. Later, the insurgents began to make an effort to establish a permanent presence in sections of Nicaragua itself. While the pressure generated by cross-border raids might have been sufficient to motivate Managua to cut off aid to insurgents in El Salvador, it held out little hope of compelling the Sandinistas to effect basic reforms or, even less, of changing the political system. For these things to occur, a protracted-popular-war strategy was necessary, a fact that was recognized only belatedly. The point is that a coherent strategy depended upon a clarification of the main goal and that vital clarification was largely in the hands of an external-support state that could not decide what *it* wanted.

While various motives may help explain the withholding of political support by external actors, a major reason is that political support is more risky than moral support. This is because governments whose very existence or territorial integrity is challenged by political support for its adversaries are more apt to adopt diplomatic and economic policies detrimental, if not hostile, to those giving such support. Since efforts by external powers to champion the goals of insurgents in the international arena may lead other states to follow suit and perhaps motivate them to give tangible assistance to the insurgents, threatened governments see political support as far more damaging and intolerable than the general sympathies and platitudes associated with moral support. Giving material support to insurgents is even more offensive to governments.

Material Support

Material support consists of tangible resources that are either used on behalf of the insurgents or given to them directly. Obviously, material support is important and often crucial for insurgents. Although the popular image of material support tends to focus on military-related resources, it actually covers a wide spectrum, consisting at the nonmilitary end of such things as financing, basic necessities (food, clothing, medicine, shelter, etc.), supply or use of radio stations, and political, ideological, and administrative training. Money has many purposes, especially paying for the acquisition of military supplies, the salaries of full- and part-time members of an insurgent movement, and the expenses associated with sustaining a political apparatus, especially its representatives abroad. Assistance in the form of basic necessities can be quite important because they are directed toward needs that must be met if defections from and demoralization of the insurgent movement are to be avoided. This is particularly true of insurgents who are committed to a prolonged struggle based on popular support. In these situations, radio stations (or airtime) and instruction in politics, ideology, and administration can greatly enhance the organizational dexterity and esoteric and exoteric appeals that, as we have seen, are instrumental in insurgent efforts to gain and retain popular support.

There are many ways that outside powers can help in insurgent warfare. To begin with, the supporting state may use its own forces to assist the insurgents, either directly or indirectly. Examples of the direct use of force include Iran's periodic artillery support of Kurds across the border in Iraq in the 1970s and Jordan's occasional artillery support for Palestinian guerrillas in 1968–1969; the indirect use of force is illustrated by China's instigation of hostilities along its borders with North Vietnam in response to Vietnam's campaigns against Chinese-supported guerrillas fighting the Vietnamese-backed government in Kampuchea in the 1980s. Both direct and indirect use of military forces from supporting states risk escalating internal conflicts to interstate wars, so it is not nearly as prevalent as the provision of advisers, intelligence, training, communications equipment, weapons, ammunition, and other combat-related supplies, which are essential in cases where the insurgents are unsuccessful in obtaining them from the target government on the battlefield (or otherwise) and/or where the insurgents have decided to increase their military operations in scope, intensity, and duration. An example in which an inability to obtain outside support for expanded military forces led to failure, according to Edward E. Rice, is the Mexican Revolution of 1910–1920. A contrasting situation in which acquisition of external military supplies played a key role in success occurred in Vietnam from 1965 onward, when a North Vietnamese decision to conduct mobile-conventional attacks led to the development of an elaborate logistical system (based on massive Russian and Chinese supplies) that stretched from North Vietnam, through Cambodia and Laos, to South Vietnam.[9]

SANCTUARY

The Vietnamese conflict also exemplifies the vital role that sanctuaries can play in insurgencies, since all three states adjacent to South Vietnam contained bases used for training, arms stockpiling, operational planning, and providing safe havens for leaders and facilities for rest and recuperation.[10] The contribution of the sanctuaries to the North Vietnamese and Vietcong war efforts was obvious to all who participated in that conflict; thus, it was not surprising that major bombing campaigns and ground operations were directed at them.

The Vietnam conflict represented one of two situations in which sanctuaries are particularly important. The first is when the insurgents decide to escalate hostilities to widespread and large-unit guerrilla attacks or, beyond that, to mobile conventional frontal assaults. Both levels of fighting require nearby bases and depots to provide substantial and sustained logistical support. The second situation in which sanctuaries are crucial is when insurgents are denied permanent bases inside the target country because of effective government countermeasures. Under these conditions, the sanctuaries are literally the last fallback position of the insurgents because without them military activity will cease or be inconsequential (e.g., the PLO after the 1982 Israeli invasion of Lebanon).[11]

The importance of sanctuaries for insurgent movements has been long recognized by students of insurgency. One astute veteran observer of insurgencies, Bernard B. Fall, argued that "in brutal fact, the success or failure of all rebellions since World War II depended entirely on whether the active sanctuary was willing and able to perform its role."[12] But, while one might agree with the general thrust of this proposition, three qualifications should be kept in mind when examining external support. First, there are exceptions where the insurgents accomplished their goal with minuscule or no sanctuaries; second, the presence of sanctuaries may be less important in explaining developments than other factors; and, third, the specific contributions of sanctuaries vary from case to case.[13]

Castro's insurgency illustrates the first point, since it succeeded without a contiguous sanctuary. In fact, the importance of all forms of external support was minimal because the Batista government was so weak that it collapsed in the face of low-level guerrilla warfare.[14] The insurrection in Oman during the 1960s and 1970s is a case of factors other than sanctuaries being more important in explaining events, especially the demise and containment of the insurgency. Although the PFLO had an active sanctuary across the border in the People's Democratic Republic of Yemen that sustained its guerrilla operations for several years, a palace coup in Oman in 1970 brought to power a new sultan who dramatically changed the government response by instituting political, economic, and military reforms that shrewdly exploited the PFLO shortcomings in the areas of popular support and organization. In a word, an energetic and enlightened government response offset the impact of the sanctuary and the other advantages the insurgents enjoyed.[15]

As far as the third qualification is concerned, a number of situations demonstrate that the contributions of sanctuaries can vary considerably. At one end of a continuum is the most valuable form of sanctuaries, namely, extensive fixed bases with headquarters, supplies, training areas, hospitals, and so forth. Current and recent examples include the use of Cambodia, Laos, and North Vietnam by the Vietcong, Pakistan by the Afghan guerrillas, the Tindouf area in Algeria by the Polisario, Lebanon by the Palestinian fedayeen prior to 1982, and Angola by SWAPO. Somewhere in the middle are smaller facilities and camps used to support terrorism and/or low-level guerrilla warfare. Iran, for instance, provides facilities for a number of groups, including al-Dawa (the Call), a Shiite terrorist group opposed to the Iraqi regime, the Bahrein National Liberation Front, dissident Iraqi Kurds, and several smaller groups. Until recently, India permitted the southern state of Tamil Nadu to function as a limited sanctuary for Tamil insurgents fighting in Sri Lanka, and Thailand did the same in its border areas for Kampuchean insurgents. At the lowest end of the sanctuary continuum is an absence of fixed bases but tolerance for the transit of weapons and personnel. Although modest in comparison to the more complex sanctuaries, transit privileges and facilities are hardly insignificant for insurgents who are fighting in landlocked countries like Afghanistan or who are denied easy access to the sea (e.g., the Kurds in Iran and Iraq, the Thai National Liberation Front, UNITA in Angola, and so on). For them, overland shipment of supplies is a veritable lifeline.

A final point with respect to sanctuaries concerns their location. For the most part, sanctuaries in adjacent states are preferable to those a considerable distance away. Although more vulnerable to government counterattacks, sanctuaries in contiguous states facilitate and expedite the marshaling and moving of men and supplies to battle zones far more effectively than distant santuaries do, something that is very important as insurgents move toward higher levels of military activity. In fact, the absence of contiguous sanctuaries may preclude serious military escalation by insurgents, and their loss will normally result in de-escalation.

Without a contiguous sanctuary, groups such as the Tamils in Sri Lanka and the New People's Army and the Moro Liberation Front in the Philippines are handicapped severely when it comes to expanding their small-scale guerrilla attacks to large, sustained, and widespread guerrilla campaigns. Accordingly, they must depend on the hope that government ineptitude and demoralization in the army will eventually result in political abdication. If the government and army do not falter, the lack of an adjacent sanctuary can be a glaring, if not fatal, deficiency.

That the loss of contiguous sanctuaries can lead to a de-escalation of military activity could be seen in the sharp regression of Palestinian guerrilla attacks that occurred following the expulsion from Jordan in 1971 and the almost total absence of cross-border guerrilla and terrorist attacks after the exodus from Lebanon in 1982. Indeed, the hollow nature of the PLO's rhetoric about armed struggle in the 1983–1990 period is directly related to the lack of sanctuaries in the confrontation states surrounding Israel.

The Precariousness of External Support

An accurate description of the types, donors, and contributions of external support, while important, is only part of the picture, since there can be many costs, risks, and uncertainties in donor-client relationships. The fact is that few, if any, external states engage in open-ended assistance programs for altruistic reasons; they render support because it serves their interests at specific points in time. As a result, it is not unusual to find that they often decrease or terminate assistance or, in some instances, switch sides if it suits their purposes. This is particularly so when the ultimate goal of the insurgents and the aims of the external supporter are incongruent. For example, during the 1960s and early 1970s Kurdish insurgents known as the Pesh Merga were able to carry out a persistent, albeit moderate, level of guerrilla warfare against various governments in Iraq. While one of the major reasons the Pesh Merga was able to persist was because of material and sanctuary support from Iran, the durability of this relationship was always in doubt because the Shah of Iran did not endorse the ultimate goals of the Kurds. Essentially, the Kurds tended to vacillate between the goal of outright seccession and the reformist aim of autonomy, both of which were unpalatable to the shah because their achievement would serve as an example to his own restive Kurdish population. As far as the shah was concerned, the Kurds were a useful instrument for pursuing his own aims of compelling Iraq to agree to border rectifications favorable to Iran, especially with respect to the boundary line in the Shatt-al-Arab waterway. As things turned out, Baghdad agreed to make concessions and the shah reciprocated by ending his support for the Kurds. Since the Kurds had made the mistake of concentrating their forces, they suddenly found themselves vulnerable to Iraqi military attacks, which they could not withstand in the absence of the external support from Iran. In the end, they were sacrificed on the altar of Iranian state interests.[16]

Situations in which there is ambiguity with respect to external political support are also risky for insurgent movements. In the case of assistance to the Afghan insurgents, many key external supporters have never clearly endorsed the political goals of any of the insurgent groups. Moreover, although they appeared to back the intermediate aim of expelling the Soviets from the country, there were questions about whether this meant Soviet military units and the Soviet-backed government or just the former. The implication for the insurgents was clear. If most or all of their external supporters were willing to settle for a Soviet military withdrawal that left a Marxist government in power, the insurgents could have found themselves locked in a conflict with that government but without the benefit of badly needed outside aid. Similar situations existed in Angola and Mozambique, where the Republic of South Africa aided insurgents, not because of a commitment to the ultimate aims of the latter but because it wanted quid pro quo agreements (i.e., an end to Angolan support for SWAPO attacks in Namibia and Mozambican support for the African National Congress in return for South Africa's termination of assistance to UNITA in Angola and RENAMO in Mozambique).

A final and somewhat different twist to the ambiguity of external support was illustrated when India allowed its southern state of Tamil Nadu to provide all four types of support to Tamil secessionists in Sri Lanka while the central government in New Delhi actually opposed the goal of secession (because its achievement could lead India's Tamils to pursue a similar aim at some point). When it appeared that the short-term political benefits of placating the population of Tamil Nadu might be outweighed by Tamil success in Sri Lanka, the Indian government accepted an invitation to deploy peacekeeping forces to Sri Lanka, which ended up conducting counterinsurgency operations against the Tamil insurgents.[17]

Even where governments unequivocally support the political goal of the insurgents, there are no long-term guarantees that external support will continue. A classic example is the People's Republic of China's moral, political, and material assistance to the Popular Front for the Liberation of

Oman and the Thai National Liberation Front, especially during the heady days of the Cultural Revolution in China. As the Cultural Revolution subsided, a new Chinese leadership reassessed its foreign policy and decided to focus on containing Soviet expansionism. Pursuant to this end, Beijing decided to repair damaged relations with a number of official governments, including those in Thailand and Oman, by eliminating or severely curtailing assistance to dissidents opposed to these and several other governments.[18] Even Libya's self-proclaimed champion of Third World liberation movements, Muammar el-Qaddafi, has not been above this kind of volte-face; witness the surprise 1984 Oujda agreement with Morocco, which led to his withdrawal of support from Polisario in return for an end to King Hassan's opposition to Libya's role in Chad.[19] In all these cases, new or reformulated national interests stemming from political reassessments took precedence over previous ideological affinities and seemingly shared goals with insurgent groups.

Another negative aspect of external support, one that often occurs in disunified insurgent movements, is the proclivity of some donor states to contribute to internecine strife in the movement by backing one group at the expense of its rivals. This can result from an outright desire to establish hegemony over the insurgents, from a perceived need to check the influence of other donor states, or, as is so often the case, from both. A classic case is the previously mentioned Syrian assistance to elements of the P.L.O., which has been motivated by a combination of factors, including a historical conception that the area the insurgents are seeking to "liberate," Palestine, is really part of southern Syria. In addition there are strategic sensitivities about threats to the regime in Syria posed by potentially unfriendly insurgent groups and their allies in nearby Lebanon, many of which oppose the ideology of Syria's ruling Ba'ath Party. Finally, there are fears that some groups might reach a settlement with Israel that would isolate Syria and thus undercut its effort to get back the Golan Heights (captured by Israel in 1967). The interplay of these factors has led Syria not only to sponsor its own group in the PLO, Saiqa, but also to frequently instigate and support hostilities against PLO groups that are following or contemplating policies inimical to Syrian interests. Such hostilities have taken the form of using various Palestinian groups against each other (e.g., support for the Abu Musa rebels against Yasir Arafat's Fatah in 1983–1988) or the use of Saiqa and Palestine Liberation Army units controlled by Syria against PLO groups (e.g., during the Lebanese civil war in 1976). What this example suggests is that when insurgent movements suffering from disunity and factionalization are the recipients of external support, close attention should be paid to whether the assistance deliberately favors one group over others, what the motives behind the assistance are, and what the consequences are for the insurgency.

The examples above reveal that both authoritarian and democratic governments of states providing external support can be unreliable donors over the long term, although it would seem that the underlying values and institutions of pluralist governments make them more apt to engage in policy reassessments that can lead to a decrease or complete termination of aid. With respect to values, there is frequently discomfort, if not outright aversion (which can be heard in the public debate), to interfering in the internal affairs of other states. As with other issues, support for insurgent movements in other countries is not exempt from close and critical scrutiny by the media and various branches of government; witness the impact of the American press and Congress on the policy of supporting UNITA in Angola and the Contras in Nicaragua. While it is premature to reach a firm historical judgment about the relative reliability of authoritarian and democratic external-support states, the analyst of insurgency needs to be particularly alert to domestic political events in democracies that may affect external support for insurgencies.

Summary

To summarize, the same global factors that have accounted for the increased availability of external support for insurgents (i.e., superpower, Sino-Soviet, and regional rivalries) have had the somewhat paradoxical effect of making such support precarious because in specific situations political calculations can lead to the conclusion that new circumstances and opportunities may make the continuation of support an obstacle to achieving other foreign policy aims. The implication for analysts is obvious. Careful attention must be paid to the types of external support rendered and their effect on the insurgency, and the durability or continuation of the support must also be examined in terms of the motivations of donor states and changes in the domestic, regional, and international political contexts that affect donor-state motivations. Although exact predictions may not be possible, the more analysts are able to set forth underlying factors or developments that could adversely affect external support, the more complete their overall assessment. While the academic merit of such an undertaking is self-evident, it also has practical implications for the parties to the conflict. For the insurgents, a better understanding of the motivations of donor-nation's may lead to a quest for support from multiple sources, to efforts to prevent changes that could result in a decrease or end to support, or to adjustments in strategies and plans. For governments trying to cope with insurgents, a better understanding of donor motivations may result in foreign policy initiatives designed to cultivate or bring about the events and circumstances that will undercut external support.

Notes

1.   Two recent examples where the capability to arm insurgents has reportedly not kept pace with an increase in recruits are the Contras in Nicaragua and the

Tamils in Sri Lanka. According to Enrique Bermúdez, the operational military commander of the Nicaraguan Democratic Force, only a quarter of his 14,000 troops had adequate ammunition and boots for combat; see *Washington Post*, February 18, 1985. Both Indian intelligence officials and Western diplomats noted in early 1985 that many Tamils could not fight because of a shortage of weapons, according to the *Washington Post*, February 5, 1985.

2.   While historians may debate whether the Cold War began before or shortly after the Bolshevik seizure of power in Russia or in the aftermath of World War II, no one denies that insurrections in Greece and Iran in the late 1940s and in Malaya, the Philippines, and Vietnam in the 1950s intensified suspicions and fears in the West about perceived Sino-Soviet expansionism. Although support from the Soviets and Chinese varied considerably in these cases, the insurgencies suggested that the Western powers were vulnerable to wars of national liberation in the Third World. Accordingly, by the 1960s both Moscow and Beijing openly endorsed the notion of support for wars of national liberations. On Soviet-bloc support, see Richard Shultz, "The Role of External Forces in Third World Conflicts," *Comparative Strategy* 4, no. 4 (1983):79–104.

3.   In general, support for insurgents in neighboring states appears to be a less risky and costly way to pursue national objectives than interstate conventional warfare. Moreover, since many Third World states suffer from crises of political legitimacy (i.e., weak political communities, systems, and/or authorities), they are vulnerable to pressures generated by armed insurgents. The problem with such an approach is that two can play the same game. Hence, governments that have legitimacy crises of their own invite similar actions by their adversaries as time goes by. Where the states initiating external support have greater problems, as in Angola and Mozambique, compared to the Republic of South Africa, they may end up experiencing greater threats to their own stability than they create for their adversary.

4.   Both American and French private groups have provided aid to the Afghan resistance. It has included, among other things, money, blankets, radio transmitters, and medical care. See, for instance, Claude Malhuret, "Report from Afghanistan," *Foreign Affairs* (Winter 1983–1984):426; and *Christian Science Monitor*, December 28, 1984.

5.   In early February 1985, the Nicaraguan Democratic Force had collected some $5 million in the absence of U.S. aid. Part of it was from private sources. See *Washington Post*, December 10, 1984, and February 18, 1985; and *New York Times* June 15, 1984.

6.   Numerous insurgent groups have received training at PLO bases. A succinct account may be found in Claire Sterling, *The Terrorist Network* (New York: Holt, Rinehart and Winston, 1981), pp. 122–126.

7.   See Bard E. O'Neill, *Armed Struggle in Palestine* (Boulder, Colo.: Westview Press, 1978), pp. 195–196.

8.   The question of whether the primary U.S. aim in supporting the Contras was to destabilize the country and bring about the downfall of the Sandinista regime or to compel the Sandinistas to end their support of the insurgents in El Salvador has never been satisfactorily clarified. The uncertainty and problems surrounding this ambiguity are discussed in the *New York Times*, April 7, 1983.

9.   Edward E. Rice, *Wars of the Third Kind* (Berkeley: University of California Press, 1988), pp. 79–80. Numerous other writers have called attention to the impor-

tance of external material aid; see, for instance, Virgil Ney, "Guerrilla Warfare and Modern Strategy," in Frank Mark Osanka, ed., *Modern Guerrilla Warfare*, (New York: Free Press of Glencoe, 1962), pp. 31–32; Bernard B. Fall, *Street Without Joy* (Harrisburg, Pa.: Stackpole Books, 1963), p. 294; Ted Robert Gurr, *Why Men Rebel* (Princeton, N.J.: Princeton University Press, 1970). pp. 269–270; Julian Paget, *Counter-Insurgency Campaigning* (New York: Walker & Co., 1967), p. 25; Frank Trager, *Why Vietnam?* (New York: Frederick A. Praeger, 1966), p. 77.

10.   On the importance of sanctuaries, see Ney, "Guerrilla Warfare and Modern Strategy," p. 10; Peter Braestrup, "Partisan Tactics—Algerian Style," in Osanka, ed., *Modern Guerrilla Warfare*, pp. 376, 380–382; John J. McCuen, *The Art of Counter-Revolutionary War* (Harrisburg, Pa.: Stackpole Books, n.d.), p. 37; Roger Trinquier, *Modern Warfare* (New York: Frederick A. Praeger, 1964), pp. 97–98; Richard L. Clutterbuck, *The Long, Long War* (New York: Frederick A. Praeger, 1966), p. 7; and Otto Heilbrunn, *Partisan Warfare* (New York: Frederick A. Praeger, 1962), pp. 51, 60–61.

11.   A good example of this situation is the predicament of the insurgents in Sarawak as depicted in Douglas Hyde, *The Roots of Guerrilla Warfare* (Chester Springs, Pa.: Dufour Editions, 1968), pp. 86–88. In more recent times, the Palestinian guerrillas have relied on sanctuaries in Jordan and Lebanon because they could not establish permanent bases in Israel, the West Bank, and the Gaza Strip; see O'Neill, *Armed Struggle in Palestine*, pp. 163–164.

12.   Fall, *Street Without Joy*, p. 294.

13.   J. J. Zasloff, *The Role of Sanctuary in Insurgency: Communist China's Support to the Viet Minh, 1946–1954* (Santa Monica, Calif.: The Rand Corporation, 1967), p. 80, contends that Fall and others state their case on sanctuaries too strongly. However, in this writer's opinion, Zasloff goes too far in suggesting there is no crucial relationship between external support and success. Whether the Vietcong and North Vietnamese could have succeeded without sanctuaries is very doubtful.

14.   Dickey Chapelle, "How Castro Won," in Osanka, ed., *Modern Guerrilla Warfare*, pp. 333–334.

15.   See Bard E. O'Neill, "Revolutionary War in Oman," in Bard E. O'Neill, William R. Heaton, and Donald J. Alberts, eds., *Insurgency in the Modern World* (Boulder, Colo.: Westview Press, 1980), pp. 213–233.

16.   On the shah's termination of aid to the Kurds, see Paul R. Viotti, "Iraq: The Kurdish Rebellion," *ibid.*, p. 202.

17.   The mutual commitments to end external support for insurgents between South Africa and Mozambique are summarized and discussed in the *New York Times*, October 10, 1984, and November 30, 1988. The agreement involving Angola is discussed in the *Washington Post*, October 14, 1984.

18.   William R. Heaton, "China and Southeast Asian Communist Movements: The Decline of Dual Track Diplomacy," *Asian Survey* (August 1982):779–798; and "People's War in Thailand," in George Edward Thibault, ed., *The Art and Practice of Military Strategy* (Washington, D.C.: National Defense University Press, 1984), pp. 850–852; O'Neill, "Revolutionary War in Oman," pp. 223–224.

19.   *Christian Science Monitor*, September 7, 1984.

VIII The Government Response

O$_F$ ALL THE VARIABLES THAT HAVE A BEARING ON THE progress and outcome of insurgencies, none is more important than government response. Professor Walter Sonderlund put it succinctly: "As soon as the challenge is in the open the success of the operation depends not primarily on the development of insurgent strength, but more importantly on the degree of vigor, determination and skill with which the incumbent regime acts to defend itself, both politically and militarily."[1] Implicit in Sonderlund's comment is the notion that governments can control their own destiny, largely because they are normally in an advantageous position during the incipient stages of violence because of their higher degree of political institutionalization and their control of the instruments of coercion (i.e., the police and military). Whether governments lose, maintain, or enhance their initial advantage depends, in the main, on how they mobilize and use the political and military resources at their disposal, a subject that has spawned a considerable body of counterinsurgency literature. In this chapter, the most important aspects of that literature will be integrated with my own ideas and findings.

There are, of course, many ways to organize information and thinking about this diverse subject matter. For our purposes, the preceding components of the framework will be used. The goals, techniques, and strategies of insurgents, as well as their efforts and achievements in the areas of organization and popular and external support, enable us to focus our analysis on what it is that governments are responding to, and when linked to government response, they also remind us of the dynamic interplay among all the factors.

It should be noted before proceeding that the general use of the term *response* does not mean that the government is always in a reactive mode with respect to particular threats, issues, and problems. In fact, governments that anticipate difficulties and initiate preventive measures are in a much better position than those that wait for problems to emerge and then react. Both effective reaction and anticipation depend on an informed and comprehensive understanding of the situation on both sides of the conflict.

Responding to Insurgent Goals, Strategies, and Means

As noted in previous chapters, insurgents pursue various goals, use a variety of techniques or methods, and pose different threats to governments. Consequently, a key point to be addressed when evaluating a counterinsurgency program is how well the government knows its enemy. As self-evident as this may seem, historical and contemporary data reveal instances in which governments have misdirected policies because they misunderstood or falsely portrayed the goals, techniques, strategies, and accomplishments of their opponents. Whatever the reasons (inflexibility, sloppy thinking, ignorance, biases, bureaucratic imperatives, or psychological aversions to acknowledging one's own weaknesses), the outcome is flawed, costly, and sometimes fatal policies and behavior.

To begin with, it is important to find out if the authorities have made a conscious effort to identify what type of insurgency they are dealing with, by carefully examining all information at their disposal—statements, publications, and internal documents of the insurgents, as well as intelligence from human and electronic sources, if it is available. Failure to do this can lead to false pictures of their adversary. For instance, reformists can be erroneously identified as egalitarians; secessionists as egalitarians; anarchists as egalitarians; and so forth. The penchant of some beleaguered governments to simply portray all of their adversaries as Marxist egalitarian revolutionaries is a well-known manifestation of this mistake.

When a government misunderstands the type of insurgent movement it is facing, it can blind itself to policy options that could end the insurgency at lower costs. For example, a government that correctly views reformists as those who want a more equitable distribution of economic and political power can then see the possibility of a compromise settlement; mislabeling reformists as egalitarians, traditionalists, or anarchists rules out possible accommodations. In turn, ruling out accommodations runs the longer-term risk of transforming increasingly frustrated reformists into one of the other types of insurgents, as happened in the Dhofar insurgency in Oman.[2]

Careful analysis may also reveal goal disagreement within an insurgent movement and thus enable the government to craft policies that may satisfy some insurgent groups, thereby exacerbating divisiveness in the insurgency. Being aware of different insurgent goals can also lead to actions aimed at sowing discord among insurgents by publicly stressing their incompatible goals or by infiltrating the insurgency with agents provocateurs who try to intensify distrust among the groups. By contrast, a government approach that treats diversified insurgents as "birds of a feather" is self-defeating because it precludes strategic and tactical responses that can exploit differences between insurgents.

Accurate assessments of insurgent goals, of course, only begin the process of fully understanding an opponent's profile. Early in the struggle it is also important to ascertain the strategy of the insurgents and the prominent forms of violence they employ. In some cases, such as Vietnam, the declarations, writings, and behavior of insurgents clearly revealed their strategy, while in others, such as Afghanistan, the strategy must be inferred because of its nebulous, ad hoc character. Whatever the case, governments that take the time to carefully examine insurgent strategies are better prepared to conceptualize a broad and relevant counterstrategy.

Once analysts understand the insurgent strategy, they can focus on the most important requirements for insurgent success associated with that strategy and look at ways to frustrate insurgent efforts to fulfill those requirements. To illustrate, if the insurgents have chosen a Maoist protracted-popular-war strategy, informed government strategists will be attuned to the need to devise political, social, and economic policies and programs to undercut the propaganda and organizational efforts of their enemies. Since, as we have seen, insurgent activity in the first phase of a protracted-popular-war strategy is largely nonviolent and political in nature, it may go undetected or be accorded little significance because of the government's lack of a basic understanding of the strategy. By contrast, knowledge of what transpires early in an insurgency using this strategy can alert the government to shed its apathy and complacency, to move quickly to improve and extend its own administrative capability, and to uncover and neutralize the work of insurgent political cadres. If this is done, the insurgency may be contained early on; if not, the insurgency may progress to the point where the stage has been set for guerrilla warfare. Should that occur, the costs of countering the protracted-popular-war strategy will sharply increase. This is precisely what happened in the Philippines during the 1970s when the Marcos government, preoccupied with various political enemies and the Moro Liberation Front's seccessionist insurrection in the south, casually dismissed the threat posed by the fledgling New People's Army, which was quietly going about the business of organizing and gaining support for an armed struggle that rapidly became a serious threat once violence commenced.

Where insurgents have adopted other strategies, the strategic orientation of the government will differ correspondingly. The military-focus approach would call for a response that emphasizes the military dimension. Conventional warfare threats must be countered with conventional forces. This, of course, was the basic idea underlying the Union's strategy of seeking to decisively defeat Confederate armies in the American Civil War. The

North's difficulties in that conflict stemmed not from an improper strategy but from problems of implementation, not the least of which was mediocre leadership (e.g., General George B. McClellan's indecisiveness in the early years).[3] Where the military-focus strategy of the insurgents emphasizes guerrilla warfare, which has most often been the case in recent times, the government emphasis must be on counterguerrilla campaigns (the characteristics of which are discussed below). Emphasizing counterguerrilla operations does not mean that political, social, and economic factors are neglected altogether. The role these matters play must be assessed and appropriate policies designed to address whatever problems they pose or are likely to pose. Finally, conspiratorial and urban warfare strategies necessitate a government response that concentrates on political efforts and on intelligence and police work in the cities rather than on expenditure of resources in the rural areas. Examples here include the responses to the Tupamaros in Uruguay, the Monteneros in Argentina, and the Red Brigades in Italy.

While an accurate assessment of an insurgent movement's strategy is important for the design of an effective general counterstrategy, more specific guidelines and principles for government behavior are related to the political techniques and forms of warfare adopted by the insurgents. All of these have received ample attention in the writings on insurgency, particularly those that set forth "lessons learned." There is thus a large collection of propositions, suggested antidotes, and policy prescriptions associated with the different threats.

The political threat posed by insurgents varies in scope and complexity from case to case. It involves organizational activity, propaganda, demonstrations, and the like and can have either internal or external dimensions (or both). Since the political aspects of insurgent movements falls within our categories of popular support, organization, unity, and external support, which are dealt with later in this chapter, we shall defer further comment until then and confine our remarks here to the question of coping with the different forms of warfare (violence) that insurgents may adopt, starting with terrorism.

Experience and the experts suggest that the most effective way to deal with internal terrorism and small-scale *urban* guerrilla attacks against soldiers and policemen is to emphasize police work, good intelligence, and judicial sanctions.[4] Since terrorists operate in very small units or cells and are normally highly secretive, regular military forces are of marginal use, because of their conventional training and orientations. Moreover, as is well known, regular military forces often resort to indiscriminate violence when frustrated by their inability to cope with elusive terrorists. Two recent examples were the acknowledgments by both the Peruvian and Sri Lankan governments that their armed forces were responsible for large-scale violence against civilians in the mid-1980s when they responded to terrorism.[5]

To avoid situations like this, wise governments turn to specially trained police and intelligence agencies for a solution.[6] However, as brutal episodes involving the Peruvian Guardia Civile have also shown, even the police can get out of hand in the absence of discipline and a respect for the law. Accordingly, to be effective, professional police and intelligence work must be disciplined. It is not just coincidence that terrorism subsided and became less threatening in Northern Ireland and Italy when disciplined police forces were emphasized.[7] Keeping the military out of the day-to-day business of countering terrorists in favor of special police forces can be done even when the latter are part of the military establishment. One way, adopted in Italy for the *carabinieri* and in Spain for the Guardia Civile, is to transfer units involved in antiterrorist actions to the control of the Interior Ministry.

Police and intelligence agencies are also the main instruments for combating transnational terrorism. In today's world the problem of transnational terrorism places a premium on international police cooperation and intelligence sharing. In fact, even where terrorism is limited to internal attacks, international cooperation is important because supplies and other forms of aid for terrorists often come from the outside. The obvious question is whether governments facing terrorists with international links are willing to work with police and intelligence agencies of other countries. Where they are, the situation can improve markedly as French-Spanish cooperation against Spain's Basque terrorists has shown. In that case, a change in French policy in 1986 led to the arrest and jailing of nearly five hundred ETA suspects in southwestern France, where the terrorists had found a safe haven.[8] As for officials and citizens who are threatened while abroad, governments may resort to various defensive and offensive measures. Defensively, steps can be taken to enhance the security of embassies, consulates, airline offices, and the like (e.g., access control, weapons detection, and the posting of armed guards). Offensively, special operations can be mounted against terrorists located in other countries. As the Israelis have shown, these may involve attacks against the bases and headquarters of terrorists and special operations such as the dispatch of hit teams to eliminate terrorist operatives.[9] However, it is important to note that such actions risk international opprobrium and an expansion of warfare if the third countries involved decide to retaliate.

Guerrilla warfare in the rural areas presents problems different from terrorism. Since guerrilla units are larger and better armed than terrorist units, specialized police units are inadequate and vulnerable. In those rare cases in which guerrilla units are isolated in areas with open terrain, government regular forces can eliminate them with conventional attacks. By contrast, they are difficult to detect and engage when, as is often the case, they operate in favorable terrain and emphasize hit-and-run attacks, dispersal, and reliance on the population. Under these conditions, guerrillas often frustrate regular military forces because, as the United States and Soviet

Union found out in Vietnam and Afghanistan, heavy firepower and large-unit maneuvers are irrelevant, are not cost-effective, and are sometimes counterproductive.[10]

Numerous cases suggest that the centerpiece of successful counter-guerrilla campaigns are small-unit operations—that is, sustained and aggressive patrols and ambushes in guerrilla-infested zones. The main targets are not pieces of territory that are to be seized and held but rather the insurgents themselves, as well as their supporters, sources of supply, and organization. McCuen has argued that the proper response to low-level guerrilla warfare is the positioning of armed units in a large number of small posts where they can protect and mix with the local people, supported by backup mobile air, naval, and ground forces that assist ambush patrols that engage guerrillas and conduct harassment operations against insurgent units in underpopulated hinterlands.[11]

When insurgents begin to conduct successful large-scale guerrilla operations (e.g., the Vietcong in 1965–1966), governments obviously face a more serious threat. McCuen's analysis suggests that smart governments first consolidate the areas they hold (lest they also be subverted) and gradually expand from there with the object of gaining control of the population, food, and other resources.[12] Once this is done, government forces can venture forth from their base areas and seek to defend *vital* lines of communication (the French in Indochina mistakenly tried to defend all lines of communication and thus ended up in a large, static defense force), to inflict losses on guerrilla units, and to neutralize the insurgents' political apparatus. Once again, the key components are patrols, attacks, and ambushes by dispersed units operating day and night, supported by mobile forces. Air artillery and commando harassment of insurgents in remote areas where bases are likely to have been established may also make an important contribution to the antiguerrilla efforts. Populated areas cleared of guerrilla bands should be reorganized by military civic action teams that are prepared to play a defensive role in conjunction with forces operating in the region. If forbidden zones (i.e., areas that can be fired into at will) are to be created, it is important that they not be set up where there are innocent civilians; otherwise, such military actions may prove to be counterproductive because they risk creating more insurgents than are eliminated.[13]

In order to free regular military forces for counterguerrilla operations and to provide security for government officials, civic action teams, and the people, local self-defense forces may be established. Where they are not, civilian officials who are in charge of social and economic programs can be intimidated or eliminated by insurgent violence; witness the plight of unprotected mayors in El Salvador in 1988 who either resigned or were assassinated.[14] When local militias are established to prevent this kind of thing, their effectiveness will be partly contingent on whether they constitute a disciplined force perceived to be a servant of the people, as in the case of the *firqats* in Oman, or are instead ill-disciplined units guilty of excesses against the people, as in the case of the Civilian Home Defense Force in the Philippines.[15]

Governments confronted by *conventional* warfare are in a more serious situation, since the insurgents have calculated that the balance of forces has shifted in their favor to the point where they can deploy larger and more heavily equipped units against government forces in sustained battles (e.g., the terminal phases of the Chinese civil war). One analyst argues that the government's first step should be to stabilize its own base areas, even if this means sacrificing large parts of the country. After securing base areas, large mobile strike forces, supported by air and artillery, can be directed at insurgent bases, as was done with the assaults on guerrilla strongholds during the Greek civil war. If the government is lucky, the insurgents may choose to defend their bases, thus violating a cardinal insurgent principle that warns against engaging a superior force in positional battles. If insurgents decide to revert to guerrilla warfare, the government can then respond likewise, taking appropriate steps summarized previously.[16]

The last point suggests that *adaptability* is crucial when responding to the various types of threats posed by insurgents. This is easier said than done in many cases because insurgent threats may not only overlap but also vary from region to region. In view of this, an effective response involves a sophisticated military strategy that avoids one form of warfare applied indiscriminately in all sectors and instead adopts a flexible policy that coordinates a variety of countermeasures in different areas, depending on the nature of the threats. For example, it would be a mistake for a government facing a substantial conventional threat in one sector and low-level guerrilla activity in another to extend its search-and-destroy operations against conventional formations to the guerrilla area, because such a move would constitute a costly and perhaps counterproductive overreaction. The reason for this is that guerrillas can easily blend back into the population and thus raise the possibility of regular military units striking out against the people, many of whom may be quite innocent. Past experience suggests that under such circumstances it is more appropriate to conduct conventional operations in one area and patrols in the other. The height of folly would be to rely almost solely on conventional operations while neglecting small-unit operations in key populated areas of the country (e.g., the Westmoreland strategy in Vietnam).

Up to this point, our discussion has concentrated on the different orientations with respect to the use of force against terrorism, guerrilla attacks, and mobile-conventional warfare. As we know, however, since the use of force is part of a larger political-military struggle, success depends on its integration with political, judicial, administrative, diplomatic, economic, and social policies. This is particularly true when it comes to dealing with terrorist and, most important, guerrilla threats because the success or failure of these forms of warfare is largely determined by nonmilitary factors, all of which the government can influence. To better understand this and to complete the counterinsurgency picture, we must now focus on the relationship between government response and the other criteria of the framework for analysis.

Government Response and the Evaluative Criteria

THE ENVIRONMENT

The physical environment, as we saw in chapter 4, can be a tremendous asset for insurgents pursuing protracted-popular-war or military-focus strategies. Large areas with heavy jungles and/or mountains and poor roads, as in the Philippines, Vietnam, Afghanistan, and China, will remain conducive to guerrilla operations for the forseeable future, despite improvements in the areas of defoliation, detection technology, air mobility, and the like. Although the government cannot completely neutralize the advantages conferred on the insurgents by these physical settings, it may be able to reduce those advantages by adopting an appropriate counterinsurgency strategy and skillfully using its own assets. Essentially, government forces need to isolate areas favorable to guerrilla operations by consolidating their own areas of control and then surrounding and moving gradually into the areas with rugged terrain. The British demonstrated that this was possible in Malaya and Kenya in the early 1950s, although it required substantial resources and patience. Parenthetically, it should be recalled that the identification of the Malayan Communist Party with the Chinese minority facilitated British efforts.

Many countries, of course, do not have ideal topographical conditions for guerrilla warfare. Although they may have some rugged areas with good cover and few, if any, roads, governments may be able to isolate such zones and decisively reduce their contributions to insurgent efforts. The insurgency in Oman in the 1960s illustrates this point well. For the most part, the activities of the insurgents were centered in the southern province of Dhofar, a mountainous area with boulder-strewn canyons, abundant foliage, and a poor road and communications system, all of which favored guerrilla operations. But on closer inspection, the physical setting of Dhofar also revealed some serious flaws that could be exploited by the government. Among these was the confinement of the insurgents' transportation and communications lines to the mountains because the latter were bounded on the east by the coast and on the west by the hot, desolate, and inhospitable Rub al-Khali (the Empty Quarter). Following the Qabus coup in 1970, the Sultan's Armed Forces, aided by Iranian expeditionary forces, took two steps to exploit these vulnerabilities: first, they built roads and extended lines of communications that allowed the army to set up permanent bases in the mountains, and second, they constructed a series of fortified lines that bisected the guerrillas' north-south supply routes and isolated their units. Consequently, what initially was a favorable area for guerrilla operations turned out to be something much less than that. Although this was done on a smaller scale than in China, the Omani actions were similar in many ways to those of the Chinese Nationalists during their fifth "extermination campaign" against Mao's base area in south-central China (which led to the famous Long March in the 1930s).[17]

Another illustration of government adaptability and initiative to neutralize a physical environment that had been supportive of guerrilla operations for several years occurred in the Western Sahara. Unlike Dhofar, the terrain there was an expansive desert devoid of foliage. Relatively unhindered by a mediocre government air force, the Polisario guerrillas took advantage of their knowledge of the desert to conduct numerous attacks, some of which were quite large and actually reached into Morocco proper. Following a reassessment of the situation, the Royal Armed Forces (FAR) decided to concentrate on defending the so-called useful triangle, an area that contained the majority of the population and phosphate deposits, by building a series of walls (made of sand, dirt, and rocks) that contained intermittent military outposts and detection devices. Although costly, the walls significantly blunted Polisario's guerrilla and mobile-conventional operations because insurgent units seeking to circumvent or attack them were relatively easy to detect in the open terrain.[18] Incidentally, it is worth recalling that a similar effort to construct a barrier along the border between South and North Vietnam (the McNamara line) during the Vietnam War was rendered ineffective by the insurgents' ability to penetrate or go around the line via Laos. In that case, the size of the area and the dense foliage would have been too costly to overcome.

Both the Omani and Western Saharan situations nonetheless demonstrate that in some situations governments can turn elements of a once unfavorable physical environment to their advantage through calculated policy decisions and effective implementation. The general questions suggested by these two situations are, of course, whether the government is aware of the impact of the physical makeup of the country on the insurgency and what, if anything, is done to offset the advantages it gives the insurgents.

While an understanding of the implications of the physical setting for the two sides facilitates, and is frequently a requisite for, a sound government response, understanding the human milieu is vital. A careful and unbiased assessment of demography, social structure and values, economic trends, the political culture, and the structure and performance of the political system is, as we have seen, necessary for uncovering the causes of the insurgency and identifying obstacles that both sides face with regard to implementing their strategies and policies. From the government's perspective, a comprehensive review can reveal critical social, economic, and political problems that need to be addressed; it can also provide insights into the feasibility of various antidotes. The more complete the assessment, the better it is, since partial reviews run the risk of focusing on only part of the problem and ignoring the interrelatedness of demographic, social, economic, and political factors. In the current insurgency in the Philippines, for instance, a profile of the social structure and economic distribution pattern has suggested a need for land reform. The fact that land reform may not be a panacea, however, becomes evident from an examination of basic demographic trends, which portray an overpopulation problem that may render the effects of land reform inconsequential. This, of course, further suggests that the population dilemma must be dealt with and that other policies may be necessary to cope with the disappointments that will be engendered when hopes associated with land reform are not fulfilled.[19] The likelihood of accomplishing any of this appears dubious in the midterm because the political system allows entrenched wealthy elites to use their leverage to block fundamental changes.

On a more positive note, the insurrection in Oman in the 1960s and 1970s represents a case in which an assessment of the human milieu by the government and its British advisers set the stage for adopting more effective policies. In Oman the human environment in the 1960s was conducive to insurrectionary behavior because the ethnolinguistic differences between the *jebali* (mountain people) and the coastal population were exacerbated by the lack of government administration and commitment of resources to the *jebal* (mountainous areas). Under such conditions, insurgent political organizers found it relatively easy to exploit existing social antagonisms. An energetic and enlightened reversal of the government's policies in the 1970s, which emphasized an administrative and military presence, as well as the provision of health, educational, and agricultural services in the *jebal*, eventually mitigated the hostility of the *jebali* toward the sultan. What these developments in Oman showed is that governments are capable of affecting various dimensions of the socioeconomic milieu in positive ways once they understand the opportunities and challenges it presents.

A comparison of the Omani situation with that in Afghanistan further suggests that an appreciation of social values and structures can help prevent counterinsurgency blunders. Reforms in Oman were effective not only because they met some identifiable material needs but also because they did not involve a substantial government intrusion into local affairs that would have challenged tribal values and structures. In Afghanistan, by contrast, ambitious land, educational, and marriage reforms in 1978 played a key role in igniting violent resistance. In places such as El Salvador, Guatemala, and the Philippines such "enlightened" reforms would have been undoubtedly greeted with popular approval; in Afghanistan they met with scornful and violent disapproval because of the threat they posed to widely accepted and deeply entrenched social values and structures legitimized by tradition and religion. The lesson for governments is that officials responsible for counterinsurgency policymaking need to understand the tolerance of the social system with respect to both the kind and degree of policy initiatives that they are considering.

The final aspect of the human environment, the political culture and system, is no less important to governments facing insurgencies. This comes as no surprise, since the resolution of social and economic problems that are often the root causes of insurgencies is contingent upon political decisions. Regardless of the type of political system they operate in, political leaders need to be sure that it functions well enough to keep them informed of the extent and intensity of popular demands, which groups espouse them, and how strong the groups are. The basic point here is that blocked channels of communication and expression can, as the Shah of Iran belatedly found out, be a major problem because of the misleading and poorly informed images of the popular mood that they may create. In a word, problems that are unknown are hard to solve.

Aside from the issue of whether social and economic demands are effectively articulated, processed, and communicated, the functioning or effectiveness of a political system itself may be a concern. A major issue here may involve demands for participation in national decision-making by various groups. The essential questions are who wishes to participate and what kind of participation they have in mind. Generally speaking, the larger and more educated the groups seeking participation, the greater problem they present. Smaller groups are easier to manage. The matter of what kind of participation is also important. Not all demands for participation are for Western-style formulas. In the context of the political culture and style of Persian Gulf countries, for instance, participation is more apt to mean a role in the consultative process than "one man, one vote" open elections, political parties, and so on. If this continues to be so and the professional middle class increasingly demands participation, the real answers may not be the adoption of Western institutions but the adaptation of local ones. The idea of co-opting potential or actual dissidents is, after all, hardly a new one.

Much more, of course, could be said about the political system and insurgency. Entire books devoted to the subject of instability have sought to identify specific functions necessary for system maintenance and how the functions are performed in specific cultures in order to assure stability. One point the studies make is the same as ours—namely, that flaws in the political system can be fundamental underlying causes of instability, which are at times translated into insurgent behavior. The logical prescription here is that governments dealing with insurgencies should take a hard, open-minded look at the political process as part of their assessment of the human environment. It may be another matter whether they can satisfactorily rectify major flaws that an analysis of the political process reveals (e.g., the inordinate leverage of privileged groups like the military, police, or land-owners). Reform may well be improbable, but the absence of an open-minded look at the political process will make it impossible.

While common sense suggests that governments will naturally take the rational step of thoroughly assessing the human environment prior to making policy choices, such an assumption has been disproven many times (most recently by the blunders of the Afghan government, which woefully misunderstood its own society, according to Soviet specialists). The government's assessment of the human environment is thus a significant area of inquiry for all analysts. Assessments that are superficial, incomplete, distorted, and/or erroneous often contain the roots of political and military policies that are ineffective or have failed altogether, especially when it comes to neutralizing insurgent efforts to acquire and organize popular support.

POPULAR SUPPORT

As noted previously, effective government actions and policies are closely related to insurgent efforts to gain popular support, especially in cases in which the insurgents are trying to obtain active assistance for terrorists and especially guerrillas. It has been common to refer to this as the battle to win the "hearts and minds of the people." In assessing government efforts to counteract insurgents, it is important to remember our discussion of the various techniques that insurgents use to gain support. Two basic questions need to be asked. First, is the government attuned to the fact that normally the elites and the masses have different interests and respond to different insurgent appeals, thus raising the possibility of the government driving a wedge between the two by adopting policies tailored to each? Second, how is the government responding to whatever techniques are being employed by the insurgents?

In cases in which the charismatic attraction of the insurgent leader is thought to play a key role in gaining support, governments often seek to capture or eliminate him (e.g., Soviet attempts to kill Jonas Savimbi).[20] But, since the security surrounding such a personage rarely permits this, other approaches may be tried, including propaganda and disinformation campaigns designed to discredit him. In addition, agents who have penetrated the insurgent apparatus may try to stir up jealousies and rivalries. Where charismatic leaders are operating in a culturally diverse environment, such efforts sometimes emphasize the ethnic, religious, and/or racial differences between the charismatic leader and groups he is seeking to influence favorably, thereby sowing distrust, if not dislike, between them.

Esoteric appeals based on either religion or secular ideology can be countered by posing alternative ideologies or, short of that, general values. To help dissuade intellectuals from joining the insurgents, persuasive and compelling alternative values, arguments, and ideas need to be presented, and the basic points of the insurgents' theories must be skillfully critiqued and refuted; simple psychological warfare operations directed at the masses will not suffice for the intellectuals. Rather, the insurgents' ideas and implementation of the ideas must be shown to be detrimental to the interests of the educated classes. An example would be sophisticated critiques of Marxist class analysis and reminders of the fate of the intelligentsia under Marxist rule, all of it designed to discourage discontented intellectuals from casting their lot with the insurgents. The terrible repression and economic failures of recent regimes that came to power as the result of successful insurrections or political protest movements trumpeting ideologies or theologies intolerant of other views (e.g., Marxist regimes and the Islamic Republic of Iran) can be adduced as compelling evidence to underscore this point. For the most part, the purpose of this persuasion is to deter members of the educated stratum from backing insurgents; once intellectuals have joined or otherwise actively supported an insurgency for ideological reasons, it is difficult to win them back, because of the psychic investment they have made. This is especially so when nationalist or religious ideas are involved.

Nationalism, as we have seen, has a particularly potent appeal in many insurgencies. Whether nationalist ideas are part of a larger comprehensive ideological thought system or not, they continue to play a part in galvanizing popular support for many insurgent movements. Since nationalist appeals are especially powerful because they exploit the natural tendencies of people to distrust and dislike foreigners who rule over them, and because they ascribe psychological (or cultural) traumas, economic deprivation, political disenfranchisement, and repression to foreign rule, it is difficult, if not impossible, for colonial or imperial regimes to counter effectively with esoteric appeals of their own. Consequently, such regimes generally try to survive by resorting to repression and/or attempts to meet the material needs of the people. In cases in which their dominions are multicultural, imperial governments have frequently pursued "divide and rule" policies. While such measures may be successful for a time, over the longer term they have been generally ineffective. This is meant not to pass judgment on the merits or demerits of imperial or colonial regimes but to recognize they have been exceedingly vulnerable in the post–World War II era, something that was discovered by the French in Vietnam and Algeria; the Portuguese in Guinea, Angola, and Mozambique; the Ian Smith government in Rhodesia; and the Soviets in Afghanistan.

Religious appeals also present a difficult problem for governments because, unlike the appeals of secular ideologies, which are primarily directed at elites, they tend to have much greater influence on the attitudes of the masses; witness the role of Islam in Afghanistan. Where this happens, governments may try to cultivate support from other, more moderate leaders and make the case through propaganda or disinformation campaigns that insurgent religious leaders are disingenuous, selfish individuals who hypo-critically violate the most sacred norms of the faith. This, of course, is pre-cisely what the Afghan government tried to do.[21] However, as that case also shows, success will be elusive in the absence of government rectitude, since claims regarding moral superiority have little impact when the claimant is engaged in excessive brutality and/or subscribes to a doctrine (e.g., Marx-ism) that has well-known antireligious tenets. For the analyst, the task at hand is to ascertain whether the government seeks to establish or reinforce its legitimacy with its own esoteric appeals, how its ideas are disseminated, and whether or not they are perceived as relevant and credible.

The manner in which the government responds to exoteric appeals is even more important, for, as we have seen, popular support from the masses is primarily motivated by concrete grievances such as land reform, injustice, unfair taxation, and corruption. It is over these issues that the battle to win hearts and minds is most directly joined. History suggests that the most effective way a government can undercut insurgencies that rely on mass support is to split the rank and file away from the leadership through calcu-lated reforms that address the material grievances and needs of the people. Implicit in this is the notion that the government is able to distinguish be-tween the motivations of insurgent leaders to change the political commu-nity or the political system and authorities, which cannot be accommo-dated, and the motivations of the masses, which tend to focus on material needs and demands.

Arthur Campbell has noted that in the Spanish guerrilla war against Na-poleon the guerrillas had great difficulty getting aid from the people of Huesca because of the material benefits provided by the French and their restraint with regard to taking things from the people. Likewise, he cited the kindness, administrative reform, and good management of General Suchet in Aragon as factors that undercut support for the guerrillas. In contrast, the repression of General Augereau's forces in Catalonia is said to have played into guerrilla hands and facilitated their quest for popular backing.

Another example of the differential effects of contradictory ap-proaches by elements of the same governing authority involved the German administration in the Ukraine during World War II. For the most part, the Germans were their own worst enemy, especially since the Ukrainians had no love for Stalin and seemed ready to help the Germans. As it happened, the German exploitation and repression against the Ukrainians eventually turned them against the Third Reich. Benevolent German administration and effective reforms, such as those carried out by Colonel General Schmidt (which proved effective in harnessing popular support), were few and far between and were undercut by general Nazi policies.[22]

In the postwar era, there have been a number of cases in which con-scious and determined government socioeconomic reforms reduced active support for insurgents. Besides the previously mentioned Qabus reforms in

Oman, one could point to both Israeli policy in the West Bank in the late 1960s and early 1970s and the Huk insurgency in the Philippines in the 1950s. The Israeli case is interesting because the Palestinian Arabs of the West Bank, which had been occupied by Israel in the 1967 war, detest the idea of being controlled by a Jewish military government. Yet, the West Bank populace gave little active support to the Palestinian resistance, even though the latter had experienced a surge in popularity throughout the Arab world in 1968–1969. Among the reasons for Israel's success was an improvement in the standard of living in the area, which, the Israelis calculated (correctly as it turned out), would give the people a stake in stability and make them reluctant to support guerrillas and terrorists. The success of the Israelis along these lines was ruefully conceded by the insurgents, with left-wing ideologues attributing it to the "false consciousness" of the people.[23]

In the Philippines, the government faced an increasingly serious threat from the Communist Huk insurgency in the early 1950s, largely because of its poor relations with the people. However, with the election of a new president, Ramon Magsaysay, and good advice from an American, Edward G. Lansdale, a number of social, economic, and military reforms were instituted to exploit the inherent division between the reformist rank and file and the revolutionary elites in the Huk movement. This generated support for the government and contributed to its eventual victory.[24] It is instructive to contrast this situation with the neglect, corruption, and gross economic favoritism of the Marcos government in the 1980s, all of which played a key part in the striking increase in popular support for the Huk's successor, the New People's Army.[25]

Although less effective than exoteric appeals as a means of gaining popular support, insurgent terrorism can have some impact if it is selective. The major problem for the government is to protect its officials, who must be in place if social and economic reforms are to be implemented. Both rural and urban-based insurgents recognize this and make officials special targets for assassination, kidnapping, and the like. Many examples come to mind, including the Algerians, the Vietcong, the Tupamaros, the Monteneros, and, more recently, groups such as the IRA, Red Brigades, Basque ETA, FMLN in El Salvador, Sendero Luminoso in Peru, the Palestinians, Shiites in Lebanon, Al-Dawa in Iraq, the *mujahidin* in Afghanistan, and the African National Congress in South Africa. To protect their officials from terrorist attacks, governments have found that patient intelligence and police work designed to uncover, detain, or eliminate terrorists is more effective than reliance on the military. Although acts of terrorism may not be eliminated altogether, their incidence and the human costs can be dramatically reduced. As both the British in Northern Ireland and the Italian government have demonstrated, effective intelligence, combined with disciplined police work and determined follow-up by judicial officials, can not only reduce terrorism but may also lead to informers from insurgent ranks turning against their former colleagues.[26] When this happens, the insurgents' popular support base normally shrinks.

Pluralist democracies find it quite difficult and stressful to cope with terrorism because their inherent commitment to due process restricts their actions and thus places a premium on patience, determination, and discipline. In contrast, authoritarian states, especially those that exercise extensive control over their citizens' behavior, find it easier to cope with terrorism. The fact that little or no terrorism took place in the Soviet-bloc countries when Communist parties monopolized power is hardly surprising, given the pervasiveness of secret police and intelligence agencies, controlled judicial processes, and a willingness to employ indiscriminate force, if necessary. Authoritarian governments in the Third World have also used harsh and indiscriminate measures to eliminate or reduce terrorism (e.g., Uruguay, Argentina, Syria, Iran, and Iraq). Unlike the Soviet-bloc countries, however, they run a greater risk of a resurgence of terrorism or popular resistance in the longer term because they lack the organizational, material, and technological resources of the Soviets and their allies. Indiscriminate brutality (e.g., death-squad activities) risks driving terrorists underground, while simultaneously creating seething hatred among those who are among its more innocent victims.

Recognizing that reliance on coercive measures to eliminate popular support for insurgents is both precarious and costly, some hard-line authorities adopt concurrent noncoercive measures. In Iraq, for instance, the Ba'athist government of Saddam Hussein met the challenge of various Shiite insurgent groups, especially Al-Dawa, not only with harsh coercion (including mass executions of insurgents and their families) but also with political and economic measures designed either to win support from the Shiite community at large or to dissuade it from rendering support to the insurgents. These measures included such things as the appointment of Shiites to high-ranking political posts, renovations of urban slums, the building of mosques, and well-publicized visits by President Saddam Hussein to Shiite religious shrines and residential areas.[27]

Whereas the Iraqis have had success with such policies, the Soviets in Afghanistan have not, in part because widespread support for the insurgents grew so rapidly after the 1979 Russian invasion. The Soviet reaction, as noted earlier, was an excessively violent one, designed to eliminate popular support in the rural areas through the obliteration of towns and villages and the destruction of crops. This situation, as well as a similar one in Eritrea, raises a question that only history will answer: Can the physical extermination or expulsion of civilian communities on a widespread scale succeed in coping with the problem of popular support for insurgents? The propaganda of the Afghan government in the mid-1980s, stressing support for Islam, accommodation of ethnic nationalism, and economic development, indicated that the Soviets and their Afghan allies had begun to doubt the effectiveness of indiscriminate violence. The Soviet withdrawal from Afghanistan in 1989 confirmed the validity of their doubts.

Where governments do not take an overly coercive approach, insurgents sometimes try to provoke repression and an overreaction by government forces against the general population. As pernicious as this age-old ploy to gain popular support may seem, it can be effective where governments rely on the military to cope with terrorism, since regular military forces, which are not trained for this, often become frustrated and rely on the kind of large-scale violence for which they *are* trained and equipped. Excessive reactions, such as the previously mentioned responses of the Peruvian armed forces to the SL and the Sri Lankan army against the Tamil insurgents in 1984–1985, have too often been indiscriminate and ended up creating more support for the insurgents. Where most of the military is drawn from an ethnic or religious group other than that of the insurgents, as in the largely Sinhalese army in Sri Lanka, the danger of overreaction is even greater. Furthermore, even when such behavior does not increase active popular support for the insurgents, it can result in an eventual demise and even punishment of the authorities. Such was the case in Argentina, where the indiscriminate campaign against the Monteneros and other insurgents had the long-term effect of creating pressures on later governments to bring those responsible to trial. To avoid such problems, prudent governments can, as the British in Northern Ireland and the Israelis in the West Bank demonstrated, reassess and alter their policies.

In Northern Ireland during the late 1960s, the British initially reacted to IRA violence by relying on military units and harsh policies such as internment without trial, which was perceived as unjust, indiscriminate, and abusive. When this backfired, contributing instead to increased Catholic support for the IRA, the British rethought their policy, opting for more judicious treatment of suspects, enhanced discipline for military units, and a gradual turnover of the antiterrorist mission to police forces that received support (especially intelligence) from the military. Although imperfect, this turnabout, combined with increasingly indiscriminate IRA terrorist attacks, resulted in decreased Catholic support for the IRA.[28]

Despite their efforts, the British found their policies continuously jeopardized by illegal acts of violence carried out against Catholics by preservationist insurgents from the Protestant community (e.g., the Ulster Volunteer Force). Rather than ignore these actions or look the other way, and thereby facilitate IRA recruiting efforts, the British directed police and judicial efforts against the terrorism of Protestant extremists in the same way as they did against the IRA. Despite controversial episodes in 1988 involving the alleged murder of IRA operatives in Gibraltar and a "shoot to kill" policy directed at unarmed IRA suspects, the British performance remained a more disciplined one than it was in the late 1960s.

The Israelis faced a somewhat similar problem in their conflict with the fedayeen during the height of the armed struggle in 1968–1969. In this case, however, the main source of the problem was more a matter of spontaneous violence by irate Jewish civilians against innocent Arabs (in reaction to Palestinian acts of terror) than it was actions of the military or police. Typical of such violence was a response by Jewish citizens after an explosion in a Tel Aviv bus station on September 4, 1968, which killed one and wounded fifty-one. In retaliation, a Jewish mob attacked Arabs in the terminal, beating eight severely, and turned on Arabs arriving in buses, none of whom were among the suspects in the incident. The following day, one of Israel's most respected newspapers, *Ha'arez,* called attention to the counterproductive nature of such behavior when it said that the perpetrators "must be considered active, unwilling allies of the Arab terrorists." Recognizing the validity of this point and concerned that such violence could lead victims to support the Palestinian resistance, the Israeli government undertook an intensive education drive to prevent recurrences. In addition, government leaders visited Arab representatives in an effort to convince them that such actions did not reflect official policy or attitudes. The crackdown on illegal reprisals extended to the security establishment. In November, two frontier policemen were sentenced to life imprisonment for murdering two local Arabs, and three months later it was announced that an Israeli captain would be tried for killing an Arab woman and wounding several others.[29]

As a consequence of the attention and effort devoted to the violent reprisals, such behavior decreased and became exceptional rather than normal, until the hard-line Likud came to power in 1977 and ushered in an era of regressive counterinsurgency policies. Among other things, these involved a less discriminate use of force and increased collective punishments, which, in turn, increased Palestinian resentment and led to the *intifada* in 1987. This dramatic regression for the Israelis was capped by the well-publicized and indiscriminate brutal acts by Israeli Defense Force units that were psychologically and tactically ill prepared for riot duty.[30] This reaction created a groundswell of support for the PLO, a fact acknowledged by all observers, save perhaps the ideologically blinded. In a word, the Israelis have provided good—and bad—examples of how governments cope with insurgent attempts to provoke excessive repression.

The final method used by insurgents to gain support is by demonstrating their potency through military successes and by providing services. This is obviously a broader method, which ultimately comes down to images and the population's perceptions. Where insurgents can demonstrate relative military and organizational achievements, their chances for gaining support increase, especially if the government is inept, lethargic, and incompetent. While it may sound trite, people generally tend to gravitate toward the side perceived to be winning. This is particularly true of fence sitters, who have been insufficiently moved by esoteric or exoteric appeals to make a commit-

ment. As for the government response to insurgent terrorism, guerrilla warfare, and mobile-conventional warfare, successful counteraction will depend on the various responses discussed earlier, plus traditional military
requirements—adequate training, discipline, logistics, transportation, command, control and communications, and, very crucially, astute and flexible
leadership at all levels. Since these factors often can affect battlefield outcomes, analysts need to be alert to performance—on both sides—in terms
of these traditional military requirements. The failure of the Afghan and the
Soviet military to subdue the *mujahidin* was, among other things, the result
of poor leadership, inflexibility, and an overly centralized control system
that denied local commanders the initiative required to combat guerrillas.[31]
Battlefield reverses for government forces in El Salvador in the early 1980s
and in the Philippines in the mid-1980s can also be explained partially by
failures in many of these areas, especially leadership.[32]

The nonmilitary aspect of demonstrating potency by providing services is intended to take advantage of people's concrete grievances. As we
have seen, insurgents try to show they can meet the needs of the people and
can provide order and control. This leads us to next consider the government's response to the insurgents' organizational abilities.

ORGANIZATION AND COHESION

Successful government campaigns to undermine insurgent efforts to
obtain, maintain, or increase popular support and to cope with terrorism
and guerrilla warfare are closely associated with both a program to address
the needs of the people and administrative competence and capability. Programs without good administrators are hollow. Efficient administrators
without programs are powerless, and those with bad programs may exacerbate whatever problems already exist. These qualifiers aside, it is true that
dispensing basic services, addressing important grievances, and providing
security against insurgent violence depend on a good organization that can
marshal and wisely use human and material resources. Well-trained and
well-motivated political and military officials are essential if both the usual
tasks of governing and the special undertakings required to cope with terrorism and guerrilla warfare are going to get done effectively. Those undertakings can involve such things as detention without trial, resettlement of
sections of the population, control and distribution of food, curfews, restric-
tions on movement, issuing and checking identification cards, and imposing
penalties on people possessing unauthorized weapons. Sir Robert Thompson has argued that harsh measures like these can only be applied in areas
under government control. To apply them sporadically in regions under
insurgent control would leave the people with little choice but to support
the insurgents. Beyond this, other experts make the point that to be morally
acceptable, governments must impose collective sanctions within the context of providing security against insurgent reprisals. A sound administra-

tive apparatus is vital in assuring that these guidelines are followed and are applied in a judicious, fair, and consistent manner.[33]

Resettling portions of the population, for example, may become necessary if the government is to sever the links between the insurgents and the populace. While this is not a desirable course of action, resettlement may be necessary if terror and/or guerrilla attacks persist and are attributed, at least partially, to the support given insurgents by certain segments of the population. If the government is going to be effective in relocating sections of the population, it must give good explanations to those affected and must assure people that the material benefits of the new locale supersede those of the old one. Civic action and political organization become extremely important during resettlement. The Briggs plan for relocating the Chinese squatters in Malaya, the Kitchener resettlement scheme during the Boer War, and the relocation program during the Mau Mau uprising are examples where moving segments of the population was instrumental in denying the insurgents the support of the population. Conversely, the resettlement carried out by the regime of Ngo Dinh Diem in South Vietnam failed, largely because it was too fast, overextended, and characterized by poor regulatory procedures, ineffective government, inadequate police forces (both quantitatively and qualitatively), and a lack of attention to alternative ways for people to earn a living.[34]

Whenever the government undertakes security measures directed at individuals or groups, it can expect the insurgents to make use of legalistic appeals to try to protect their personnel and to portray the regime as a violator of civil and human rights. Essentially, the insurgents will seek to have those under detention treated as peacetime offenders.[35] This rebel ploy, which makes it even more difficult for the government to avoid alienating its citizens, is another reason why the government needs trained officials to implement policies in a judicious and limited fashion.[36]

If the security measures suggested above are to be fairly applied, the government must have accurate information about the insurgent organization, including the identification and location of its members and its intended activities. This requires an effective intelligence apparatus that extends to the rural areas. The best way for the government to obtain the necessary information is to establish rapport with the people by means of good administration and prudent and diligent police work. That, in turn, calls for well-trained interrogation experts who can minimize violence by knowing the right questions to ask and competent agents who can penetrate the insurgent apparatus.[37] The best agents are members of the insurgent organization who will betray its secrets and provide "contact" information (what is going to happen in the future).[38] Since the army and police both have a need for intelligence, their cooperation at all levels is imperative. Besides expediting the flow of information, coordination enables military forces to respond as quickly as possible against guerrilla and terrorist units.[39] Governments with diffused power but little coordination among agencies find quick responses hard to come by.

In light of the fact that the insurgents themselves are a potentially valuable source of intelligence, their treatment by government forces is of no small concern. Although it is not likely that members of the hard core (the true believers) will defect, it is possible that the less-dedicated insurgents may be induced to surrender, especially if guerrilla fortunes are not bright. Psychological-warfare programs that stress the declining fortunes of the insurgency, contrast the harsh life-style of insurgents with people in government-controlled areas, and promise amnesty, security, and material benefits can play a key part in enticing defections, as the British found out in Malaya and Oman. But if violence is used against defectors, psychological-warfare programs will fail (for obvious reasons).

The successful accomplishment of the political and security tasks noted above depends on the existence of a complex and extensive administrative apparatus. It is no mere coincidence that a main feature of the successful turnarounds of counterinsurgery programs like the ones against the Huks, the PFLO in Oman, and the Malayan Communist Party (MCP) was an improvement in the political-administrative capacity of the government. Where the government lacks the ability to establish an efficient administration relatively free of corruption, it runs the grave risk of seeing the insurgents implant their own organizational structures and gain momentum. Both developments become more costly to overcome as time goes by. In the Malayan emergency in the early 1950s, British inattention to the Chinese squatters in areas bordering the jungle enabled the MCP to organize a support base sufficient to sustain a tenacious insurrection. To defeat the MCP, the British eventually had to expend considerable resources to resettle and administratively control the squatters.

The poor performance, corruption, and neglect that characterized the administration of the South Vietnamese government of Ngo Dinh Diem in the formative years (1958–1964) of the Vietnam War were exploited by the Vietcong, who set up a political and military infrastructure that ably supported local and increasingly larger regional-force units. By 1965, the victories of the Vietcong led to American and then North Vietnamese involvement on a large scale and to the incredibly costly trial by arms that followed. As a participant on the American side, it was this writer's opinion then that for anyone attempting to understand the problems, the abysmal political and military performance of the South Vietnamese government in the countryside was as important an element as the introduction of North Vietnamese forces. Had the Saigon government done a better job dealing with what was still essentially a southern threat in the early years, the outcome could have been quite different. At a minimum, it might have removed the mantle of legitimacy and credibility from the Vietcong. If North Vietnam had then proceeded to introduce its own main-force units, the move would have been viewed as an outright invasion rather than being perceived as an effort to assist freedom fighters against American forces.

More recently, the same organizational failure has been played out in the Philippines and Afghanistan. There is a consensus among observers, including high-ranking Filipino officers, that a poor, inefficient, repressive, and corrupt Marcos government administration paved the way for the increased popularity and growth of the New People's Army, which set up political structures in many parts of the country.[40] Likewise in Afghanistan, Soviet and Afghan government failures in the countryside were due principally to their political and administrative shortcomings, a situation that Afghan leaders Babrak Karmal and later Najibullah candidly admitted a number of times during various conclaves of the People's Democratic Party of Afghanistan. Recognition of the problem, however, was not followed by a solution because, as in many Third World states, a combination of entrenched political and bureaucratic interests, a dearth of trained administrators (due, in large part, to purges), and insecurity in the rural areas continued to exist.[41] Whether a belated Soviet long-term plan to compensate for the Afghan government's organizational deficiencies by training officials in the Soviet Union and then returning and dispatching them to the countryside in Afghanistan would have made an impact will never be known.

Effective organization presumes a reasonable degree of unity within the government. Like insurgents, governments can suffer debilitating effects from severe political and ideological discord and/or poor coordination of the various civilian and military organizations under their jurisdiction. The phrase "severe political and ideological discord" refers to situations in which high-ranking officials and political elites pursue fundamentally different policies for instrumental (i.e., using policies to build political coalitions) or theoretical reasons, or both. Since under such circumstances the primary reason for disunity is often domestic power struggles, the insurgency may receive secondary attention, if that. The familiar results can be paralysis, haphazard behavior, and agencies failing to share vital intelligence data and working at cross-purposes (e.g., civilian and military officials trying to cultivate popular support through civic action, while various police and security forces are committing atrocities). The situation in El Salvador in the early 1980s, which was marked by bitter strife between the extreme-right and centrist politicians, is a case in point. This rift not only led to contradictory policies but also resulted in the outright murder of numerous centrist and leftist political leaders (as well as innocent civilians) by right-wing death squads—developments that benefited the insurgents. Likewise, the chronic and frequently violent disunity between the Khalq (masses) and Parchamite (banner) factions plagued Afghanistan's ruling People's Democratic Party (PDPA) following its ascension to power in 1978. That disunity was a major cause of the failure of the government's policies is well known to those who follow Afghan affairs, having been copiously reported or acknowledged by journalists, diplomats, PDPA leaders, and high-ranking Soviet advisers.[42]

Dealing with disunity is no easier for governments than insurgents when factions or groups have roughly equal (albeit asymmetrical) power, as in Afghanistan. In less-severe cases where the central governing authorities have preeminent power but have to cope with rivalries among officials and bureaucratic agencies, good leadership qualities appear to be more important than organizational structures. At a minimum, leaders cannot afford to be detached, because that simply perpetuates a bad situation. The top leadership must at least clearly articulate a common sense of purpose and objectives, provide general guidelines, actively coordinate the actions of various agencies, and emphasize initiative, flexibility, and adaptability on the part of local civilian and military officials. While this is quite obviously a challenging agenda, to the extent governments can carry it out, they are better off. Whether regimes are pluralist or authoritarian, there is a need to steer a middle course between overcentralization and undercentralization. As the Soviet Union found out in Afghanistan, overcentralization undermines the initiative and flexibility at local levels that are vital for coping with guerrilla and terrorist threats. Conversely, as the United States found in Vietnam, decentralization can yield interservice rivalry and poor interagency coordination.

To some degree, the nature of the political system must be considered. Authoritarian systems need to be especially alert to problems of overcentralization as they seek to unify their efforts, while pluralist systems are more vulnerable to excessive decentralization. An extreme case of the latter is Turkey, where efforts to cope with both egalitarian and traditionalist insurgents in the 1970s were poor, due in large part to the fact that the multiparty system produced virtual paralysis in the political, economic, and security spheres. The outcome was stagflation, rising terrorism, and an eventual military takeover that met with popular acquiescence, if not approval.[43]

As a general rule, the chances of having both a broad counterinsurgency strategy and a coordinated and effective organizational structure to implement it would seem to be greater under civilian than under military control, even though there are obviously exceptions (e.g., mediocre military rule is better than incompetent and corrupt civilian rule). The reason is that military professionals are naturally preoccupied with the management of violence, while civilian politicians are apt to have broader outlooks conducive to seeing more dimensions of the problem and to appreciating various nonmilitary responses. Hence, it comes as no surprise that military governments see coercion, sometimes in extremis, as the central feature of a counterinsurgency strategy. The excessive and indiscriminate brutality of military juntas confronted by insurgents in Argentina, Guatemala, Pakistan, and Uganda, to name but a few in the past two decades, is well known.

In Pakistan and Uganda, the violence contributed to insurgent success; in Argentina, human costs were clearly higher than necessary; and in Guatemala, the long-term outcome is in doubt.

While there are ample cases of civilian governments being every bit as myopic about overreliance on force as their military counterparts, there are, as we have seen, also many examples of successful counterinsurgency campaigns run by civilians in which force was but one component of strategy. Rarely do we find examples of military governments pursuing multifaceted strategies in which the use of force is judicious. Hence, other things being equal, civilian governments stand a better chance of success than military governments as far as the organizational response to insurgents is concerned.[44]

EXTERNAL SUPPORT

Governments can make a number of possible responses in those cases in which external support for insurgents, particularly in the form of material aid and sanctuaries, is playing an important role. Which ones governments choose will depend on calculations of their capabilities relative to external supporters, as well as potential costs and risks. Since dealing with external support involves interstate relationships, government actions can be analyzed in terms of the familiar instruments of statecraft: diplomacy, communications (information and propaganda), economics, and the military. It almost goes without saying that before deciding on which instrument (or combination of instruments) to use and how to use it, the governing authorities need to have a clear picture of exactly what types of external support are being provided and the impact that aid is having. This is necessary if the government is to avoid misdirecting its resources, because in some cases external support is not the major reason for insurgent success, and in others it is of little or no consequence. The American exaggeration of Soviet and Cuban assistance to the FMLN in El Salvador in the early 1980s, which diverted attention from the real (i.e., indigenous) reasons for insurgent successes, illustrates the former; the NPA in the Philippines and the Sendero Luminoso in Peru exemplify the latter.

If external support is important, one option is to rely on diplomacy. Several actions are possible. On the positive side, quiet negotiations to persuade the external-support state to terminate or alter its support in return for various political concessions may succeed if the supporter can be convinced that more important interests can be served by an agreement. This appears to have been what transpired with respect to China's support for the Thai National Liberation Front in the late 1970s. While we are not privy to minutes of meetings between the Thai and Chinese officials that led to marked improvements in state-to-state relations, it is probably safe to assume that a Thai desire to see an end to Beijing's support for Thai insurgents was not only discussed but linked to better relations with Thailand, which, in turn, would serve China's far larger aim of containing Vietnamese and Soviet influence in Asia.[45] Successful diplomacy like this, of course, depends on identifying and skillfully exploiting important common interests. Where this is impossible, coercive diplomacy can be used.

Various courses of action are associated with coercive diplomacy, including the threat or imposition of political, economic, and military sanctions, several of which will be considered when we come to the other instruments of statecraft. Political sanctions can include breaking diplomatic relations with external-support states and building coalitions with friendly states that will oppose the external-support state on various issues in international forums. Where external supporters are major powers, an important government objective is frequently to gain support from other major powers. However, since major powers pursue a wide range of interests and goals, many of which are more important than those related to a particular insurgency, they are often reluctant to join coalitions or impose sanctions against other major states that are external supporters, because to do so might jeopardize the resolution of more-important issues with these states. For example, although various European governments shared American concerns about Soviet assistance to various insurgents like the Vietcong in Vietnam or the FMLN in El Salvador, they avoided taking strong stands on behalf of the Vietnamese, Salvadoran, and U.S. governments because to do so might have undercut what they considered to be the far more significant process of rapprochement with the Soviet Union. Since bilateral issues involving major states usually transcend concerns about each other's dealings with third states, governments threatened by insurgents may not succeed in generating international political sanctions. Accordingly, they frequently place greater reliance on other instruments of statecraft.

The principal aim of the communications instrument is to provide information that will convince various audiences that external support to insurgent groups is not in their best interests. There are three targets of information campaigns: insurgents and their external supporters, other nations not directly involved in the conflict, and groups inside the external-support states. As far as the insurgents and their active supporters are concerned, the aim is to create distrust between insurgents and external supporters by stressing differences or past antagonisms between the two (e.g., ideological, racial, ethnic, religious, and historical animosities). Afghan government propaganda about putative American anti-Islamic policies, which seeks to drive a wedge between the *mujahidin* and their U.S. supporter, is one illustration; Angola's public castigation of UNITA's support from the "racist" South African government is another. It should be noted, however, that no matter how accurate and skillful such propaganda may be, there is little, if any, evidence that by itself it has had an appreciable impact on insurgents and external supporters.

Information directed at uninvolved nations may be more effective, as the Angolan government has shown. By emphasizing the fact that UNITA's principal external support has come from a South African government whose racial policies have been condemned internationally, the MPLA government has managed to discredit Jonas Savimbi to the point where many states have been reluctant to render any kind of external aid to UNITA. In fact, some states that might not otherwise have done so have been critical of Savimbi.

Propaganda directed at groups inside external-support states, particularly in pluralist democracies, may also be somewhat effective; witness the Nicaraguan government's successful 1984–1985 campaign to influence American political leaders and the attentive public by criticizing both the Contras' human rights abuses and their attempt to overthrow the Sandinista government.[46] Other examples of efforts to deny external support to insurgent groups through the use of international publicity efforts are the depiction and excoriation of terrorist acts of the PLO by Israel and of the IRA by Britain. That the existence, content, and effectiveness of communications efforts vary considerably from situation to situation does not mean they can be overlooked by analysts, since in specific cases they could be important.

The use of the economic instrument of statecraft to undercut external support may also have a positive impact in deterring or undermining external support for insurgents in some cases. One of the purposes of Saudi Arabia's largesse vis-à-vis neighboring Arab states, some of which are ideologically opposed to the monarchy, such as Syria and Iraq, has been to keep them from assisting insurgent groups that could pose a threat to the Saudi regime. A more familiar and negative use of the economic instrument is the threat to curtail or terminate trade and foreign aid, or actually doing so. The problem with this approach is that most governments, particularly in the Third World, simply do not have sufficient capability and leverage to make this work. Hence, they often try to get others who do have leverage to bring it to bear on their behalf. American economic sanctions against Nicaragua and Cuba, because of their support for egalitarian insurgents in El Salvador or elsewhere, would be a case in point. Here again, however, success is not guaranteed, because as Cuba and Nicaragua also illustrate, alternate sources of trade and aid are often available, even though they may not be preferable. All in all, the use of the economic instrument has not been very successful as a means of undercutting external support for insurgents. Still, the analyst must be alert to the possibility of doing so and judge such options according to their merits and effectiveness.

The frequent failure of the diplomatic, communications, and economic instruments of statecraft to eliminate external support has, not surprisingly, led governments to threaten or use force against external supporters. There are various options available, and which, if any, are chosen will depend on cost and risk calculations related to the possible escalation of hostilities. The most risky option is the use of conventional armed forces against external support states or insurgent sanctuaries in such states. Actions here can range from cross-border artillery or air attacks to incursions of various size by ground forces. At one time or another, Israel has done all of these against Jordan and Lebanon, with one or two aims in mind: inflicting serious losses on Palestinian insurgents and/or compelling the external-support state to crack down on the insurgents. Where Jordan was concerned, there was success on both counts because Israel had decisive military superiority, Jordan had no strong ally willing to come to its assistance, and the Jordanian regime was itself threatened by elements among the fedayeen. While this fortuitous combination of circumstances resulted in the expulsion of the Palestinians from Jordan, similar attacks by Israel in Lebanon in subsequent years were not nearly as successful, because, unlike the Jordanian military, Lebanon's was not strong enough to defeat the Palestinians, who had support from the Lebanese leftist and Druze militias.[47] Although the Israelis did crush the PLO militarily with large conventional operations in 1982 and scattered its political apparatus to various corners of the Middle East, they ended up trading their Palestinian adversaries for Shiite insurgents who proved to be much tougher. What the Israeli experience suggests is that while conventional operations can be very effective antidotes to external support under some conditions, they may meet with far less success than hoped for or lead to unanticipated costs under others.

Many, if not most, governments find conventional military reactions too dangerous, either because the external-support state is strong enough to respond in kind or has support from major powers that might intervene on the external state's behalf. Not wishing to risk the potential costs of interstate conventional warfare, they opt for lesser uses of force. Afghan or Soviet troops, for example, would no doubt have crossed the border in the 1980s to clean out *mujahidin* sanctuaries in Pakistan if it were not for fears that the United States might come to the aid of Pakistan. Accordingly, they limited their response to frequent air and artillery attacks, which they usually denied took place. During the Vietnam War, the South Vietnamese and the Americans did much the same thing, since they were concerned that large ground assaults into North Vietnam might have been countered by the introduction of Chinese forces to aid Hanoi.

Where conventional military responses are deemed too perilous, unconventional attacks by commandos and covert operations may be adopted to exert pressure on external-support states. Among the possible targets are insurgent bases, camps, and offices, and the military and economic assets of the external-support state. American Special Forces operations in Laos and Cambodia during the Vietnam War, Israeli raids against fedayeen bases and Jordan's irrigation system (the East Ghor Canal) in the Jordan Valley in the late 1960s, and South African attacks inside Botswana in March 1988 are examples.[48] While such operations may contribute to a crackdown on the insurgents, they seldom are sufficient, since they are episodic rather than sustained actions. Because of this, governments have turned increasingly to the support of insurgents inside the external-support state; they consider this "mirror response" a far more effective way of intensifying the pressure and raising the costs to the external supporter. This stratagem, as noted in the previous chapter, is quite common and has yielded positive payoffs to the Republic of South Africa, most notably with respect to Mozambique.

Whether the South African–Mozambique situation can be replicated in many other places remains to be seen and will depend on the balance of forces inside the external-support state. Where the external-support state's economic and military capabilities are weak and insurgents opposing them measure up reasonably well in terms of at least some of the criteria discussed so far in this study, the insurgents may be able, as they are in Mozambique, to conduct sustained attacks and inflict troublesome costs on the external-support state. Accordingly, if the policy of aiding insurgents in external-support states is adopted, analysts must carefully scrutinize the strengths of the insurgency in the external-support state to ascertain how likely the policy is to succeed.

Flexibility and Integrity

Before summing up, two crucial qualities that are extremely important with respect to the government response need to be underscored, namely, flexibility and integrity. The absence of one or both can create untold difficulties.

FLEXIBILITY

Since insurgencies differ in many ways, there is no model government response or counterinsurgency program that can be applied in all cases. This does not mean that lessons, ideas, and policies in one situation may not be transferred to another. The key questions are which lessons, ideas, and policies might be borrowed and how they might be adapted under somewhat different circumstances. Those responsible for counterinsurgency strategy and planning can thus benefit enormously from serious study and analysis of other governments' experiences.

By itself, this is not sufficient, however. To avoid mindless borrowing, careful assessment of the overall situation regarding the local insurgency is necessary. That is, the situation, problems, and challenges with respect to the environment, popular support, organization, unity, and external support must be set forth as cogently, comprehensively, and clearly as possible. Once this is done, an overall counterinsurgency strategy *tailored to relevant problems* can be devised. This suggests that the relative roles of military, social, economic, and political measures will vary according to the problems presented by different insurgencies. By way of example, the kinds of social

and economic reforms and/or civic action programs associated with successful counterinsurgency programs in places like Malaya and the Philippines
in the 1950s and Oman in the 1970s would not have been crucial or even
important in places like Greece in the late 1940s or Belgium and Italy in
recent times, because in these cases the insurgents lacked significant popular
support.[49] What this means is that sensible counterinsurgency strategic
thinking and programs need to be flexible and adaptable. Whether the
thinking and programs are flexible and adaptable in particular cases is a
question analysts need to answer.

INTEGRITY

Closely related to the question of flexibility is the matter of integrity,
a quality that profoundly affects all aspects of the government response.
Webster's definition associates *integrity* with honesty, completeness, and
incorruptibility. Needless to say, an absence of these attributes has a corro-
sive effect on situational estimates, generating either pessimism or, as seems
to be more often the case, undue optimism. Ignoring or downplaying problems, for whatever reasons, usually leads to faulty, misguided, incomplete,
and sometimes irrelevant policy responses. While many examples could easily be adduced here, noting the Vietnam War is more than sufficient. By
now there is clear and persuasive testimony to the fact that self-deception,
often deliberate, was a pervasive problem on the South Vietnamese–United
States side.[50] Inflating the enemy's casualties, portraying defeats as victories,
and ignoring the shortcomings of various Saigon regimes turned on nonexistent lights at the ends of tunnels and engendered a sense of complacency
that undercut needed social, economic, political, and military changes.
While the point about integrity may be common sense and simple, its importance cannot be emphasized enough. Governments that make an honest
effort to know themselves and their enemies are in a better position to identify threats and to contemplate effective responses. Those which indulge in
"killing the bearer of bad tidings" court disaster. This being so, the analyst
should be especially alert to the absence or presence of integrity when evaluating all dimensions of the government response.

Summary

The importance of a thorough evaluation of the government's response cannot be overstated. What the government does or neglects to do
and how it performs has a direct bearing on the strategies and forms of
warfare insurgents choose and the nature and extent of challenges insurgents must cope with as they seek to accomplish their aims. The more government responses are informed, prudent, relevant, determined, and disciplined, the greater the burden on the insurgents.

Responses marked by such qualities do not come easily. As we have seen, they depend on many things, not the least of which is the recognition that an insurgency is a political *and* military phenomenon. It is not an either/or situation. The question is which dimension is most significant and what to do about it. To answer those questions, governments should have a comprehensive profile of their adversary fully in mind. A rigorous assessment of the goals, strategy, and forms of warfare of insurgents and the advantages and disadvantages inherent in the physical and human environments is crucial for devising a sensible, relevant, and effective counterinsurgency strategy. Where popular support is important, knowing precisely what techniques the insurgents are using to obtain support is indispensable for properly focused policies designed to neutralize their efforts. No matter how hard insurgents try, they will be frustrated if the government has a competent and capable administration that dispenses services, controls the population, and effectively coordinates a multitude of political, economic, and security policies.

Where external support is part of the overall equation, the government evaluation of its exact nature and role should inform its choices and uses of diplomatic, economic, propaganda, and military means to counter it. In the final analysis, a careful and systematic examination of the government's response in terms of the considerations set forth in this chapter will no doubt yield most of the key answers to the question of why the insurgency is progressing or regressing.

Notes

1.   Walter C. Sonderland, "An Analysis of Guerrilla Insurgency and Coup d'État as Techniques of Indirect Aggression," *International Studies Quarterly* (December 1970):345.

2.   Bard E. O'Neill, "Revolutionary War in Oman," in Bard E. O'Neill, William R. Heaton, and Donald J. Alberts, eds., *Insurgency in the Modern World* (Boulder, Colo.: Westview Press, 1980), pp. 216–217.

3.   On McClellan, see Stephen W. Sears, *George B. McClellan: The Young Napoleon* (New York: Ticknor and Fields, 1988).

4.   John J. McCuen, *The Art of Counter-Revolutionary War* (Harrisburg, Pa.: Stackpole Books, n.d.), pp. 128–142.

5.   On indiscriminate violence against civilians by the police and military in Peru, see Mario Vargas Llosa, "Inquest in the Andes," *New York Times Magazine* (July 31, 1983):23; Cynthia McClintock, "Sendero Luminoso: Peru's Maoist Guerrillas," *Problems of Communism* (September–October 1983):29–30; *Christian Science Monitor,* February 20, 1985; and *Washington Post,* September 19, 1985. On Sri Lanka, see Jared Mitchell, "A Nation Losing Control," *Macleans* (February 18, 1985):31; *Far Eastern Economic Review* (September 6, 1984):18; and *Christian Science Monitor,* February 8, 1985.

6.   Recent successes by European governments against terrorism (e.g., Belgium, France, and Britain) have been linked to the replacement of untrained local police by police who are full-time specialists on terrorism; see *Christian Science Monitor*, March 8, 1988.

7.   In an off-the-record discussion, a major British commander in Northern Ireland pointed out that while the police were emphasized in counterterrorist operations, they lacked some important capabilities, especially in the area of intelligence information. Consequently, the military provided crucial support. This led to a situation he characterized as a police-military partnership. On Northern Ireland's and Italy's experiences, see *Northern Ireland: Problems and Perspectives*, Conflict Studies no. 135 (London: Institute for the Study of Conflict, 1982), pp. 20–21, 32–33; Vittorfranco S. Pisano, "The Italian Terrorist Experience: 1968–1984," *ISUPP Strategic Review* (Pretoria: Institute for Strategic Studies, University of Pretoria [ISUPP], June 1984), pp. 2–15; Franco Villalbal, "The Organizational Structure of the Italian Counter-terrorist Forces," *International Defense Review* (June 1985): 915–917; *New York Times*, October 1, 1981, and September 29, 1983; and *Christian Science Monitor*, March 25, 1985.

8.   The impact of French-Spanish cooperation on the Basque ETA is reported and discussed in the *Christian Science Monitor*, February 24, 1988, and January 31, 1989; and *New York Times*, January 13, 1989. Discussions by the author with Spanish and American officials in May 1988 corroborated the main conclusions of these accounts.

9.   On the Israeli countermeasures against transnational terrorists, see Bard E. O'Neill, *Armed Struggle in Palestine* (Boulder, Colo.: Westview Press, 1978), pp. 78, 86–89; Christopher Dobson, *Black September* (New York: Macmillan Publishing Co., 1974), pp. 110–113; David B. Tinnin and Dag Christensen, *The Hit Team* (New York: Dell, 1976).

10.   The author's observation while serving as an intelligence officer in Vietnam in 1965–1966 was that large search-and-destroy operations against guerrillas (as opposed to regular North Vietnamese divisions and regiments) were futile exercises in which the guerrillas faded into the background during sweeps and then returned when the attacking forces withdrew. Many military and civilian officials have been critical of the clumsy U.S. strategy. See, for example, Charles Maechling, Jr., "Counterinsurgency: The First Ordeal by Fire," in Michael T. Klare and Peter Kornbluh, eds., *Low-Intensity Warfare* (New York: Pantheon Books, 1988), pp. 42–43. Amazingly, the Soviets duplicated this error in Afghanistan. See, for example, *New York Times*, June 5, 1988.

11.   McCuen, *The Art of Counter-Revolutionary War*, pp. 119–124, 166–181. The French mobile operations in the Atlas Mountains in Algeria are cited by McCuen as a model that might be emulated. Moreover, he suggested that counterorganization using native tribes could prove useful in some underpopulated areas, the French experiences with the Moi and Thai tribes in Indochina being examples.

12.   *Ibid.*, pp. 195–205. The failure of the French to heed General Latour's advice that they consolidate their own bases before searching for the Vietminh during the first Indochina war had disastrous consequences.

13.   *Ibid.*, pp. 205–245; Douglas Hyde, *The Roots of Guerrilla Warfare* (Chester Springs, Pa.: Dufour Editions, 1968), pp. 205–231; and Richard L. Clutterbuck, *The Long, Long War* (New York: Frederick A. Praeger, 1966), p. 176. Examples

of costly failures to organize the population after an area had been cleared were the French Odine operations in Indochina (cited by McCuen) and Operation Hammer in Sarawak (cited by Hyde). In Oman, by contrast, the role of civic action teams and the extension of the government administration played a key part in consolidation of the populace; see O'Neill, "Revolutionary War in Oman," p. 226.

14.   The campaign against mayors in El Salvador is reported in the *Christian Science Monitor,* January 13, 1989. Earlier reports indicated army claims to have organized 21,000 civil defense troops of mixed quality; see *Washington Times,* June 27, 1988. However, a *Christian Science Monitor* report indicated that 35 percent of El Salvador's municipalities had no local government.

15.   Michael Richardson, "Insurgency in the Philippines: No. 2—The Militia: Help or Hindrance," *Pacific Defence Reporter* (September 1985):15; O'Neill, "Revolutionary War in Oman," p. 226.

16.   *Ibid.,* pp. 235–245, 258–309.

17.   *Ibid.,* pp. 219–220; Edward E. Rice, *Wars of the Third Kind* (Berkeley: University of California Press, 1988), pp. 98–99.

18.   John E. Bircher III, *Conflict in the Western Sahara: A Dilemma for United States Policy,* Strategic Study (Washington, D.C.: National War College, 1985), pp. 14–15, 21–22; *Le Monde* (Paris; June 21, 1984, and March 16, 1985); *Washington Post,* August 15, 1985; *Christian Science Monitor,* April 12, 1989.

19.   *New York Times,* July 31, 1988.

20.   *INFORMAFRICA* (Lisbon; March 11, 1989), reprinted in *FBIS/AFR* (Africa), no. 89089 (May 10, 1989), p. 14.

21.   Official government-controlled statements by the Afghan government, speeches by former President Babrak Karmal, and the media in the 1980s continuously identified the regime as the defender of Islam and the insurgents as enemies of religion. A typical example is the speech by Karmal to an extraordinary session of the Revolutionary Council on November 9, 1985; see the text in *FBIS/SA* (November 12, 1985), p. C5.

22.   Arthur Campbell, *Guerrillas* (New York: The John Day Company, 1968), pp. 10–17, 73–89; Frederick Wilkins, "Guerrilla Warfare," in Franklin Mark Osanka, ed., *Modern Guerrilla Warfare* (New York: The Free Press of Glencoe, 1962), pp. 10–11; Walter D. Jacobs, "Irregular Warfare and the Soviets, " *ibid.,* p. 61; Brooke McClure, "Russia's Hidden Army," *ibid.,* p. 96–97; Ernst von Dohnanyi, "Combatting Soviet Guerrillas," *ibid.,* pp. 102–105.

23.   O'Neill, *Armed Struggle in Palestine,* pp. 69–71. Interestingly, the increased terrorism in the West Bank in 1984–1985 came at a time of economic troubles in Israel, which, in turn, had adversely affected the West Bank. One of the major concerns of Israeli political and military leaders about the future has been the potential impact of worsening economic problems on stability in the West Bank and Gaza Strip.

24.   Rice, *Wars of the Third Kind,* p. 70; Kenneth M. Hammer, "Huks in the Philippines," in Osanka, ed., *Modern Guerrilla Warfare,* p. 102; Boyd T. Boshore, "Duel Strategy for Limited War," *ibid.,* pp. 193–196, 199–201; Tomas C. Tirona, "The Philippine Anti-Communist Campaign," *ibid.,* pp. 206–207; Campbell, *Guerrillas,* pp. 129–133; Robert Ross Smith, "The Hukbalahap Insurgency," *Military Review* (June 1965):35–42.

25.   Accounts of contemporary problems in the Philippines may be found in S.

Bilveer, "The Philippines: How Much Longer Can the Center Hold," *Asian Defence Journal* (July 1985):18–33; Denis Warner, "Insurgency in the Philippines: No. 1—Deterioration Marked, Widespread and Demonstrable," *Pacific Defence Reporter* (September 1985), pp. 10–13; Steve Lohr, "Twilight of the Marcos Era," *New York Times Magazine* (January 6, 1985):30, 32, 34–35, 39, 41, 44, 46, 53.

26.   Don Mansfield, "The Irish Republican Army and Northern Ireland," *Insurgency in the Modern World*, pp. 66–67, 74–79; Pisano, "The Italian Terrorist Experience: 1968–1984," pp. 2–15.

27.   Ofra Bengio, "Shi'is and Politics in Ba'thi Iraq," *Middle East Studies* (January 1985):8–12.

28.   Mansfield, "The Irish Republican Army and Northern Ireland," pp. 66–67; Pisano, "The Italian Terrorist Experience: 1968–1984," pp. 2–15.

29.   *Arab Report and Record* (November 1–15, 1968), p. 364; (February 15–28, 1969), pp. 86–87.

30.   The commentary on Israeli response to the *intifada* is extensive and consistently paints a harsh picture; see, for instance, *New York Times*, February 8 and 19, and March 15, 1989; and *Washington Post*, March 12, 1989.

31.   *New York Times*, June 15, 1980, and *Washington Post*, July 8, August 12, September 20, and October 5, 1980.

32.   On the problems of military leadership in the Philippines, see Bilveer, "The Philippines: How Much Longer Can the Center Hold," p. 26; Warner, "Insurgency in the Philippines: No. 1," p. 13; *New York Times*, November 6, 1984. On El Salvador, see *New York Times*, August 19, 1983. Leadership and other deficiencies in the Salvadoran military led to extensive efforts to better train and equip the armed forces. By 1985 improved battlefield performance, discipline, and political sensitivity were reported by a number of observers; see *New York Times*, January 29, May 19 (Section IV), and July 28, 1985; and *Christian Science Monitor*, January 24, 1985. By the spring of 1989, numerous observers were reporting that while some attention was being given to winning "hearts and minds," other trends were unfavorable, among them the further deterioration of an already bad economic situation and the resurgence of death-squad activity; see, for example, *Washington Post*, June 12 and 27, and August 28, 1988; and *Christian Science Monitor*, August 5, 1988.

33.   McCuen, *The Art of Counter-Revolutionary War*, pp. 143–158; Ted Robert Gurr, *Why Men Rebel* (Princeton, N.J.: Princeton University Press, 1970), pp. 236–259; Sir Robert Thompson, *Defeating Communist Insurgency* (New York: Frederick A. Praeger, 1966), p. 53; Charles Wolf, Jr., *Insurgency and Counterinsurgency: New Myth, and Old Realities* (Santa Monica, Calif.: Rand Corporation, 1965), p. 22; Otto Heilbrunn, *Partisan Warfare* (New York: Frederick A. Praeger, 1962), pp. 151–158; Julian Paget, *Counter-Insurgency Campaigning* (New York: Walker & Co., 1967), p. 169; Roger Trinquier, *Modern Warfare* (New York: Frederick A. Praeger, 1964), pp. 43–50; Campbell, *Guerrillas*, pp. 232–233.

34.   On the question of resettlement and its successes and failures, see Ian F. W. Beckett, "Introduction," in Ian F. W. Beckett, ed., *The Roots of Counter-insurgency* (New York: Sterling Publishing Co., Inc., 1988), pp. 9–10; Rice, *Wars of the Third Kind*, p. 96; Clutterbuck, *The Long, Long War*, pp. 56–63, 66–72; Campbell, *Guerrillas*, pp. 36, 148, 218; Paget, *Counter-Insurgency Campaigning*, p. 36; Heilbrunn, *Partisan Warfare*, pp. 36, 153; and, McCuen, *The Art of Counter-Revolutionary War*, pp. 231–234.

35.   Trinquier, *Modern Warfare,* p. 47. A recent example is the case brought before the European Court of Human Rights by four Northern Irishmen who were detained without charges under the Prevention of Terrorism Act (which is an important part of the campaign against the IRA). In this case, the court found the law to be a violation of human rights; see *Washington Post,* November 30, 1988.

36.   Clutterbuck, *The Long, Long War,* p. 40.

37.   John Pimlott, "The British Experience," in Beckett, ed., *The Roots of Counter-insurgency,* pp. 22–23; Trinquier, *Modern Warfare,* pp. 23–27, 35–38; Campbell, *Guerrillas,* pp. 300, 323; Paget, *Counter-Insurgency Campaigning,* p. 164.

38.   Clutterbuck, *The Long, Long War,* pp. 95–100.

39.   Trinquier, *Modern Warfare,* pp. 23–27, 35–38; Campbell, *Guerrillas,* pp. 300–323; Paget, *Counter-Insurgency Campaigning,* p. 164; McCuen, *The Art of Counter-Revolutionary War,* pp. 113–119; Clutterbuck, *The Long, Long War,* pp. 95–100.

40.   Bilveer, "The Philippines: How Much Longer Can the Center Hold," pp. 26–27; *The Situation in the Philippines,* A Staff Report Prepared for the Committee on Foreign Relations, United States Senate (Washington, D.C.: U.S. Government Printing Office, 1984), pp. 12–16. That a number of prominent Filipino officials were concerned with the course of events was clear from critical assessments and new strategy proposals that had surfaced by 1989. The need to counterorganize the people and to address their grievances was clearly articulated. See Eric Guyot and James Clad, "Regaining the Initiative," *Far Eastern Economic Review* (September 22, 1988):40; *Christian Science Monitor,* April 18, 1989; Barry Crane et al., *Between Peace and War: Comprehending Low-Intensity Conflict,* National Security Program Discussion Paper Series 88-02 (Cambridge, Mass.: John F. Kennedy School of Government, Harvard University, 1988), pp. 257–258.

41.   *New York Times,* January 2, 23, and 27, March 5, 6, and 30, and August 14, 1980; *Washington Post,* November 7, 1978; January 25, March 5, and November 18, 1980; and February 27, 1981; Kabul Domestic Service (December 17, 1981), in *FBIS/SA* (December 21, 1981): C1–C2. Karmal severely criticized several ministries for their poor performance. See Kabul Domestic Service (February 24, 1982), in *FBIS/SA* (March 2, 1982): C1–C6.

42.   Acknowledgment of the severe disunity of the Afghan government and its negative impact on government performance was made by Major General Kim Tsagolov, Soviet military adviser in Afghanistan from 1981 to 1984 and again in 1987, in the weekly magazine *Ogonyok.* See David Remnick, "Soviet General Predicts Fall of Afghan Communists After Afghan Pullout," *Washington Post,* July 25, 1988; and Bill Keller, "Soviet General Declares Kabul Could Collapse," *New York Times,* July 24, 1988.

43.   Bruce R. Kuniholm, "Turkey and NATO: Past, Present and Future," *Orbis* (Summer 1983):426–433.

44.   A compelling case for civilian control is made by Pimlott, "The British Experience," pp. 17–20.

45.   The PRC'S diminished support for the insurgency in Thailand had begun by 1973. See William R. Heaton, "People's War in Thailand," in George Edward Thibault, ed., *The Art and Practice of Military Strategy* (Washington, D.C.: National Defense University, 1984), pp. 850–852.

46.   An account of the Nicaraguan effort to influence the United States by means of professional public relations efforts may be found in the *Washington Post*, October 9, 1984.

47.   O'Neill, *Armed Struggle in Palestine*, pp. 77–86, 168–169, and especially 170–173.

48.   *Ibid.*, p. 81; *Christian Science Monitor*, March 29, 1988.

49.   D. Michael Shafer has made a persuasive case that despite the American assumptions about the positive impact of assistance during the Greek civil war, brute force was the reason for success, since the Greek government ignored U.S. prescriptions, did little to improve its relations with the people, did not promote development, and did not control right-wing death squads; see his *Deadly Paradigms* (Princeton, N.J.: Princeton University Press, 1988), pp. 166–204.

50.   The problems associated with a breakdown in integrity in Vietnam are easy to document and could fill pages. Neil Sheehan's prize-winning and meticulous book *A Bright Shining Lie* (New York: Random House, 1988) brilliantly captures the essence of the problem. Also see David H. Hackworth, *About Face* (New York: Simon and Schuster, 1989).

IX Concluding Observations

ANALYZING INSURGENCIES IS A COMPLICATED MATTER, IN-
volving a dynamic interplay of many factors. To facilitate this undertaking,
I have presented the factors as part of a structured framework for analysis.
Although the framework is neither a formalized model nor a theory, I have
set forth a number of important relationships among the factors at various
points. This reflects not only the complex nature of the subject, which defies
facile generalizations, but also a deliberate aim of providing an analytical
approach that emphasizes practicality more than theory.

Each of the factors represents an area of inquiry that may be crucial
for explaining the course of events in insurgencies. How important the factors are varies from case to case and can only be determined by careful
empirical investigation. Since numerous studies give ample evidence that
combinations of important factors vary considerably between cases, there
is no one model that can be applied to all cases. In the last chapter, for
instance, we saw that the ingredients of a successful counterinsurgency program vary according to the actual or anticipated threats posed by insurgents
and the status of the insurgency with respect to the environment, popular
support, organization, unity, and external support; there is no pat formula.
Far-reaching programs that seek to win popular support through a mix of
substantive political, military, economic, and administrative policies may
be suitable for some cases in which insurgents are following a protracted-
popular-war strategy. In contrast, insurgents who follow an urban-warfare
strategy and emphasize terrorism rather than organizing popular support
may be countered by a modest but vigorous program centered on intelligence, police, and legal due process.

While acknowledging that the differences between insurgencies do
exist, it is important to recognize that there may also exist similarities that
permit particular lessons learned to be transferred from one case to another.

Whether policies are transferable depends, in large part, on the overall situation. For example, the notion of using small-unit patrols to cope with a guerrilla threat worked well in Malaya and was successfully adopted in Oman. In each case, the insurgents were minorities that could be isolated and the government side had the resources and will to stay the course. Whether patrols against guerrillas could have been as effective in, say, Afghanistan is another matter. While they would have been preferable to the large-scale search-and-destroy operations conducted by Soviet conventional forces and their Afghan allies, they would probably never have compensated for the inept and misguided political, social, economic, and administrative policies of both the ruling People's Democratic Party and the government. This underscores an important point: analysis of an insurgency must pay special attention to the interrelationships of the factors in the framework. While they help us sort out and make sense of information, the factors are by no means unrelated, discrete categories. What happens with respect to one can have an enormous impact on another (e.g., a loss of external support may undercut cohesion or vice versa). Both the potential criticality of specific factors and their interconnections make it imperative that analyses of insurgencies be as comprehensive as possible.

A comprehensive approach to the study of insurgency means that insightful and penetrating questions need to be asked about all the major components of the framework. If researchers wish to add additional questions, so much the better. Leaving out major factors can be a serious mistake, since major explanations for what has, and is, transpiring may be associated with missing elements. For instance, although a study of developments in the Polisario insurgency that gave no attention to external support might be somewhat enlightening, it would still be woefully distorted, given the crucial role that external support plays in that case. In the same context, a study of El Salvador that emphasized external support but ignored the political, social, and economic elements of the human environment could lead to the badly flawed conclusion that the insurrection could be quelled by eliminating external support. The point is that by addressing all of the factors, one is less apt to overlook a critical facet of the insurgency and to be in a better position to determine what is known and what requires further investigation and analysis.

Using the Framework

Anyone interested in insurgency can use the framework, whether they are in an academic setting, are involved in the policy process, or are firsthand observers of an internal conflict. In my experience over the past fifteen years with graduate students and highly qualified midcareer professionals from the national security policy community, I have found the framework for analysis to be an effective pedagogical tool. As those who have spent time in a classroom know, formal presentations and seminar discussions can easily lapse into "stream of consciousness" exchanges that do little to illuminate the issues at hand. And when it comes to written work, a similar problem surfaces early in the process, as students struggle to find ways to organize and present their thoughts. What the framework does is provide a conceptual format for ordering, interpreting, and presenting vast amounts of information related to one or more cases. If we are studying a single case, the concepts or factors that comprise the framework for analysis can help identify specific changes in the situation. For instance, the insurrection in country X has changed with respect to insurgent goals, strategy, and external support. Or, the insurgency in country Y has changed with respect to popular support and government response. When we analyze several cases, the concepts can help us see similarities and differences with reference to explicit criteria and what they mean in the broader context of insurgency.

The use of the framework in an academic setting can be quite flexible. For short classroom or written exercises limited by time, the basic categories may be used, whereas for major classroom projects and papers (e.g., theses, dissertations), a more detailed version of the framework may be used. Certainly, there is no reason why users cannot add their own ideas and concepts to sections of the framework. Finally, the framework is also helpful for critiques and reviews of articles and books because it gives the reviewer a scheme for quickly identifying important subjects that may be neglected and for assessing those things that are covered.

The framework can also be used by analysts and supervisors involved in the policy process. For analysts, it provides a clear organizational format for written reports and briefings. One former participant in National Security Council meetings told me after observing classroom use of the framework that clearly organized presentations during policy deliberations are invaluable because they make briefings easier to follow and are more persuasive. For high-level supervisors, the framework, even when reduced to a basic one-page outline, provides a basis for asking explicit, focused questions and for determining what is known, only partly known, and unknown. Ascertaining what is unclear or unknown can be as important as finding out what is known. For instance, a presentation may be quite solid in its portrayal of the type of insurgency, strategy employed, forms of warfare, environment, and so forth, but have little or no information or insights with respect to one important factor, such as organization. Where this happens, intelligence analysts and collectors can be asked to concentrate further attention on organization.

Frequent discussions with firsthand observers of insurgencies (diplomats, military officers, journalists, insurgents, and so on) indicate that they, too, find value in having basic general concepts in mind to aid them in collecting data and structuring their thoughts. While their ultimate purpose may not be to produce the more detailed product of an academic or government analyst, they can still benefit from an overall conceptual format, even if it is abbreviated. On a number of occasions, individuals who spent considerable time observing an insurgency and who had amassed impressive knowledge of social, political, historical, and economic details have told me the one thing they needed to help them interpret and report on their findings was a series of general concepts that generated and framed essential questions. They thought the kind of framework discussed in this book would have met that need.

Objectivity and Subjectivity

Regardless of who uses the framework, they will always confront the issue of objective versus subjective analysis. While dispassionate analysis is obviously what one aspires to achieve, it is not uncommon to find ideological and moral predispositions injected into assessments, either consciously or unconsciously, particularly when it comes to insurgencies. No frameworks are foolproof when it comes to this. Anyone so inclined can selectively use the data and skew interpretations. The key for dealing with this is the integrity of the researcher. Basically, he or she must inventory his or her own biases on the subject and make a decided effort to see to it that they do not lead to a deliberate manipulation of data to support preconceived notions or to hide unfavorable information.

To give a brief illustration, if one personally deplores the nature of a particular regime, finds some of its countermeasures repugnant, and even sympathizes with the insurgents, there could be a tendency to ignore findings that the insurgents have little support and are disorganized, and that government countermeasures are effective. For the serious analyst, as opposed to a polemicist, all of the important findings must be presented, even if they contradict the analyst's prejudgments. It almost goes without saying that the practitioner, regardless of the side he or she is on, also has a great need for objective assessments. Falsifying or ignoring data yields delusions, which can lead to short-term catastrophes and long-term defeats.

In a number of discussions with individuals who have been participants on either the government or insurgent side or who have been in supporting roles in various situations, the utility of the framework has been demonstrated. Initially, those with partisan interests tend to exaggerate their own successes and ignore their own shortcomings. When compelled to evaluate the situation point by point in terms of the framework, they find they must confront uncongenial information. By the end of the exercise, they frequently comment that the process of deliberately trying to answer a range of neutral questions as objectively as possible is extremely beneficial in a practical sense, especially because the critique of one's own side and acknowledgment of an adversary's strengths is indispensable for improving their own situation.

Summary

There can be little doubt that in the years ahead insurgencies will continue to pose important domestic and foreign policy challenges for many nations, including the superpowers. Aside from participants, these insurgencies will be of interest to a wide range of people—decision-makers, government analysts, scholars, students, and journalists. All will find that the analysis of insurgency is a complex and challenging undertaking and must be approached in an organized way and with an open mind. If the framework for analysis set forth in this book facilitates that undertaking, my main purpose has been achieved.

INDEX

Afghanistan: Afghan resistance, 96–97, 99–101; Baluchi in, 14; external assistance for insurgents, 113, 149; government response, 146, 149, 161; guerrilla warfare in, 56, 71; Hezb-i-Islami of Gulbuddin Hekmatyar in, 18; Islamic Conference Organization, 100; Muhammad Gailani's National Islamic Front for the Liberation of Afghanistan, 18; *mujahidin,* 139, 143; Pathans in, 14; People's Democratic Party of Afghanistan (PDPA), 146–47; popular support for insurgents, 73, 76; *pushtunwali,* 81–82; reforms versus tradition, 134–35; socio-political structure in, 65; Soviet invasion of, 8, 9, 79, 137–38, 147; Soviet repression of terrorism in, 140, 161; Soviet withdrawal from, 140–41; terrorism in, 80, 140

Algeria: anticolonial insurrections in, 60, 137; assistance to Polisario rebels in the Western Sahara, 7; class struggle in, 4; FLN, 62, 92; insurgents' organization, 96; popular support for insurgents in, 93, 139; protracted popular war strategy used in, 39–40; sanctuary for Polisario, 118; terrorism in, 79

Angola: Front for the National Liberation of Angola (FNLA), 102; insurrection against Portugal, 102, 137; Jonas Savimbi, 56, 75, 136, 150; Popular Movement for the Liberation of Angola (MPLA), 100, 102; Ovimbundu tribesmen in, 60, 74, 102; support for SWAPO and ANC against South Africa, 112, 118; totalitarianism in, 16; Union for the Total Independence of Angola (UNITA), 19, 40, 74, 92–93, 100, 102, 107n.8, 114, 122, 149–50

Argentina: government repression of terrorism in, 140–41, 147–48; Montenero insurgents in, 12, 57, 96, 128, 139, 141

Belgium: conflicts between Flemings and Walloons, 14; Fighting Communist Cells, 47; pluralism in, 16

Cambodia: American Special Forces operations in, 151; totalitarianism in, 16

Castro, Fidel: charismatic attraction of, 75; ideology of, 43–45

Causes of insurgency: Communist party involvement, 4; domestic factors related to insurgency, 2; intergroup antagonisms, 4; international factors, 2; lack of economic development, 3–4; lack of national integration, 3;

THE AUTHOR

Bard O'Neill has a doctorate in international relations from Denver University. He is professor of international affairs at the National War College, Washington, D.C., where he is also director of Middle East studies and director of studies of insurgency and revolution. Also an adjunct associate professor at Catholic University, Washington, D.C., he teaches graduate courses in the Department of Politics.

A 1979 Senior Research Fellow at the National Defense University, O'Neill has served as a consultant to various high-ranking officials in the Departments of State and Defense. As director of Middle East studies, he has led various study groups to meet with heads of state and cabinet members in Israel, Jordan, Egypt, Saudi Arabia, Iran, and other countries. O'Neill has written and edited several books and articles including *The Energy Crisis and U.S. Foreign Policy, Armed Struggle in Palestine*, and *Insurgency in the Modern World* and "Israel" for *The Defense Policies of Nations*. He and his family live in Springfield, Virginia.